Issues in Finance and Industry

This is the first of two volumes in honour of Ajit Singh, the other one being *Issues in Economic Development and Globalization*

Issues in Finance and Industry

1 Introduction: Ajit Singh (Philip Arestis and John Eatwell)
2 Principles versus Rules (John Eatwell)
3 Finance and Growth in Developing Countries: Sound Principles and Unreliable Evidence (Valpy FitzGerald)
4 Micro-Finance, Macro-Finance and Egalitarian Development (Robert Pollin)
5 Financial Liberalization: The Current State of Play (Philip Arestis and Malcolm Sawyer)
6 Global Financial Regulation versus the Engines of Financial Instability (Robert H. Wade)
7 The Developmental Potential and Political Economy of Private Remittances: What Do We Know, and What Do We Need to Know? (Ilene Grabel)
8 Ownership, Institutions and Technological Intensities: Automotive and Electronic Component Firms in East Asia (Rajah Rasiah)
9 Competition and Industrial Rates of Return (Anwar Shaikh)
10 Accounting for Business Combinations (Geoff Meeks and Geoff Whittington)
11 Takeovers after *Takeovers* (Andy Cosh and Alan Hughes)

Issues in Economic Development and Globalization

1 Introduction: Ajit Singh (Philip Arestis and John Eatwell)
2 The Third World Industrial Revolution in Historical Perspective (Ha-Joon Chang)
3 Explaining Differential Performance: The Institutional Factor in Indian and Chinese Development (Ashwani Saith)
4 The Renaissance of China and India: Implications for the Advanced Economies (Robert Rowthorn)
5 The Rise of China and India: Implications for Developing Countries (Deepak Nayyar)
6 China's Impact on Sub-Saharan African Development: Trade, Aid and Politics (John Toye)
7 The Contradictions of Capitalist Globalization (Peter Nolan)
8 Europe's Future: Income Convergence to Fight Unemployment (James K. Galbraith)
9 Heckscher-Ohlin in Theory and Reality (Adrian Wood)
10 Growth Rates, Economic Structure, Energy Use and Sources of Demand (Codrina Rada von Arnim and Lance Taylor)
11 Macro Adjustment Policies and Horizontal Inequalities (Arnim Langer and Frances Stewart)
Appendix: Ajit Singh Publications
Epilogue by Alice Amsden

Also by Philip Arestis

THE POLITICAL ECONOMY OF ECONOMIC POLICIES (*co-editor with Malcolm Sawyer*)

MONEY AND BANKING: Issues for the Twenty-First Century (*editor*)

MONEY, PRICING, DISTRIBUTION AND ECONOMIC INTEGRATION

RELEVANCE OF KEYNESIAN ECONOMIC POLICIES TODAY (*co-editor with Malcolm Sawyer*)

WHAT GLOBAL ECONOMIC CRISIS? (*co-editor with Michelle Baddeley and John McCombie*)

POST-BUBBLE US ECONOMY: Implications for Financial Markets and the Economy (*with Elias Karakitsos*)

FINANCIAL DEVELOPMENTS IN NATIONAL AND INTERNATIONAL MARKETS (*co-editor with Jesús Ferreiro and Felipe Serrano*)

ADVANCES IN MONETARY POLICY AND MACROECONOMICS (*co-editor with Gennaro Zezza*)

ASPECTS OF MODERN MONETARY AND MACROECONOMIC POLICIES (*co-editor with Eckhard Hein and Edwin Le Heron*)

ON MONEY, METHOD AND KEYNES: Selected Essays by Victoria Chick (co-editor with Sheila Dow)

IS THERE A NEW CONSENSUS IN MACROECONOMICS? (*editor*)

POLITICAL ECONOMY OF BRAZIL (*co-editor with Alfredo Saad-Filho*)

FINANCIAL LIBERALIZATION AND ECONOMIC PERFORMANCE IN EMERGING COUNTRIES (*co-editor with Luiz Fernando de Paula*)

Also by John Eatwell

AN INTRODUCTION TO MODERN ECONOMICS (*with Joan Robinson*)

WHATEVER HAPPENED TO BRITAIN?

KEYNES'S ECONOMICS AND THE THEORY OF VALUE AND DISTRIBUTION (*editor with Murray Milgate*)

THE NEW PALGRAVE: A Dictionary of Economics (*editor with Murray Milgate and Peter Newman*)

THE WORLD OF ECONOMICS (*editor with Murray Milgate and Peter Newman*)

THE NEW PALGRAVE DICTIONARY OF MONEY AND FINANCE (*editor with Murray Milgate and Peter Newman*)

GLOBAL UNEMPLOYMENT (*editor*)

UNDERSTANDING GLOBALISATION: The Nation-State, Democracy and Economic Policies in the New Epoch (*with Elizabeth Jelin, Anthony McGrew and James Rosenau*)

GLOBAL FINANCE AT RISK: The Case for International Regulation (*with Lance Taylor*)

INTERNATIONAL CAPITAL MARKET: Systems in Transition (*editor with Lance Taylor*)

GLOBAL GOVERNANCE OF FINANCIAL SYSTEMS: The Legal and Economic Regulation of Systemic Risk (*with Kern Alexander and Rahul Dhumale*)

Issues in Finance and Industry

Essays in Honour of Ajit Singh

Edited by

Philip Arestis

and

John Eatwell

palgrave
macmillan

First published 2008 by
PALGRAVE MACMILLAN

Palgrave Macmillan in the UK is an imprint of Macmillan Publishers Limited, registered in England, company number 785998, of Houndmills, Basingstoke, Hampshire RG21 6XS.

Palgrave Macmillan in the US is a division of St Martin's Press LLC,
175 Fifth Avenue, New York, NY 10010.

Palgrave Macmillan is the global academic imprint of the above companies and has companies and representatives throughout the world.

Palgrave® and Macmillan® are registered trademarks in the United States, the United Kingdom, Europe and other countries.

ISBN-13: 978–0–230–55360–6
ISBN-10: 0–230–55360–5

This book is printed on paper suitable for recycling and made from fully managed and sustained forest sources. Logging, pulping and manufacturing processes are expected to conform to the environmental regulations of the country of origin.

A catalogue record for this book is available from the British Library.

A catalog record for this book is available from the Library of Congress.

10 9 8 7 6 5 4 3 2 1
17 16 15 14 13 12 11 10 09 08

Printed and bound in Great Britain by
CPI Antony Rowe, Chippenham and Eastbourne

Contents

List of Tables and Figures

Tables

Figures

सत्यमेव जयते

प्रधान मंत्री

Prime Minister

MESSAGE

I am delighted to learn that Queens' College is hosting a special dinner to mark the retirement of my dear friend Ajit Singh. I truly wish I could have been there with all of you. I know I would have been happy spending an evening with old friends around a familiar table.

I have known Ajit Singh over the years as a truly perceptive economist with a wide range of interests. He has combined a deep commitment to scholarship and theoretical research with a willingness to work with governments and international organizations. This has enabled him to acquire a truly informed view of the dynamics of development and globalization. His grasp of the micro economics of industrial organization and change as well as his understanding of the macro economics of development have helped him traverse a wide field of research in development and industrial economics. I have greatly benefited from Ajit Singh's understanding of the processes of development in an increasingly globalized world.

I am sure Queens' College will miss him both as a teacher and a researcher, for Ajit has not only distinguished himself as a researcher but has earned a special place in the hearts and minds of several generations of students at Cambridge for his qualities as a teacher. I wish him a long and productive life and the best of health in the years to come.

New Delhi
August 23, 2007

(Manmohan Singh)

Note: This letter from Dr Manmohan Singh, Prime Minister of India, is reproduced with permission.

Foreword

This volume presents papers by scholars pursuing broad themes paralleling Professor Ajit Singh's highly productive research career. My own characterization of the integrating theme is this: how behaviour in financial capital markets affects real sector economic performance, and in particular, how it affects growth – the growth of business corporations in Singh's early papers and, more recently, the growth of whole developing nations. In advancing this theme, Singh bridged the domain of business finance specialists on the one hand with the specialties of industrial and development economics on the other.

A number of Singh's contributions deal directly with the economics of corporate mergers. Indeed, my first encounter with Singh's research came from reading his 1971 book, *Takeovers*. In the seminal literature on that subject, it ranks just behind Robin Marris's 1964 book, *The Economic Theory of Managerial Capitalism*. The Marris book and a parallel article by Henry Manne in the United States suggested that takeovers and the threat of takeover forced company managers on to a shareholder wealth maximization path from which they might otherwise stray to pursue their personal goals. These theories gained a considerable following. Singh was an early sceptic.

Another related theme in Professor Singh's work is careful research showing that less profitable firms were more likely to be taken over, as the Marris–Manne theories predicted. The change, however, in the probability of takeover with varying profitability was small, and was overshadowed by the tendency for large companies to avoid takeover much more successfully than small firms. One implication was that managers had an incentive to enter mergers with little rationale other than enhancing company size and reducing the likelihood of losing their independence through takeover. This conjecture led to further research by Singh and others on the actual post-fusion consequences of mergers. The weight of assembled evidence revealed that mergers did not on average lead to longer-run profit increases, supporting Singh's findings and contradicting the assertions of those who saw mergers as an unambiguous efficiency-increasing force in the capitalist milieu.

This sceptical view is consistent with research by David Ravenscraft and myself on US mergers, and with many others' investigations, but it is contested furiously by some scholars, especially by those whose specialty is financial economics. Indeed, no subject on which I have done research evokes more passionate disagreement than the question of the consequences of mergers. That Singh and other sceptics have been influential is suggested by the results of a survey of 111 economists, mainly members of the European Association for Research in Industrial Economics (EARIE). One survey question asked for agreement or disagreement with the statement, 'Mergers usually do not increase accounting profit ratios in the long run.' Among the respondents, 10.8 per cent agreed completely (or 38.7 per cent with provisions), while 22.5 per cent expressed indifference.[1] But 22.5 per cent disagreed with qualifications and 2.7 per cent disagreed completely. Among sixteen more-or-less factual questions on 'the way the industrial world is', the merger question had the highest coefficient of disagreement. Still, as Bill Clinton, Tony Blair and Gordon Brown might attest, it is no small measure of success to win affirmative votes in a vigorously contested contest.

Paralleling Singh's work on mergers was a stream of research with several Cambridge colleagues on other aspects of business corporations' financial performance. It had two notable characteristics. First, it was among the first, if not the first, systematic empirical research that attempted to correct for the biases imparted to comportation financial statistics by various accounting conventions; and second, it constituted some of the first empirical testing of Gibrat's Law, which hypothesizes that firm size distributions evolve over time through random growth processes.

Yet another important strand of Professor Singh's research agenda merits mention. In recent years it has become fashionable for developing nations, whether capitalist, socialist, or socialist-turned-capitalist, to cultivate a vibrant stock market as a symbol of modernity. In Mongolia, where vast expanses and primitive communication raise transaction costs appreciably, it was proposed seriously that investors should be equipped with special-purpose radio transceivers permitting stock sales and purchases from any place in the nation. The announcement that Red China was creating a stock market elicited from Singh a critical response. It reflected his fear that speculation and an excessively short-term orientation on the part of common stock purchasers might deflect nations from capital investment strategies that maximize real long-term growth. Indeed, egregious bubbles, as in the Albanian Ponzi scheme of

[1] Karl Aiginger, Dennis C. Mueller, and Christoph Weiss, 'Objectives, Topics and Methods in Industrial Organization in the Nineties: Results from a Survey', Working Paper, University of Vienna, June 1997.

the 1990s, might succeed only in giving capitalism a bad reputation. Yet, as Singh further investigated the evolution of stock markets in developing nations, he was surprised to learn, as, I suspect, were many others, including myself, that large corporations in ten developing nations relied heavily on common stock issues to finance their growth. Recognizing this, he urged measures to ensure that stock markets and related institutions (such as pension funds) pursued policies encouraging individual saving and investment for the long term – both crucial ingredients for economic growth.

Another way of characterizing the central theme of Professor Singh's contributions is to say that what he seeks is financial market behaviour that will advance the economic welfare of all participants in a national economy, not merely the wealth of successful speculators and corporate empire-builders. And, in this, there is consistency with Singh's essential character as a considerate, giving and eminently admirable person.

F. M. Scherer
Harvard University

Notes on the Contributors

Philip Arestis is University Director of Research, Cambridge Centre for Economics and Public Policy, Department of Land Economy, University of Cambridge.

Andy Cosh is Assistant Director of the Centre for Business Research, University of Cambridge, UK.

John Eatwell is President of Queens' College, Cambridge, and Professor of Financial Policy and Director of the Centre for Financial Analysis and Policy at Judge Business School, University of Cambridge.

Valpy Fitzgerald is Professor of International Development at Oxford University, as well as a Professorial Fellow at St Antony's College, Oxford. He is also Head of the Department of International Development, Oxford University.

Ilene Grabel is Professor of International Finance and Director of the graduate programme in Global Finance, Trade and Economic Integration at the Graduate School of International Studies at the University of Denver, Colorado, USA.

Alan Hughes is Director of the Centre for Business Research, University of Cambridge, UK.

Geoff Meeks is Professor of Financial Accounting at Judge Business School, University of Cambridge, UK.

Robert Pollin is Co-Director, Political Economy Research Institute (PERI), University of Massachusetts-Amherst, USA.

Rajah Rasiah is Professor of Technology and Innovation at the University of Malaya, Kuala Lumpur, Malaysia.

Malcolm Sawyer is Professor of Economics at Leeds University Business School, UK.

F.M. Scherer is Aetna Professor at the John F. Kennedy School of Government, Harvard University, USA.

Anwar Shaikh is a Professor in the Department of Economics, Graduate Faculty, New School for Social Research, New York, USA.

Robert H. Wade is Professor of Political Economy and Development at the Development Studies Institute (DESTIN), London School of Economics and Political Science, UK.

Geoff Whittington is a Research Associate at the Centre for Financial Analysis and Policy, Judge Business School, University of Cambridge, UK.

1
Introduction: Ajit Singh

Philip Arestis and John Eatwell

Ajit Singh studied, initially as an undergraduate, at Government College, Chandigarh, Punjab University. He read Sanskrit (for nationalist reasons) and Mathematics as his subjects. In order to understand how India could become a modern, prosperous country, he also studied Economics. In 1958, Ajit went to the US to study Economics. An important motivation for going to America was that the educational system there permitted one to work one's way through university, whereas in the UK, the usual destination of students from India at the time, studying could only have been at his parents' expense.

In the US, Ajit studied for a Master's degree in Economics at Howard University. Not only was Howard very cheap, even for foreign students in those days, but the graduate school also functioned in the evenings. That enabled Ajit to work during the day at the India Supply Mission and thus to pay his way. After completing his Master's degree at Howard, Ajit went to Berkeley in September 1960 to begin a PhD. In 1961–2, the Economics Department awarded him the much-coveted Alice J. Rosenberg Research Fellowship at Berkeley, on the basis of his academic performance in his first year.

At the invitation of Robin Marris, Ajit went to Cambridge (UK) for the calendar year 1963. This led to a post at the Department of Applied Economics and subsequently, in 1965, to an Assistant Lectureship in the Faculty of Economics, and to an official Fellowship at Queens' College at the same time. In 1968, Ajit was appointed to posts as a Lecturer in the Faculty of Economics and Politics and as Director of Studies in Economics at Queens' College. He was given tenure in 1971 by the University of Cambridge. In 1991, he was appointed to an *ad hominem* University Readership and promoted to a personal Chair in Economics by Cambridge University in October 1995. Ajit Singh also held, between 1987 and 1994, the Dr. William M. Scholl Visiting Chair in the Department of Economics at the University of Notre Dame in the US. He was a senior economic adviser to the governments of Mexico and Tanzania and a consultant to various UN developmental organizations, including the World Bank, the ILO, UNCTAD and UNIDO. He was appointed to a Fellowship at the Cambridge MIT for 2002–3, and in 2004 was elected as an Academician of the British Academy of Social Sciences.

As many developing countries – particularly the NICs – have achieved a significant degree of industrialization since the 1960s, work on the corporate economy, takeovers and the stock market has acquired a far wider field of application. In the 1990s, Ajit examined the question of the desirability of establishing a stock market in a centrally planned economy. Although that work was undertaken with special reference to China, its argument is more general and applicable to many Third-World countries as well. (That work was the subject of an Economic Focus in *The Economist* magazine, 2 September 1989, p. 69.) At the same time, Ajit and collaborators provided the first systematic study of corporate financial structures in the NICs. The purpose of that research programme was to analyse the relationship between corporate organization, corporate finance, and economic and industrial development. More generally, it was to discover what kinds of financial systems and property rights were most conducive to industrialization in developing countries, as well as promoting international competitiveness in advanced economies. With the recent change in the political balance of power between the North and the South, and the East and the West, and the onslaught of international financial institutions – with their recipes for liberalization, privatization and deregulation for rich and poor countries alike – that work had also had significant and timely policy implications at the microeconomic and structural levels. These latter aspects have been further developed and applied in the case of East and South-East Asian and Latin-American countries.

By the mid-1990s, Ajit had established an international reputation in the following three areas, and presumably in recognition of this he was promoted to an *ad hominem* professorship in the Economics Faculty in 1995.

Modern business enterprise and the theory of the firm:

Corporate organization; corporate finance and governance in advanced countries and emerging markets; takeovers, mergers and the stock market; the financial system and its efficiency in promoting economic growth and development in both advanced and emerging countries.

Deindustrialization and long-term structural changes in the UK and other advanced economies:

North–South competition; employment and unemployment in the North and the South; liberalization and globalization of financial, labour and product markets.

Industrialization of the Third World:

Economic development and economic policy in developing countries since 1950.

All these areas of Ajit's expertise continue to be very important in the real world and have significant implications both for economic theory and for policy, and Ajit remains active in all of them.

The focus of Ajit's previous research under the first two areas was advanced countries. Thus, his well-known work on corporate growth, mergers and takeovers in the stock market was based on corporate data from the UK and the US. Similarly, his pioneering studies of de-industrialization were based on the experiences of advanced countries. However, since the mid-1990s, Ajit's work has concentrated increasingly on emerging countries. The subjects he was exploring in the first of the three areas have acquired a new stature on the international agenda. It has been argued by the Bretton Woods institutions and by leading US government officials, including Alan Greenspan and Larry Summers, that the fundamental causes of the Asian crisis of 1997–99 lay in the 'Asian way of doing business'. More specifically, crony capitalism in the sense of close relationships between governments, business and finance, and deficits in corporate governance and competition were blamed for the crisis. In his research, Ajit takes serious issue with these claims and suggests that the reform strategy advocated by the international financial institutions is increasingly being questioned as to whether it is a step in the right direction. Ajit's research also shows that capital account liberalization advocated by the IMF with greater or less vigour for developing countries is not helpful for development.

Not only does Ajit's research on aspects of corporate behaviour in emerging markets have direct policy implications, it is also significant for economic theory. His three IFC technical papers on corporate finance indicated that, contrary to *a priori* reasoning, developing-country corporations finance their growth much more from external than from internal sources (that is, retained profits). In relation to external sources, they have surprisingly large recourse to stock markets, indeed much more so than advanced country corporations.

This anomalous finding, which has been referred to as the 'Singh paradox', is generating further research. Similarly, Ajit and his associates have found that, contrary to theoretical speculation and anecdotal evidence, emerging markets display greater intensity of product market competition than do advanced country markets. Using the methodology of persistency of profitability studies, widely employed in assessing the intensity of competition in advanced countries, Ajit and his collaborators suggest that emerging market firms display a lower persistence of profitability than advanced countries, in both the short and the long run.

Nicholas Kaldor's influence on Ajit's work is most evident in the book of essays, *Competitiveness Matters: Industry and Economic Performance in the US*, co-edited with Candace Howes, on industry and economics performance in the US economy. The book includes contributions by leading American economists working in this area, as well as a substantial introductory chapter by Ajit and Howes. The latter reviews and advances further the debate on the concept of competitiveness and its application to the US economy. This chapter also interprets, *inter alia*, US deindustrialization issues in terms of the analyses and concepts of Cambridge economists. In addition, Ajit contributes an essay analysing the relationship between the Anglo-Saxon financial system, the market for corporate control and international competitiveness.

Kaldor's influence is also manifest in Ajit's recent work on the Indian economy. The relevant papers on this topic suggest that the faster growth of services compared with manufacturing – characteristic of the Indian economy in recent decades – does not necessarily indicate a structural imbalance with harmful consequences for the country's long-term economic growth. The IT sector, which has been the mainspring of the rapid growth of service provision, meets all the Kaldorian criteria by which manufacturing is regarded as an engine of growth. The Indian IT sector meets these criteria particularly well and should therefore be regarded as an additional engine of economic growth for the economy. These papers, alongside others, also consider issues of premature deindustrialization, and of a growth in unemployment in the formal sector, which many emerging countries are experiencing.

In recent years, Ajit has been participating in a new research field concerning law, finance and development. The main research in this area since the later 1990s has been carried out by economists from Harvard University – Professor A. Shleifer and his associates, R. La Porta, F. Lopez-de-Silanes and R. W. Vishny, collectively known in the literature as LLSV). On the basis of a large number of studies published in leading international journals, LLSV have suggested that a country's 'legal origin' (crudely basic legal philosophy) determines its corporate law, which in turn determines the level and terms of finance advanced to corporations, and ultimately determines the rate of economic growth. LLSV's findings, based mainly on a cross-section of fifty countries during a single year in the mid-1990s, are controversial. Ajit, the economist, in collaboration with two lawyers (Professor Simon Deakin of Cambridge, and Professor John Armour of Oxford) are the principal investigators in an interdisciplinary, ESRC-funded research project. Their research has collected, for the first time, time-series information for thirty-five years (1970–2005) for four 'mother' countries in relation to legal origin (that is,the UK, the US, Germany and France). Their results indicate that, contrary to the legal origin theory, time-series evidence suggests that common law countries manifest no greater degree of shareholder protection than civil law countries, and that there was no relationship – again, contrary to the legal origin analysis – between shareholder protection and stock market development. These results call into question the advocacy of the Anglo-Saxon model of corporate governance as a universal standard because of the assumed greater legal protection afforded to shareholders.

To sum up, as an economic researcher, Ajit Singh has been guided by the W. B. Reddaway dictum (paraphrased here) *that it is better to be technically crude and relevant than to be technically sophisticated and irrelevant.* This has meant that Ajit has often taken up big questions where knowledge is quite incomplete and yet requires an urgent policy response. Thus, his current research on ongoing industrial revolutions in India and China and their impact on the West has an immediacy and cannot wait several years for the relevant data to be assembled and processed in order to provide policy guidance. Further experiences suggest that big questions such as these require institutional and historical analyses as well as economic theory and appropriate econometric methodology. Ajit Singh's main conclusions are as follows:

(i) it is a social imperative for India and China to continue with their respective industrial revolutions;
(ii) the faster growth of services over manufacturing manifested in India's recent growth experience is not a structural imbalance with

harmful consequences for long-term growth, as some economists would argue: IT-related services are as much an engine of growth as manufacturing;

(iii) although India and China provide competition for advanced countries in manufactures (comprising as they do about 20 per cent of world output), they also continue to provide a stable and growing source of demand;

(iv) those who argue that the recent doubling of the world labour force as a consequence of liberalization and globalization is harmful for workers in the advanced countries, fail to take into account the demand-side potential in India and China, as above, as well as the long-term dynamism of the US economy, based on oligopolistic competition between their large corporations providing an institutionalized mechanism for technical progress in new product development; and

(v) it is, however, argued that current global financial imbalances require an international cooperative approach to rebalancing, rather than imposing adjustment on large new entrants to the global market.

Throughout his academic career at Cambridge, Ajit Singh has taken a very active part in policy work related to economic development in poorer countries. He has also been much concerned with North–South economic interactions and how these can be improved to the mutual benefit of both rich and poor countries. At a practical level, this work has involved advocacy, policy advice and interactions with ministers, officials and civil society in developing countries, and senior civil servants in international organizations. In this context, Ajit's 2005 paper, 'Special and Differential Treatment: The Multilateral Trading System and Economic Development in the Twenty-first Century', in Kevin P. Gallagher (ed.) *Putting Development First*, Zed Books, London, 2005, pp. 233–63, is significant. He argues that the concept of special and differential treatment (S&DT) for developing countries (DCs) represented an important advance in international economic law in the second half of the twentieth century – for its recognition of the notion of non-reciprocity in international economic relations. It is essentially the principle of affirmative action in the sphere of international economic relationships. This principle was reaffirmed unequivocally at the Doha Ministerial Meeting of the World Trade Organization (WTO) in 2001. It is widely acknowledged that S&DT lies at the heart of the Doha development agenda. However, since that time there has been a deep gulf between rich and poor countries on the interpretation and implementation of S&DT. This paper aims to reduce this difference between the North and the South by clarifying the analytical issues involved, including the question of the anti-development bias of the current multilateral trading arrangements, as well as issues of graduation and differentiation. The paper concludes that the strong endorsement of S&DT at Doha gives the international community a fresh chance to change course, and to put economic development at the heart of the agenda for the current and future evolution of the multilateral trading system. However, it is also argued that taking development goals seriously would require a new definition and a new conceptualization of S&DT than the narrow meaning given to it under the Uruguay Round and WTO agreements.

We are extremely grateful to Palgrave Macmillan for their encouragement to put together this volume in honour of Ajit Singh, and to the relevant staff there for making this project possible. We are, of course, equally grateful to the authors for their contributions to this volume. Queens' College, Cambridge, very generously hosted a conference to celebrate Ajit Singh's numerous contributions, not merely to this College but also to the University of Cambridge and to the discipline of economics. We thank them all for their input to this book and for the relevant celebrations.

2
Principles versus Rules

John Eatwell

Introduction

Since 2006, the UK Financial Services Authority (FSA) has instituted a wide-ranging debate on the relative virtues of 'principles-based' versus 'rules-based' regulation, a debate that is being echoed in the US, with respect both to financial regulation and (in the post-Enron, Sarbanes–Oxley world) accounting standards.[1] The position of the FSA is summarized in a document published in April 2007, entitled *Principle-based regulation: Focusing on the outcomes that matter*. This paper provided the thematic underpinning to a conference on the virtues of principles-based regulation introduced by a government minister who lauded the proposal to 'continue developing principles based regulation in the UK' (Balls, 2007).

The FSA makes its case for principles-based regulation based on the need to regulate effectively in a continuously changing financial marketplace:

> Financial markets are constantly changing. Continuous innovation and new product development are important ways in which the financial services industry generates benefits for consumers and markets. It is important that regulation can respond rapidly to the pace of change in markets and so allow them to continue to develop for the benefit of their users. We believe regulation that focuses on outcomes rather than prescription is more likely to support this development and innovation. Any set of prescriptive rules is unable to address changing market circumstances and practices at all times, and it inevitably delays, and in some instances prevents, innovation. In a quickly changing marketplace, principles are far more durable. (FSA, 2007, p. 6)

While the FSA may be right to suggest that a *successful* principles-based system may better serve the cause of efficient financial innovation, that success is dependent on the nature of the relationship between the regulator and the regulated community – as is demonstrated by the history of the FSA itself.

Analysis

The fundamental problem for both the regulator and the regulated that is at the core of the advocacy of a principles-based approach is what should/will be the response to entirely novel events. The world of finance is a dynamic environment in which new products, new markets and new institutional arrangements are being proposed and created all the time. The task of the regulator is to assess how these new events correspond to regulatory objectives. The task of the regulated is to assess how the regulator is likely to react to innovation, and what costs are likely to be imposed on the innovator.

How, then, does a regulatory regime based on 'principles' compare with one based on 'rules'?

Principles

Suppose the principles regime is indeed based on a set of defined principles, P, on the basis of which all actions are judged. A regulated entity, planning an innovation, will need to assess the likelihood of regulatory disapproval and/or sanction based on the expectation of how the regulator will apply the principles. That expectation will be formed from having observed the regulator's behaviour in the past, yielding a set of precedents, A_P, and on any consultation, dialogue or insider information, D_P, that might give a clue as to the regulator's mindset. On the basis of this information, the innovator will have some expectation of the likely regulatory cost of innovation, C_P, in a principles-based regime:

$$C_P = E[C \mid P, A_P, D_P]$$

On the basis of the expectation of C_P, the potential innovator may decide that the innovation will be ignored/welcomed by the regulator; or that it will be forbidden; or that it is worth a try and may be successful.

If all actions may be related readily to the principles, $A_P = f(P)$, then the expected cost of innovation may be written as:

$$C_P = E[C \mid P, D_P]$$

Estimation of the regulatory cost of innovation is dependent on the stated principles, and dialogue and mutual understanding as to their application.

Rules

Suppose, next, that the regulator operates by articulating a series of precise rules defining what is, and what is not, allowable. In some cases these rules may anticipate an innovation, and the likely cost of innovation in the rules-based regime, C_R, is readily assessed. However, in many other cases, existing rules will not apply to the innovation. The innovator therefore has to assess how the regulator will react, how old rules will be adapted and what new rules will be introduced to cover the new circumstances. The only way the regulated entity can do this is to infer from the regulator's prior actions (rules already set), A_R, and from any dialogue or insider knowledge, D_R, the form of the 'rules generating function' $A_R = g(X)$, where $X$is a set of inputs into the generating function. So the expected cost of innovation will be:

$$C_R = E[C \mid X, A_R, D_R]$$

or *if* X can be found from the inverse of the generating function (rules are not arbitrary) then $X = g^{-1}(A_R)$:

$$C_R = E[C \mid X, D_R]$$

However, it seems unlikely that any such precise inverse will exist that is applicable to innovations, by definition not previously embodied in A_R. This is perhaps the reason why even those regulators typically identified as 'rules-based' that operate a highly litigious regime, none the less also enunciate some basic propositions that provide guidance as to the content of the set X. Indeed, it may be supposed that, as between two regulators attempting to regulate financial systems displaying a common set of actual and potential market failures, then the set X is none other than the set of principles, P, so that the cost of innovation in the rules-based regime is:

$$C_R = E[C \mid P, D_R]$$

Principles and rules

This analysis suggests that the two regimes reduce to what is essentially a common cost structure, differentiated only by the nature of the dialogue,

D, characteristic of either case. It is not the principles or the rules that differentiate the two regimes, but the nature of the relationship between regulator and regulated that the particular regime generates. This analysis has been conducted from the perspective of the cost of innovation by firms. A similar result could be obtained by assessing how the regulator's objectives are attained under the two different regimes.

Before turning to the issue of dialogue and mutual understanding, what other factors may determine the relative expected costs of a principles regime and a rules regime?

First, in a principles-based regime it will be inefficient to attempt to explain every action from 'first principles'. Hence there will be an extensive set of rules (precedents), perhaps fairly broadly drawn, that essentially provide indicative guidance as to the way in which principles will be applied in the future and as to the existence of safe harbours. If the system is to work efficiently it is important that the regulator provides detailed information on these precedents.

Second, the principles-based regulator is likely to be at pains to outline some of the factors determining the form of f so that the regulated community knows how principles are likely to be applied. The arguments by the FSA that its regulation is 'risk-based' and focused on 'outcomes' rather than processes are of this kind.

Third, it may well be that in a rules-based regime X is not clearly enunciated by the regulator (even to itself), and hence is not known to regulated entities. The attempt to estimate X and g from the existing rulebook as far as an innovation is concerned will be a speculative exercise in which the bold will be testing the regulator continually. This is a recipe for complex and persistent litigation, and an incentive to provide some guidance as to the content of X and the form of g.

None the less, the fundamental distinction between a principles-based and a rules-based regulator is the difference between the nature of the dialogue between regulator and regulated. In stark form: whether the development of regulation is 'bottom-up' or 'top-down'.

In a principles-based regime there is a common interest that, in the light of an innovation, the regulated community knows how the regulator will react. This is obvious in the case of the regulated. But it is also the case for the regulator. If the regulator has knowledge (or at least a reasonable expectation) of how the regulated community forms its expectation of the cost of innovation, then the regulator can have some confidence that, in the majority of cases, its principles will be adhered to and its objectives met. Thus the regulator has a considerable incentive to maintain a comprehensive dialogue with the regulated community.

If it were possible (which it is not) that regulator and regulated were of one mind, then the regulator would be satisfied as to outcomes, and the regulated could minimize the net regulatory cost of innovation at zero. Given that the objectives of regulator and regulated are different, they may never be of one mind, but a thorough understanding of the goals and actions of both sides will allow the regulatory cost of innovation to be kept to a minimum.

In a rules-based regime it is likely that there will be only limited dialogue outside the courtroom. A major motivation of firms will be to innovate in a manner that either is encompassed by existing rules or evades them. A major motivation of the regulator will be to deploy existing rules in a manner that anticipates change, since the making of new rules is typically an arduous and expensive procedure. In this adversarial environment it is difficult to build a community of common interest. Firms and trade associations will lobby regulators, rather than work with them.

Systemic risk

Much of the dialogue between regulator and regulated will concentrate on areas of activity in which the firm is typically better-informed than the regulator. The firm is operating in the markets every day, knows how other market participants are likely to react to its innovations, and relies on detailed and accurate market information to conduct its business. The dialogue is a process in which the regulator is the pupil and the regulated firms are the teachers. The degree to which the regulator can trust the regulated is an important component of the regulatory process.

This relationship is reversed in the case of systemic risk. Systemic risk arises from risk externalities, and cannot be estimated accurately, or even known by firms, especially in the face of extreme events. The regulator should, at least to some degree, be informed as to the risks emanating from the structure of the market. The regulated cannot know this. The consequences of this asymmetry are:

> First, in a principles-based regime the regulator must be a trusted provider of information regarding systemic risk, and must demonstrate that regulatory actions are linked to the risks involved; and
>
> Second, in so far as the firms do not have information, or do not trust and/or respond to the information they are given, then the regulator, whether principles-based or rules-based, must necessarily impose rules to manage systemic risk.

A further complication appears when the risks are international. Once regulators are operating across more than one jurisdiction they must inevitably rely on broad principles (such as the standards advanced by the Committee on Banking Supervision of the G10). Yet regulating systemic risk also requires rules: hence the highly detailed formulation of Basel 2.

The role of dialogue in the development of UK financial regulation

Financial regulation before 2000

The perceived need to advance the cause of principles over rules at the time of writing is an a-historic puzzle, since the UK has always promoted a principles-based regulatory regime. In the nineteenth century, and for most of the twentieth century, banking regulation and general oversight of all financial activities in the City of London was conducted by the Bank of England in an informal, non-statutory process, 'the bank exercises its influence mainly by informal communication and persuasion behind the scenes ... it is better to sit round a table and agree a course of action than to stay away and force the authorities to exercise legal powers that might be awkward to administer with precision and answerability' (Sayers, 1964).

The 1986 Financial Services Act enshrined a commitment to principles-based regulation, inherited from the informality and self-regulation prior to 1986. The Bank of England's approach to the regulation of the banking sector had placed a strong emphasis on the values (principles), and on close contact between Bank officials and the regulated banks. In other financial services, a self-regulator or a professional body acts rather like a club. Members have to obey the club's general 'ethos' embodied in its principles, as well as specific rules. The concept of 'fit and proper' derives from this era.

This general approach was carried forward in the dual structure established in the 1986 Act: an overarching Securities and Investments Board (SIB) that defined the core principles of financial regulation and supervised the implementation of those principles by the self-regulatory organizations (SROs) covering the various facets of the financial services industry (the Personal Investment Authority (PIA), the Investment Management Regulatory Organization (IMRO), and the Securities and Futures Authority (SFA)).

Within the post-1986 SROs, the culture of principles-based regulation was preserved by the dominant role of the practitioners. They were the guardians of the ethics of the 'club'. They represented the market as a whole, and were committed to preserving its integrity. Firms could be confident that principles were being interpreted by individuals with insider knowledge of how firms operate. The decision-making and enforcement role of practitioners imbued principles-based regulation with considerable certainty.

The Financial Services and Markets Act, 2000

The establishment of the Financial Services Authority (FSA), and the structure of the new regulator as proposed in the Financial Services and Markets Act, 2000 (FSMA), were motivated by a number of factors:

First, the perceived failure of the Bank of England as a regulator. In the cases of Johnson Matthey, Barings and BCCI, the Bank was deemed by the Labour Party leadership to have performed poorly. This was particularly the case with respect to Barings. Prior to the Barings collapse the then Bank of England Governor, Eddie George, had written in *The Observer* newspaper (24 July 1994) that:

> We now have an expert team monitoring derivatives who are getting better every time they go in to see a firm. What they are reporting back from the most active players in the market is very reassuring. These people know what they are doing whether it's at director level or the chaps on the desk.

Just three months later, Barings was destroyed by a rogue derivatives trader. An investigation by the Board of Banking Supervision (a Bank of England committee chaired by the Governor!) reached the damning conclusion that not only did management of Barings not understand the derivatives business done in their name, but also that:

> the Bank should explore ways of increasing its understanding of the non-banking businesses (particularly financial services businesses) undertaken by those banking groups for which it is responsible for consolidated supervision ... It should also seek to obtain a more comprehensive understanding of how the risks in those businesses interrelate to one another and to such groups' banking businesses. (Bank of England, 1995, para.14.35)

In other words, the Bank of England did not understand the firms and markets it was supposed to be regulating.

Second, the liberalization of financial markets, both domestic and international, that had occurred over the preceding two decades, had resulted in a substantial integration of markets that had previously been segmented, and in the development of a number of firms that spanned those markets (Eatwell and Taylor, 2000, ch.1). In this new, increasingly seamless world, the segmentation of the regulatory function made no sense. Confining regulators to limited domains could result in both under- and over-regulation. Under-regulation because not only could particular activities 'fall through the gaps', but also limited perspectives of segmented regulators might result in major risks to the financial system being overlooked, or at least the full significance of the risk being underestimated. And over-regulated because regulators with limited reach might attempt to control risks that emanated from outside their domain, by imposing constraints where they *could,* rather than where they *should.* The old structure of the Bank of England, SIB, and the various SROs, plus the Department of Trade and Industry (DTI), all regulating supposedly distinct parts of the market, some defined by institutional boundaries (banking, insurance) others by functional boundaries (the SROs), was deemed to be inadequate to deal with the new financial environment. A single regulator that could take into account the ever-greater integration of markets and firms, at home and abroad, was necessary, both to regulate more effectively, and, by doing so, to give London a significant competitive edge.

Third, not only was the regulation of securities and investment markets by SIB and the SROs (SFA, IMRO, PIA) believed to be segmented inappropriately, it was also believed that the SRO system was flawed in at least two other important ways.

On the one hand, post-1986, the responsibility for regulatory development has shifted increasingly to the SIB, undermining the self-regulatory intent if not the rhetoric of the 1986 Financial Services Act, and resulting in what was a statutory system of regulation in all but name. None the less, there was a desire to maintain the 'principles-based' approached that had informed the Financial Services Act.

But on the other hand, in discussions within the Labour Party there was also considerable suspicion of the role of practitioners in the SROs. Didn't they 'look after their own'? This suspicion is reflected in the Labour government's FSMA, where the role of practitioners is severely reduced compared with the SIB/SROs regime. Where the active participation of practitioners was later incorporated in the operations of the FSA, as on the Regulatory Decisions Committee, their membership was carefully restricted to less than 50 per cent of the Committee. In the FSMA itself, practitioners are characterized simply as an interest group to be consulted (HMSO, 2000, clauses 8 and 9). The FSMA was designed both to embody what had become the reality of statutory regulation, and to eliminate the practitioner involvement that was seen as a hangover from the pre-1986 era of self-regulation, irrelevant to a new regime committed to openness and hostile to perceived conflicts of interest. What, then, of the future of dialogue and mutual understanding between regulator and regulated?

The goals of the FSMA were: to place at the heart of the new, statutory regulation a dedicated professional team, replacing the practitioner role in the SROs, and hence eliminating the concept of self-regulation for good; to create an effective integrated regulator, overcoming the weaknesses of segmentation, and it was hoped, the perceived deficiencies of the Bank of England; *and to preserve a principles-based approach to regulation and to the development of rules.*

The statement by the FSA chief executive in his introduction to the FSA's *Better Regulation Action Plan* (December 2005) that:

> we aim where we can to change the balance significantly towards a more principles-based approach. We believe this can produce better outcomes for both consumers and the financial services industry by encouraging a focus on how best to act in a particular situation, rather than simply following a mechanistic process.

The subsequent campaign by the FSA suggests that the latter goal has not been attained.

Regulatory dialogue under the SROs and the FSA: the end of self-regulation and the sidelining of practitioner input

The introduction of the FSMA and the creation of the Financial Services Authority confined practitioner input to the regulatory process to membership of the Regulatory Decisions Committee and to Advisory Panels. In doing so it eliminated a significant component of the regulatory dialogue that had characterized the preceding SIB/SRO framework. This has contributed to the decline of principles-based regulation under the FSA, with a significant loss of regulatory efficiency, necessitating the campaign to re-assert the principles-based approach.

In what follows, the SRO that regulated securities and futures markets, the Securities and Futures Authority, will be used as a means of comparison with the procedures of the FSA.

The SFA Board was largely made up of practitioners, with a minority of 'independent' members, typically nominated by financial organizations such as the London International Financial Futures and Options Exchange (LIFFE). The Board members sat on a number of committees with clear functional roles such as Authorization, Conduct of Business, Enforcement and Capital (devoted to policy development). The task of the committees was to guide and work with the staff of the SFA.

It is important to note that the characterization of the SFA as a 'self-regulatory' organization is a significant misnomer. The Financial Services Act of 1986, and the subsequent development of principles, rules and procedures by SIB and by the SROs,[2] meant that the SFA operated as a quasi-statutory body, in a manner totally different from the self-regulatory environment pre-1986. On the evidence of the 1986–2001 experience, it is quite wrong to identify self-regulation with practitioner leadership of the regulatory body. Practitioner leadership can operate perfectly well within a statutory framework.

Moreover, examination of the decisions and procedures of the SFA makes it clear that far from 'looking after their own', the practitioners were typically tougher than the SFA staff. Practitioners who were given responsibility for regulatory decisions 'went native' as regulators. Their commitment was to 'the industry', and they identified an effective regulatory framework with maintenance of standards of integrity and fair market dealing that would be to the ultimate benefit of the industry as a whole.

The practitioners also brought a high level of expertise to guiding the work of the staff of the SFA. These were people who worked in the markets on a daily basis, and were at the leading edge of their various disciplines. Their understanding of the financial markets, and their interpretation of the actions of market participants were of the highest order.

The practitioners who were a significant element in the operational performance of the SFA constituted a powerful link between the regulator and the regulated community. While remaining part of the regulated community, they were also guardians of the 'club's' principles and reputation. Their presence provided the dialogue that is an indispensable component of principles-based regulation. The elimination of direct practitioner involvement in regulatory decision-making, dictated by the terms of the FSMA, altered fundamentally the balance between principles in rules, in favour of rules.

The change brought about by the FSMA, and by the manner in which the Act was put into practice by the FSA, is clear in the very different enforcement procedures in the SFA as compared with the FSA.

The Enforcement Committee of the SFA, comprising a majority of practitioner members, met every two weeks, and as well as reviewing disciplinary cases in progress, processed an average of around three or four cases – so about eight cases a month.

The Regulatory Decisions Committee of the FSA (RDC) and the Enforcement Committee of the SFA differed in composition and role. Practitioners were in a minority on the RDC, the independent members being nominated by the Board of the FSA, but many of them, while being prominent in their own fields, had limited expertise in matters relating to financial markets. The task of the RDC was to act as an independent 'filter' for decision notices proposed by the professional staff of the Enforcement Division of the FSA. In effect, the Enforcement Division had to persuade the RDC of its analysis and of the case for action to be taken.

A number of factors distinguished the operation of the RDC from that of the SFA's Enforcement Committee. First, cases brought to the RDC were often accompanied by a huge amount of paperwork embodying a 'kitchen sink' approach to alleged offences, and yet were very poorly prepared. The volume of paperwork was several times greater than had been typical of SFA cases. The RDC could advise on amendment, or reject a proposed case, but could not take an active role in formulating the case, as the Enforcement Committee of the SFA had done. The RDC was therefore placed in the rather difficult position of either attempting to advise the enforcement staff to alter the manner of their presentation, or using the nuclear option of rejecting the representation outright. The RDC had no role in the content and structure of the investigation that informed the decision issued in its name. In other words, the expertise of the members of the RDC was not brought to bear on whether or how an investigation might be performed. Despite the ability of the RDC to use independent legal advice (at least post-2005), it was still the case that in reality its main information source was the Enforcement Division of the FSA, over which it had no authority and within which it had no role.

Second, almost as soon as the FSA took full responsibility for the enforcement process in December 2001, the number of cases coming from the Enforcement Division dried up. The fall in the number of cases as compared to the SFA may suggest greater selectivity (or an extraordinary increase in honest compliance within the financial services industries). But the criterion for selection is not clear, and is certainly not exposed to RDC (or practitioner) scrutiny. In this respect, the RDC does only part of the job – acting as a filter for those who will be the subject of contested enforcement actions, but having nothing to do with those cases that are dropped. Moreover, it is worth noting that, given that the FSA argues that selection of cases to pursue is 'risk-based', it is just at the point at which risk is assessed that practitioner experience would be most valuable.

Third, there has been an ill-concealed resentment among the staff towards the RDC. Given that it was the task of the enforcement staff to convince the RDC that it was worthwhile proceeding with a case, it was understandably galling to have a case referred back, often with quite stinging criticism, after all the hard work that had gone into its preparation. The recent reforms of RDC procedures, notably those introduced after the Legal & General case, have served to further limit the role of the RDC, in particular removing it from those cases in which a settlement is negotiated. This further reduces the scope of any practitioner impact in the enforcement process and strengthens the position of the staff *vis-à-vis* the RDC.

Industry guidance: restoring the dialogue and role of the practitioner?

The overall outcome is that the loss of practitioner expertise in the enforcement process has been a major loss, significantly degrading the quality of enforcement work and severely eroding the declared commitment to principles-based regulation. It is therefore no accident that the campaign to restore principles-based regulation has led to an attempt to restore the strong link between regulator and regulated. Since this is not possible under the FSA's interpretation of the FSMA, the FSA has turned to 'trade associations, professional bodies and other representative organizations … to develop Industry Guidance' (FSA, 2006b, p. 13).

Industry Guidance may receive 'FSA confirmation', and hence be deemed to have legal significance:

> There are three conceptual ways that we can recognise guidance, codes or standards developed by the industry. These different forms of recognition have different legal effects and the requirement to follow statutory processes varies. We describe these methods as:
>
> - safe harbour;
> - sturdy breakwater; and
> - implicit recognition.
>
> **Safe harbour**: has an effect on the FSA and potentially third parties. We would need to create rules in the Handbook to give Industry

Guidance this effect and follow full statutory processes, as a result this level of recognition would be more formal, and hence stronger, than a sturdy breakwater.

Sturdy breakwater: has an effect on the FSA but not on anyone else. It has the practical effect of preventing us from taking action but does not affect the rights of third parties (including firms and consumers). Our formal Handbook guidance has this effect, but so, in practice, does less formal recognition of Industry Guidance. To create a sturdy breakwater we do need to take action of some sort (e.g. make a public statement) and therefore this form of recognition is explicit.

There are some key differences between FSA guidance and Industry Guidance. Firstly, when giving formal guidance we are required to follow statutory processes, including conducting cost benefit analysis and consultation. Secondly, although FSA guidance does not bind the courts, in practice they are likely to give it significant weight. Thirdly, the Financial Ombudsman Service (FOS) is required to consider FSA guidance when deciding what is fair and reasonable, there is no such explicit requirement to consider Industry Guidance.

Implicit recognition: this has no legal effect on the FSA or anyone else. An example of this type of recognition is the provisions of the Banking Code that cover matters about which we have made no rules. Equally, we have made no rules, guidance or other statement recognising those provisions. The recognition is implicit in our inaction, because the industry has found a solution to address a market failure, rather than in actions giving explicit recognition. Implicit recognition is not subject to any statutory process.

(FSA, 2006b, pp. 7,8).

The nautical metaphors cannot hide the FSA's dilemma. There is a clear recognition that practitioner involvement is required to sustain the dialogue necessary for the effective operation of principles-based regulation, but under the statutes governing the activities of the FSA it cannot delegate the task of defining legal rights and responsibilities.

It is also relevant to ask whether trade associations are appropriate bodies to develop industry guidance. There has been insufficient time to evaluate the result of the first attempts to do so (such as LIBA's response to the FSA's desire to unbundle commissions charged as part of trade execution in institutional fund management). But the role of a trade association is inevitably different from that of practitioners charged with ultimate regulatory responsibility. Industry Guidance is a welcome halfway house, but is only a halfway house none the less.

Similarly, the FSA recognizes that principles-based regulation requires a different quality of contact between its staff and regulated firms than was the case previously (FSA, 2007, p. 12). In the case of large firms this will require 'recruiting, developing and training our staff'. In the case of small firms 'over the next few years there will be a significant change in how firms experience our interaction with them'. Again, there is the recognition of the crucial role that dialogue plays in principles-based regulation, but whether the FSA's steps achieve the necessary two-way communication remains to be seen.

Principles-based regulation of systemic risk

The regulation of systemic risk is one of the four statutory objectives the FSMA imposes on the FSA. In a speech delivered in May 2007, Ben Bernanke, chairman of the Federal Reserve Board, argued in favour of principles-based regulation:

> central banks and regulators should resist the temptation to devise ad hoc rules for each new type of financial instrument or institution. Rather, we should strive to develop common, principles-based policy responses that can be applied consistently across the financial sector to meet clearly defined objectives ... As in the United Kingdom, the principles-based, risk-focused approach to regulation has had considerable influence on this side of the Atlantic. (Bernanke, 2007)

However, it is notable that while Bernanke's speech in support of principles-based regulation focused primarily on systemic issues, the FSA's endorsement of a principles-based regime is expressed primarily through its relevance to other objectives, namely public awareness, the protection of consumers and the reduction of financial crime. Bernanke refers to three public policy objectives – financial stability, investor protection and market integrity – and cites three challenges that financial innovation poses to the attainment of these objectives – complexity, illiquidity and leverage. In contrast, of the FSA's nine 'Strategic Aims' that are to measure success in principles-based regulation, only one refers to market resilience (FSA, 2007, p. 15).

The source of the difference in emphasis is not hard to find: the regulator should have a central role in the management of systemic risk, but in the formation of the FSA this role is shared between the FSA, the Bank of England and the Treasury, under the terms of the Tripartite Memorandum of Understanding.

Financial regulation and systemic risk

The liberalization of financial markets that began in the early 1970s has transformed the financial services industry and the role of the regulator. In particular, the regulator now plays a much greater role than was previously the case in the maintenance of financial stability. A primary risk on which 'risk-based' regulation is focused is that to orderly markets – systemic risk.

Financial risk-taking is a concern of public policy because associated with the risk-taking actions of individuals there are externalities; that is, costs and benefits accruing to the society that are *external* to the calculations of the individual investor, and not accounted for in the market place.[3] A major financial failure imposes costs on society going far beyond the losses suffered by the investors. In an economy where there are important externalities, competitive markets will be socially inefficient. The task of public policy, in this case of financial regulation, is to attempt to mitigate these inefficiencies.

Financial externalities are particularly potent because they are transmitted *macroeconomically*, via interest rates, or the exchange rate, or the general level of stock prices. Financial markets are markets for stocks of current and future assets, their value today being dependent on the expectation of their future value. To the extent that expectations are shared, any factor that leads to a general shift in expected future values will have an immediate impact on financial markets, and on the major macro-financial variables, such as the interest rate and the exchange rate.

So the failure of a single firm can have an influence not only on its immediate counterparties, or even just on firms dealing in similar products, but also, through its impact on expectations, on financial markets as a whole, and then, via the interest rate or the exchange rate, the contagion may spread to the real economy both at home and abroad.

The classic example of a systemic risk is a bank run. A depositor at a particular bank would be willing to leave funds on deposit, but believes that other depositors are likely to withdraw their funds, forcing the bank to call in loans or sell securities and suffer losses, perhaps even suspending payments. Consequently, a rational investor will seek to be the first to withdraw funds, and hence all withdraw their funds as rapidly as possible, resulting in a 'run'. A run on one particular bank necessarily effects the perception of the liquidity of other banks and the run spreads to other, nominally solvent, banks.

More formally, while a depositor may be certain about the probability of suffering a liquidity shock, the depositor cannot be certain about the probability that his or her shock will occur early or late relative to others. In other words, the depositor cannot be sure where they will be in the queue to withdraw funds. Depositors therefore treat their uncertainty as 'Knightian', pursuing a max-min strategy over the set of presumed probabilities (Caballero and Krishnamurthy, 2006, p. 8). The result is the rush to withdraw funds.

However, not only has the bank run become a very rare event – whether because of the profitability of banks, the insistence of the regulators on strong balance sheets, or the perceived willingness of the public authorities to provide liquidity when necessary, but the structure of financial markets has also changed, shifting from a bank-based to a market-based financial system (Hendricks *et al.*, 2006). Financial intermediation has moved from institutions (banks) into markets, and financial crises are now manifest in markets in general rather than in the banking system in particular. A crisis may be triggered, for example, by a sharp decline in the price of one asset that sparks a widespread sell-off in the general rush for liquidity. In analytical terms, the individual agent knows the probability of a shock, but does not know the probability of being able to trade with the market counterparties on whom his or her liquidity depends. Not knowing, and being averse to uncertainty, the agent (alongside all other agents) pursues a max-min strategy over the set of possible priors, resulting in a collective bias toward liquidity (Caballero and Krishnamurthy, 2006, p. 15). The collective rush for liquidity produces the 'market gridlock' characteristic of market-based systemic crises. Liquidity dries up as traders all attempt to move in the same direction.[4]

In response to the changing nature of financial institutions and financial markets, the role of the regulator has also changed. In the traditional 'bank-run' model of systemic risk, the role of the regulator is to ensure that the bank pursues prudent policies, especially given the moral hazard created by the role of the central bank as lender of last resort. In the financial markets of today, the role of the regulator becomes as much involved with risks inherent in market structures and counter-party relationships as in the prudential activities of individual firms. The key player in the regulation of systemic risk is the financial services regulator, not the central bank (unless, of course, it is the central bank that is playing the role of regulator).

The FSA and systemic risk

The role of the FSA in the maintenance of financial stability is not only embodied within its major FSMA objective of securing 'market confidence', but also in the role assigned to the FSA in the Tripartite Memorandum of Understanding between the FSA, the Bank of England and the Treasury, specifying the responsibilities of those institutions in the field of market stability (Bank of England, 2006). The MOU defines the role of the Bank of England, *inter alia*, as:

> ii. overseeing financial system infrastructure systemically significant to the UK, in particular payments systems whether based in the UK or abroad ... The Bank is also closely involved in developing and improving the infrastructure and strengthening the system to help reduce systemic risk;
> iii. maintaining a broad overview of the system as a whole.

The role of the FSA is defined, *inter alia*, as:

> i. the authorization and prudential supervision of banks, building societies, investment firms, insurance companies and brokers, credit unions and friendly societies;
> ii. the supervision of financial markets, securities listings and of clearing and settlement systems;
> ...
> iv. regulatory policy in these areas, including that intended to promote the resilience to operational disruption of authorised firms and Recognised Bodies. The FSA advises on the regulatory implications for authorised firms and Recognised Bodies of developments in domestic and international markets

It should be obvious that there is considerable ambiguity in the assignment of these roles. This ambiguity was to be disastrously exposed by the events surrounding the failure of Northern Rock in the autumn of 2007.

While the Bank of England is supposedly responsible for 'overseeing financial infrastructure systemically significant to the UK', it is the FSA that actually has to do things. It is the FSA that must design and manage the regulations that define the market infrastructure, and ensure how resilient it might be.

Principles-based regulation and systemic risk

That individual firms are financially sound and well managed is a major contribution to the containment of systemic risk. But, by definition, systemic risks are externalities and it is simply not possible for firms to translate principles into practical measures of prudential regulation without significant guidance that they respect and value. It might therefore be expected that there would be within the FSA a significant research capacity devoted to the problem of the interrelationship between the market structure (domestic and international), product innovation and financial stability. In fact, the research capacity charged with that task works under the supervision of the Financial Stability Board of the Bank of England. It is the Bank of England that publishes the half-yearly *Financial Stability Report,* the April 2007 issue of which covered such topics as 'sensitivity of Value-at-Risk to measures of stress', 'Hedge Funds and financial stability' and 'could problems in the US sub-prime mortgage markets be replicated elsewhere?' all of which are the operational responsibility of the FSA.[5] It is highly detrimental to effective regulation in the UK that the FSA is (properly) responsible for the operational design of stability-enhancing regulation and yet does not conduct high-level research into the origins of systemic risk. This is an historical anomaly that fails to take proper account of the impact of market changes on the relative roles of the regulator and the central bank.

Bernanke's example of the need for a principles-based approach is of the development of collateralized debt obligations (CDOs). He suggests that the growing use of such complex financial instruments challenges the regulator's objectives of protecting investors and maintaining market integrity. To meet that challenge, he recommends a principles-based, risk-focused approach, with the regulator and the industry working together to develop best practice in monitoring and managing risks (Bernanke, 2007, pp. 4–5). This, in a modest way, was the task of the practitioners on the SFA's Capital Committee. It is a task that is split uncomfortably between the FSA and the Bank of England in a manner that seriously diminishes the possibility, let alone the effectiveness, of principles-based regulation in this crucial area.

Summing up

A persistent theme in the lessons drawn is the decline in necessary dialogue and understanding between regulator and regulated, and the lack of analysis of systemic risk in the day-to-day operations of the FSA.

The goals of risk-based, principles-based regulation are excellent objectives, likely both to provide exactly the regulatory framework required to improve the stability of UK financial markets, and to enhance their competitiveness. However, these tasks have been made significantly more difficult than they otherwise might have been by the failure to take full advantage of the wealth of practitioner expertise, and to face up to the changing role of central bank and regulator in today's markets. The following propositions are designed to (at least in part) address these issues.

The role of practitioners within the FSA requires fundamental reassessment. As argued above, the limitation of the role of practitioners has denied the FSA access to an important pool of expertise – expertise that could be made available relatively cheaply – and has diminished the strength of the dialogue and of mutual understanding that characterized early regulatory regimes. However, if there is to be more practitioner input into the FSA, that will only prove effective if the practitioners have real decision-making powers; that is, they are not simply corralled into an 'advisory committee' of some sort. It is when practitioners are given real decision-making powers that they 'go native' and become truly effective regulators.

There are two obvious areas in which practitioner input could prove extremely valuable. First, in the central policy function sketched above. Practitioners should be given a direct role in the development of policy – policy that, when launched, they must be able to defend to their colleagues as being in the best interests of the market. And second, there is an urgent need for greater practitioner input into the enforcement process. The shrinking role of the RDC has reduced practitioner input to contested cases. Practitioners have no role in enforcement policy or in settlement. In both areas, full practitioner involvement would greatly improve the quality and effectiveness of the enforcement function.

A financial stability research function (analysing systemic risk) should become an integral part of a central research department of the FSA. The research function within the FSA tends to be spread among various divisions of the organization. A single regulator, such as the FSA, requires a central policy research function. The existence of such a research centre would greatly increase the FSA's intellectual standing, particularly in its negotiations with firms over new regulatory initiatives. It would also lend coherence to the regulation of systemic risk.

In fast-changing markets, the efficient conduct of the dialogue between regulator and regulated is vital if principles-based regulation is to work. This is not intended to be critical of the large number of highly qualified and skilled people working at the FSA. It is, rather, a structural criticism of the way in which the organization of financial regulation in the UK has developed since 2003. The debate over principles versus rules is taking place today precisely because of these structural deficiencies. The general conclusion is that dialogue and mutual understanding play a central role in the operation of a principles-based regulatory system, both in day-to-day regulation and in the management of systemic risk.

Notes

1. The debate in the UK on principles- versus rules-based accounting standards has been a subject of sustained research by the Institute of Chartered Accountants of Scotland (2006a; 2006b).
2. While a significant proportion of policy development came from SIB, it was not the only source of innovation. The Capital Committee of the SFA played an important role in the adoption of new techniques of risk analysis, particularly with regard to capital adequacy requirements.
3. There are a number of other important market failures in the financial sector that attract the concerns of public policy, most notably the asymmetry of information between individual savers and market professionals that is the motivation of consumer protection.
4. The crisis at Northern Rock in 2007 was an example of market gridlock, not of a bank run. The bank run was not a *cause* of Northern Rock's difficulties, but a *result* of the crisis and of the preliminary response of the authorities.
5. The October 2007 issue was devoted entirely to 'Shocks to the UK Financial System' as related to 'The Structure of the UK Financial System'.

References

Balls, E. (2007) Speech at the FSA Principles-based Regulation Conference, 25 April 2007; www.hm-treasury.gov.uk/newsroon_and_speeches/2007/press.

Bank of England (1995) *Report of the Board of Banking Supervision Inquiry into the Circumstances of the Collapse of Barings*, London: HMSO.

Bank of England (2006) *Memorandum of Understanding between HM Treasury, the Bank of England and the Financial Services Authority*; http://www.bankofengland.co.uk/financialstability/mou.pdf.

Bernanke, B. S. (2007) 'Regulation and Financial Innovation', remarks to the Federal Reserve Bank of Atlanta's 2007 Financial Markets Conference; www.federalreserve.gov/boarddoc/spereches/2007.

Caballero, R. J. and A. Krishnamurthy (2006) 'Flight to Quality and Collective Risk Management', NBER Working Paper 12136, March.

Eatwell, J. and L. Taylor (2000) *Global Finance at Risk*, New York: New Press.

Financial Services Authority (2005) *Better Regulation Action Plan*, London: FSA, December.

Financial Services Authority (2006a) *Reforming Conduct of Business Regulation*, London: FSA, 31 October.
Financial Services Authority (2006b) *FSA Confirmation of Industry Guidance*, DP 06/5, London: FSA, November.
Financial Services Authority (2007) *Principles-based Regulation: Focusing on the Outcomes that Matter*, London: FSA, April.
Hendricks, D., J. Kambhu and P. Mosser (2006) *Systemic Risk and the Financial System*, New York: Federal Reserve Bank of New York.
HMSO (1986) *The Financial Services Act, 1986*, London: The Stationery Office.
HMSO (2000) *Financial Services and Markets Act, 2000*, London: The Stationery Office.
Institute of Chartered Accountants of Scotland (2006a) *Principles-Based or Rules-Base Accounting Standards: A Question of Judgement*, Edinburgh: Institute of Chartered Accountants of Scotland.
Institute of Chartered Accountants of Scotland (2006b) *Principles not Rules: A Question of Judgement*: Edinburgh: Institute of Chartered Accountants of Scotland.
McCarthy, C. (2006) 'Principles-based Regulation – What Does It Mean for the Industry?', Speech to the Financial Services Skills Council 2nd Annual Conference, 31 October 2006; www.fsa.gov.uk/pages/Library/Communication/speeches.
McCarthy, C. (2007) 'Financial Regulation: Myth and Reality', Speech to the British American Business London Insight Series and Financial Services Forum, 13 February;www.fsa.gov.uk/pages/Library/Communication/speeches.
Sayers, R. S. (1964) *Modern Banking*, 6th edn, Oxford: Clarendon Press.

3

Finance and Growth in Developing Countries: Sound Principles and Unreliable Evidence

Valpy FitzGerald[1]

Introduction[2]

Financial development and economic growth are clearly closely related, and this relationship has occupied the minds of seminal economists from Adam Smith to Joseph Schumpeter, although the channels and even the direction of causality have remained unresolved in both theory and empirics. Long-term sustainable economic growth depends on the ability to raise the rates of accumulation of physical and human capital, to use the resulting productive assets more efficiently, and to ensure the access of the whole population to these assets. Financial intermediation supports this investment process by mobilizing household and foreign savings for investment by firms; ensuring that these funds are allocated to the most productive use; and spreading risk and providing liquidity so that firms can operate the new capacity efficiently.

Unsurprisingly, this 'structural' approach to finance, rooted in the classical and Keynesian tradition, is that of Ajit Singh's critical work on the role of stock markets in developing countries, a logical extension of his better-known work on developed country markets (Singh and Weisse, 1998). Dominant economic reform strategies are designed for developing countries without due consideration of their financial systems, or indeed of those of the developed countries (which are the explicit benchmark) for that matter. Alternative financial development strategies are probably superior, but do not enjoy the benefit of orthodoxy (Singh, 2003).

Financial development involves the establishment and expansion of institutions, instruments and markets that support this investment and growth process. Historically, the role of banks and non-bank financial intermediaries, ranging from pension funds to stock markets, has been to translate household savings into enterprise investment, to monitor investments and allocate funds, and to price and spread risk. Financial

Table 3.1 Financial development by income group, 1990s (asset capitalization as percentage of GDP)

	Banks	NBFIs	Stock markets	Total
High-income countries	81	41	33	155
Upper middle-income countries	40	21	11	72
Lower middle-income countries	34	12	12	58
Low-income countries	23	5	4	32

Source: World Bank (2001).

intermediation thus has strong externalities in this context, which are generally positive (such as information and liquidity provision), but can also be negative – particularly the systemic financial crises that are endemic to market systems, as Ajit has recently pointed out so clearly (2007). Moreover, the wide range of organizational forms involved precluded any clear conclusion as to what kind of financial institutions might maximize economic growth.

None the less, as this chapter shows, recent attempts by the 'new institutional economists' to identify 'advanced' (that is, US) financial structures as a key source of economic progress seem to have created a new epistemic paradigm, strengthened by apparent support from empirical cross-country studies of the relationship between indicators of financial development and observed rates of growth.The core argument is summarized neatly by Table 3.1, from which two key conclusions are commonly drawn. First, that greater financial *depth* (that is, higher ratios of total financial assets to national income or output) is related to higher levels of productivity, and thus income per capita. Second, that higher incomes are also associated with a more advanced financial *structure*; that is, the move from banks towards non-bank financial intermediaries, and from both of these towards stock markets. The causality is assumed to run from financial development to economic growth, so that financial sector reforms – which lead to greater depth and improved structure – are held to stimulate faster growth.

The dismantling of the traditional development finance model (based on bank-based systems, directed credit, public development banks, closed capital accounts, capped interest rates, and active monetary intervention) that had been established in developing countries in the decades after the Second World War has become a core element of the economic reform and structural adjustment process led by the international financial institutions. The new standard model of financial architecture is held to reflect the imperatives of 'financial development', as revealed by the success of financial liberalization in the advanced economies that moved away from national bank-based systems towards open capital markets. These reforms are expected to raise savings and investment levels, increase the rate of growth, and reduce macroeconomic instability. However, it is far from clear that these objectives have been achieved. Most obviously, the series of financial crises that have erupted since the mid-1990s calls into question the appropriateness of financial liberalization and openings for fragile economies at early stages of industrialization; but also the decline of funding for large firms in productive sectors, and SMEs in general, is a major problem and is probably even more significant for sustainable growth and poverty reduction in the long run (Singh, 2001).

This chapter has the following structure. The next section examines the relationship between financial development and economic growth, which underpins the 'new standard model' of financial reform in developing countries. The growing empirical evidence suggests that this relationship is not so close or as unidirectional as is usually supposed, and does not provide a sound evidential basis for the prescriptions of the new standard model. I then turn to two central issues in more detail: the effect of financial reform on savings and corporate funding on the one hand; and the consequences for macroeconomic stability and investment on the other. The final section concludes with the implications of the analysis presented in this chapter for both policy design in developing countries and for our understanding of how economic ideas are spread and embedded.

Theory versus evidence on financial development and economic growth

The extremely influential study by King and Levine (1993a), and subsequent work by Levine and Zervos (1998), Levine (2000) and Levine *et al.* (2000), have all appeared to provide sound empirical evidence in support of the new standard model.[3] Levine (2000) further shows that the impact of financial development on growth acts mainly through total factor productivity rather than through capital accumulation or savings rates. Beck *et al.* (2004) even claim to show that financial development reduces income inequality and absolute poverty levels. A universal elixir.

In their canonical paper, King and Levine (1993a) regress growth in 1960–89 for seventy-seven OECD and developing countries as a

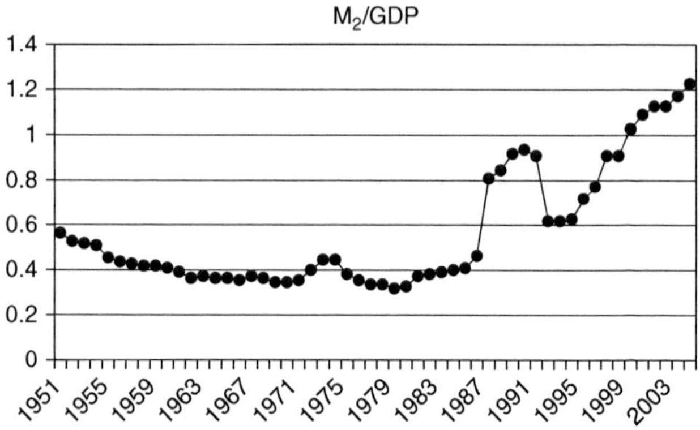

Figure 3.1 King and Levine measure of financial depth, long-run, UK
Source: IMF, *International Financial Statistics* (various years).

cross-section on *previous* financial depth (M_2/Y in 1960) in order to avoid endogeneity of the contemporary M_2/Y variable. However, the statistical significance of their financial depth variable is eliminated almost entirely by highly significant regional dummies.[4] Moreover, when contemporary correlation between financial depth and growth is accounted for, the predictive power of the model fails completely (Arestis and Demetriades, 1997). This is not just a technical econometric issue. In fact, the widely used M_2/Y is not a particularly reliable indicator of financial depth at all. It varies enormously over time as well as across countries, and responds to changing monetary policy stances and asset bubbles. Figure 3.1 applies the King and Levine (1993a) measure of financial depth to the UK over the long run. While the increase in the measure during the 1980s does clearly reflect the major financial liberalization and modernization of that decade, did the UK really become *less* financially developed between 1950 and 1980, or during the early 1990s?

This problem is brought out even more starkly by the case of Mexico, where the M_2/Y measure in fact shows relatively little variance over the long run despite major changes in Mexico's financial system, while the short-run shifts are clearly related to shifts in monetary stance related to fiscal or external shocks. As in the case of the UK, therefore, cross-section studies including Mexico are liable to be misleading, as the specific choice of base year will clearly affect the results substantially. Indeed, if we take this measure literally, Mexico had the same financial depth (a key measure of financial development, as we have seen) as the UK in the mid-1970s!

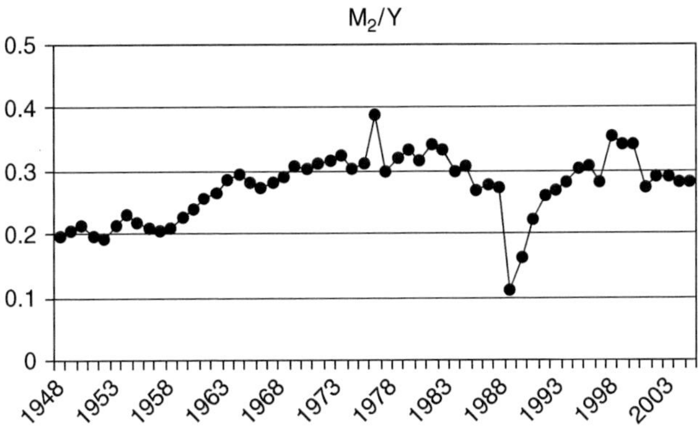

Figure 3.2 King and Levine measure of financial depth, long-run, Mexico
Source: IMF, *International Financial Statistics* (various years).

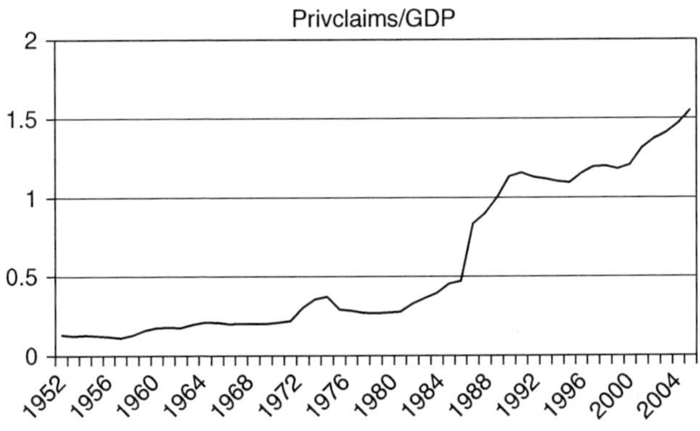

Figure 3.3 Claims on the private sector, UK
Source: IMF, *International Financial Statistics* (various years).

A broader measure of financial assets than the M_2 used in these cross-section studies should yield more reassuring results. Figure 3.3 shows the evolution of *total* financial claims on the private sector (as a proportion of GDP) for the UK since 1952. The trend is certainly more stable, and the major step-change in the 1980s is more evident, yet there are also shorter-term movements which clearly reflect asset bubbles and shifting monetary policy stances.

However, in the case of Mexico, this broader measure still exhibits considerable instability over the long run, as Figure 3.4 shows. The increase

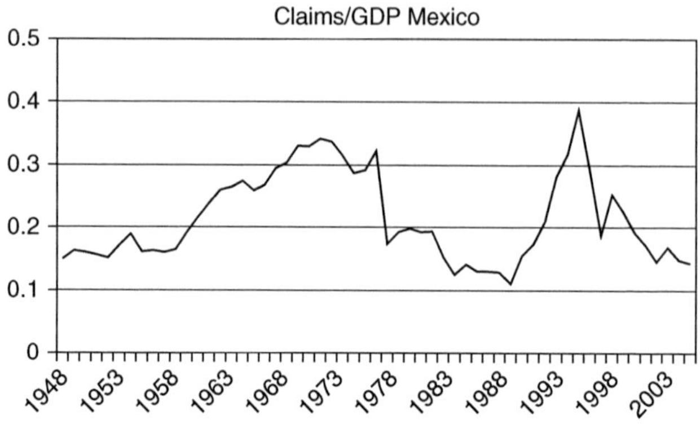

Figure 3.4 Claims on the private sector, Mexico
Source: IMF *International Financial Statistics* (various years).

of the early 1990s has been claimed as evidence of the positive effects of financial liberalization; but by the same token the second half of that decade reflects the collapse of the asset bubble and thus the decade as a whole corresponds to a cycle of external capital flows, not financial development at all. Taking the whole five decades, by this measure there has been no financial deepening at all!

It is important note that the different indicators of financial development that have a significant impact on growth reflect different characteristics of financial development. Bank credit to the private sector (as a proportion of GDP) ratio shown in Figure 3.4 is a better measure of the level of financial intermediation than the M_2/Y measure discussed above, but still has significant shortcomings that are revealed by time series but obscured by cross-section studies. Further, Levine and Zervos (1998) and the other cognate studies mentioned above do not find any explanatory power in the ratio of stock market capitalization to GDP, or in the size of stock markets relative to that of banks. Moreover, firm-level evidence shows that there are complementarities between banks and markets in developing countries (Demirgüç-Kunt and Maksimovic, 1996). An indicator of financial development that unfortunately has not been used in cross-country studies, probably because of lack of data availability in easily available multicountry databases (though readily available from central banks) is the duration of bank loans and fixed-income securities, which would best correspond to the provision of investment finance.

Part of the problem may be that these studies pool developed and developing countries; although the impact of financial development will

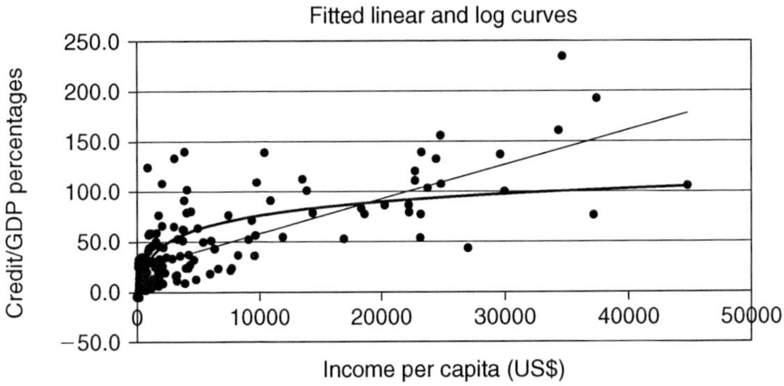

Figure 3.5 Private credit/GDP and GDP per capita, 2000
Source: World Bank, *World Development Indicators* (2005).

differ depending on the stage of economic development of a country. The level of financial intermediation may be most important for economic growth at initial stages of development, while for richer countries, its efficiency and composition may be more relevant. The original study by King and Levine (1993a) and later ones by Andrés *et al.* (1999) and Leahy *et al.* (2001), are consistent with this view: they were unable to find significant links between bank credit to GDP ratios and subsequent economic growth rates in OECD countries; even though they do find a statistically significant relationship for developing countries. The reason for this result is evident from Figure 3.5: not only is there an enormous dispersion around the fitted linear trend, but also the logged relationship shows much less variation above a per capita income level of US$10,000.

When we turn to the *structure* of finance, large differences are evident in Table 3.2. Both within the OECD and between developing regions, the level of financial market capitalization obviously differs widely, but these differences are not clearly related to either economic development or efficiency.

In fact, corporate investment finance patterns differ as a result of the evolution of ownership and regulation: they cannot be seen as a steady 'progression' towards a single US/UK model (Mayer, 1990). Banks remain the key element in the system, especially when we take into account the fact that they own most of the non-bank financial intermediaries. Pension and insurance funds emerge as major players in securitization very late in economic development. Further, a specific financial function can be carried out by different institutional forms any one country or region, which means that relative weight of statistical categories may vary widely

Table 3.2 Financial depth worldwide, 2003

		Debt Sec				
Shares of GDP	**Stk Mkt**	**Pub**	**Priv**	**Tot**	**Bank ass**	**Tot Cap**
World	0.86	0.56	0.88	1.44	1.12	3.42
EMU*	0.60	0.67	0.97	1.64	1.60	3.84
US	1.30	0.46	1.46	1.91	0.52	3.73
Japan	1.14	1.43	0.53	1.96	1.45	4.54
UK	1.37	0.29	1.05	1.34	2.22	4.93
* of which						
Germany	0.45	0.48	1.20	1.68	1.20	3.33
France	0.71	0.60	0.88	1.47	1.99	4.17
Spain	0.86	0.53	0.74	1.27	1.09	3.22
Portugal	0.42	0.72	0.81	1.53	1.18	3.14
Greece	0.60	1.29	0.12	1.41	1.02	3.03
Emerging Markets	0.47	0.23	0.15	0.37	0.78	1.63
Latin America	0.76	0.21	0.24	0.45	1.12	2.33
Asia	0.35	0.37	0.12	0.49	0.45	1.29
Middle East	0.12	0.01	0.02	0.03	0.85	1.00
Africa	0.30	0.13	0.05	0.18	0.60	1.08
Europe	0.09	0.27	0.03	0.30	0.27	0.67

Source: IMF *Financial Stability Report* (2005).

while the real difference in terms of financial provision is small. A good example of this diversity is the institutional form of housing finance (mortgage provision): in the US this is provided by securitization under government guarantee; in the UK by building society and bank loans; in Germany by insurance companies; in Spain by savings and loans associations (*cajas de ahorro*); and in Mexico by construction companies.

In consequence, financial structures are in fact very different across the world, as Table 3.3 demonstrates. It is not possible to claim that there is a unique relationship between a particular financial structure and either levels of income per capita. Indeed even though this table shows that banks remain central to the financial intermediation process in all countries other than the US – it obscures the fact that even in the US most of the non-bank financial intermediaries form part of bank holding groups.

Financial liberalization, savings and corporate funding

The proponents of financial liberalization as leading to financial development in developing countries have emphasized two main channels

Table 3.3 Financial structure worldwide

As shares of total assets	Stk Mkt	Debt Sec Pub	Debt Sec Priv	Debt Sec Tot	Bank ass	Tot Cap IV
World	0.25	0.16	0.26	0.42	0.33	1.00
EMU*	0.16	0.17	0.25	0.43	0.42	1.00
US	0.35	0.12	0.39	0.51	0.14	1.00
Japan	0.25	0.31	0.12	0.43	0.32	1.00
UK	0.28	0.06	0.21	0.27	0.45	1.00
* of which						
Germany	0.13	0.15	0.36	0.50	0.36	1.00
France	0.17	0.14	0.21	0.35	0.48	1.00
Spain	0.27	0.16	0.23	0.39	0.34	1.00
Portugal	0.13	0.23	0.26	0.49	0.38	1.00
Greece	0.20	0.43	0.04	0.47	0.34	1.00
Emerging Markets	0.29	0.14	0.09	0.23	0.48	1.00
Latin America	0.33	0.09	0.10	0.19	0.48	1.00
Asia	0.27	0.28	0.10	0.38	0.35	1.00
Middle East	0.12	0.01	0.02	0.03	0.85	1.00
Africa	0.28	0.12	0.04	0.16	0.56	1.00
Europe	0.14	0.40	0.04	0.45	0.41	1.00

Source: IMF Financial Stability Report (2005).

through which private investment is expected to rise. The first channel is through an increase in the availability of credit that would follow the removal of the interest rate ceiling as a result of increased private saving; and the second is through the enhanced screening of investment projects because of the higher cost of capital, thereby increasing the marginal productivity of investment (McKinnon, 1973). Second, ending financial repression would improve bank efficiency by ensuring positive real interest rates, eliminating excessive reserve requirements and removing mandated credit allocations (McKinnon, 1989). Extensions of the basic hypothesis focused on investment levels (Kapur, 1976; Mathieson, 1980) and quality (Galbis, 1977; Fry, 1988) as lending shifts from informal 'curb' markets into the banking system.

Early critics of this model, such as van Wijnbergen (1983) or Taylor (1983), are sceptical that increased financial intermediation will result from liberalization, because curb markets are not subject to the reserve requirement that apply to banks. Hence, if substitution takes place between bank time-deposits and curb markets, the total supply of funds available to the business sector will decline. Moreover, if banks then lend to the public sector (for example, by investing in Treasury bills), the diversion of funds away from the curb market will result in a net decline in the availability of private-sector credit. Because of limited access by small and medium-sized firms to bank credit, a shift of funds from the curb market to the banking system reduces the availability of credit for these types of firms unless liberalization of the banking system reduces bias against small borrowers.

Moreover, in most developing countries where both market and non-market imperfections exist within a broader liberalized macroeconomic framework, there are a host of factors other than the volume and cost of credit that influence firms' investment decisions. For example, evidence from four African countries (Uganda, Kenya, Malawi and Lesotho) does not support the hypothesis that an increase in financial depth increases the volume of savings or access to credit of the commercial banks in rural areas, apart from among those who already have collateral (Mosley, 1999). Conventional financial institutions are biased against small borrowers because of the high unit costs of loan administration and lack of effective collateral, which translate into low returns and high risk. This is a major problem for all developing countries as small firms account for the bulk of production and the great majority of employment. This 'gap' has traditionally been addressed by public-sector development banks and extension schemes; but these have generally been dismantled as part of financial reforms, and not replaced effectively by micro-credit schemes, which are systemically limited in their coverage and scope.

There is a general agreement that financial liberalization has led to greater allocative efficiency if this is defined as the commercial profitability of banks, but the predicted boost in saving as predicted by McKinnon and Shaw has not been observed (Williamson and Mahar, 1998). Studies by the World Bank (1989), Ghani (1992), King and Levine (1993b) and Fry (1997) did reveal positive and significant cross-section relationships between economic growth and real interest rate. However, Fry (1997) observed an inverted U-shaped relationship between national savings and real interest rates in his study of sixteen developing countries: national savings decline at both very high and low real interest rates through the effects of these rates on output growth.[5] For Argentina, no strong relationship between real interest rate and quantity of investment was reported, but an increase in financial deepening was observed (Fanelli *et al.*, 1998). Nevertheless, a positive effect on investment efficiency for Uruguay is reported by Noya *et al.* (1998).

Again, the Mexican experience shows little evidence that movement in real interest rates has a significant effect on economic performance.

While financial saving is positively correlated with real interest rates, total domestic saving appears to be unrelated to the rate of interest, which may imply some substitution of domestic non-financial assets into domestic financial savings (Warman and Thirlwall, 1994). The net effect of interest rates on Mexican investment is thus negative. Gunçavdi *et al.* (1998) observed structural change in the aggregate investment equation after financial liberalization in Turkey: as expected, the credit variable became much less important, though the cost of capital did not become significant.

In sum, there is little evidence that financial liberalization has in fact resulted in higher savings rates, which was supposed to be the main contribution to higher investment and thus growth, even though it has resulted in increased bank profitability. There are two reasons for this outcome. First, financial reform has the effect of shifting savings out of assets such as precious metals, property or currency into bank deposits and marketable securities. This will raise the recorded financial 'depth' without raising savings rates. Second, financial liberalization expands access to consumer credit in the form of factoring systems, credit cards and personal loans. These in turn *reduce* aggregate household saving because this is simply the difference between the increase in household financial assets and the increase in household financial liabilities. In many emerging markets, this net wealth effect has been compounded by simultaneous trade liberalization and real exchange rate liberalization, which cheapened imported luxury goods (Calderon and FitzGerald, 1997).

In consequence, as Figure 3.6 illustrates, there is no robust evidence that financial deepening (measured by the widest possible measure – total market capitalization) is related to higher rates of saving and thus to investment or growth for the developed countries. There is some link for developing countries but, as we have seen, the causality is more likely to run the other way: from high savings rates to high capitalization. In fact, savings rates themselves appear to depend on other factors such as demographic and tax influences on pension provision, funding of health and education, and the ownership structure of corporations or even family organization.

Of course, the effect of financial development and liberalization on investment might still be positive despite not raisings savings, through the quality of investment improving as a result of monitoring and discipline exercised by financial markets, even if absolute investment levels do not rise. Rajan and Zingales (1998) thus attempt to establish whether industrial sectors that are relatively more in need of external finance[6] develop disproportionately faster in countries with more-developed

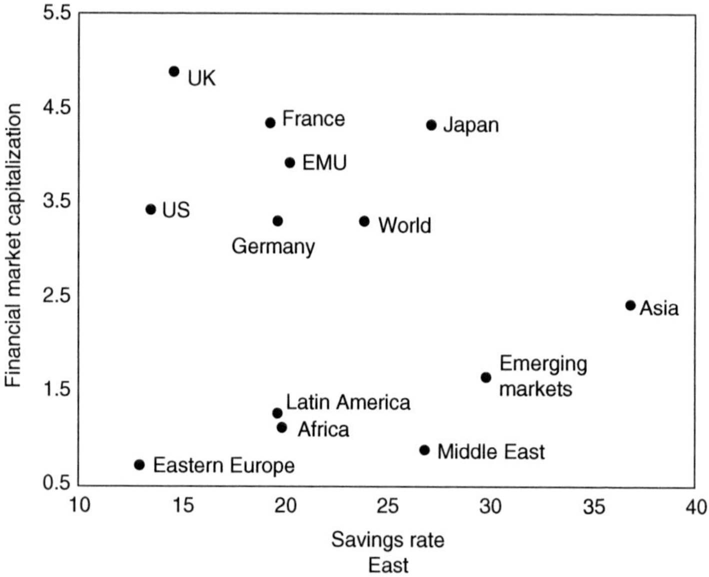

Figure 3.6 Financial market capitalization and savings rates (shares of GDP), 2003
Source: IMF, *Financial Stability Report* (2005).
Notes: 'Financial market capitalization' refers to the sum of stock market capitalization, outstanding debt securities and bank assets as a share of GDP. The 'savings rate' refers to gross national savings as a percentage of GDP.

financial markets. They use the ratio of credit to (claims on) the private sector to GDP as the financial depth indicator; but add an indicator of compliance with international accounting standards to reflect the quality of that finance. They get significant results from a panel of fifty-five countries over the period 1980–90, indicating that financial development does have a positive effect on growth through the corporate finance channel. However, there are serious shortcomings in this method: first, the unreliability of the financial depth indicator, as we have noted above; and second, the degree of financial dependence used for all countries is that for the US in the corresponding industrial sector;[7] and third, the index of compliance with international accounting standards used to instrument for 'quality of financial institutions' appears to be meaningless.[8]

The solution to this puzzle may be to look at corporate finance in more detail in order to establish the link between financial development and firms' investment. However, as is well known, corporate investment, even in advanced economies, is largely self-financed out of retained profits. The analysis of net sources of finance for physical investment in

Table 3.4 Net sources of finance, 1970–94 (percentage of physical investment)

	Germany	Japan	UK	US
Internal	78.9	69.9	93.3	96.1
Bank finance	11.9	26.7	14.6	11.1
Bonds	−1.0	4.0	4.2	15.4
New equity	0.1	3.5	−4.6	−7.6
Trade credit	−1.2	−5.0	−0.9	−2.4
Capital transfers	8.7	–	1.7	–
Other	1.4	1.0	0.0	−4.4
Statistical adjustment	1.2	0.0	−8.4	−8.3

Source: Corbett and Jenkinson (1997).

Germany, Japan, the UK and the US reveal not only the predominance of retained profits to be higher in the UK and the US despite their more developed financial markets, but the key role of banks in all cases among external sources (Corbett and Jenkinson, 1997). Only in the case of the US are bonds a significant source of corporate investment finance, and even here it should be recalled that a considerable share of these bonds are held by banks. We should not be surprised, therefore, to find that financial liberalization has little observable effect on aggregate investment levels or economic growth.

None the less, great expectations were raised by stock markets as a new source of corporate finance in developing countries in the early 1990s. In retrospect, it is clear that this boom was associated closely with capital inflows, producing an apparent correlation with economic growth (for example, Levine and Zervos 1998). These markets have since shrunk dramatically, and turn out to have low liquidity (that is, turnover) with volatile and pro-cyclical returns. Further, after the initial flotation of state enterprises, new issues have declined markedly because large domestic firms can access global capital markets and the costs are too high for SMEs.

Financial liberalization, investment and instability

The success of resource allocation efficiency depends, to a great extent, on minimizing emerging capital market imperfections such as moral hazard and adverse selection (Watson, 1993). Stiglitz and Weiss (1981) showed that an equilibrium loan market rate is characterized by credit rationing; and Mankiw (1986) indicates that there may not exist any equilibrium at all (that is, a 'collapsed market' with no lending). Asymmetric informational problems prevent banks from measuring adequately the risks associated with their lending: to compensate for these risks, banks pushed their lending rates up, leading to deterioration in the creditworthiness of borrowers. Banks thus penalise safe borrowers with a high cost of capital, while new firms with no past credit record (and/or little collateral) find funding difficult to obtain at any price. Capital markets, with high entry costs and information requirements, are even more exclusive – unless a financial intermediary can bundle securities such as credit card debt or mortgages effectively by using the homogeneity of clients to provide useful default risk indicators.

Financial market failure in the provision of long-term credit to large sections of the private sector in developing countries thus constrains the level of investment to that fundable by cash flow and trade credit; resulting in a suboptimal level of investment with consequences for economic growth. Further, the higher cost of capital induces the borrower to choose riskier projects, with a higher probability of default. Hence, the market equilibrium, if any, will be fragile. Small changes in the exogenous risk-free interest rate or a monetary contraction can have a large impact on the efficiency of the market allocation of credit. In such a situation, government intervention (in the form of a tax subsidy or a loan guarantee) can improve the situation even if the government has no informational advantage over lenders characterized by unobservable heterogeneity, as long as return exceeds opportunity cost. Market failure in a liberalized financial regime may thus call for *selective* public intervention.

Macroeconomic instability increases the variance in project returns as well as adverse selection, possibly by the banks, thus making banks risk averse. The real benefit of macroeconomic stability thus comes not from increased financial savings and greater availability of credit, but from the favourable impact on the risk-sharing relationship between borrowers and lenders (Villanueva and Mirakhor, 1990). The pace of liberalization itself is thus crucial in the sense that sudden increase in lending rate resulting from the freeing of the interest rate may render some firms unprofitable as they need to pay a higher price for their funds borrowed earlier at a lower rate. This will in turn result in non-repayment of loans. Mathieson (1980) warned that, as this leads to widespread bankruptcies in the banking system, a programme of gradual interest rate decontrol is necessary rather than sudden decontrol. Moreover, such decontrol should not be attempted until a sufficient degree of fiscal and macroeconomic stability has been achieved – financial liberalization has not been effective in itself as a means of achieving stability.

Theoretically, there are potential gains from the deregulation of financial institutions in the form of increasing growth and social welfare. But much of these depend on proper sequencing and, if poorly sequenced, deregulation can be counter-productive. The literature on sequencing of financial liberalization seeks to determine the optimal order for liberalizing the domestic real sector, the domestic financial sector, the external real sector and the external financial sector. It is generally agreed that domestic financial liberalization should come after domestic real and before external financial sector liberalization. However, it is not at all clear whether domestic financial liberalization should come before or after external liberalization, for example, trade liberalization (Gibson and Tsakalotos, 1994). Institutional factors, such as the legal infrastructure, bankruptcy code, accounting norms, disclosure rules and prudential regulations, are all important for fostering the operation of financial markets and capturing any ensuing efficiency gains, and are central elements in successful financial liberalization (Aivazian, 1998).

Finally, Sikorski (1996) points out that financial liberalization theory was predicated on an unashamed faith in the markets and the widespread belief that 'government failure' was best combated by removing the government. But this belief conflicts with what actually happens in any real economy where social institutions play a crucial role in gathering information and reducing uncertainty (Gibson and Tsakalotos, 1994). Thus deliberate institutional design is essential in order to develop the long-term, high-trust relations between market participants that determine how well a country can compete in international markets and hence, in the long run, its economic performance. For example, since information collected through monitoring the financial institutions regarding their solvency and management practices by individuals is costly and becomes a public good, it would be suboptimal in welfare terms for depositors to monitor them individually (Fry, 1997). As financial institutions know that depositors do not monitor them adequately, they have incentives to take greater risks. However, as long as central bank plays its due role of supervision and monitoring, and makes the information public, this cost should be minimized.

Nevertheless, the non-existence of markets does not necessarily imply that public intervention would result in superior outcome. Public intervention as substitute for market failure can suffer from exactly the same problems of unobservable outcomes (for example, contractual default), unobservable behaviour (for example, moral hazard) or unobservable characteristics (for example, adverse selection) as the private sector (Obstfeld and Rogoff, 1996). There other markets dealing with the problem can exist (for example, higher equity participation to tackle uncertainty problems, specialized institutions/banks for industrial credit, leasing companies). So the pertinent question is why those contingent-markets are absent and, in the case of smaller developing countries, whether these services can be provided by the international capital market.

The greatest problem for developing countries in this context is probably the absence of a domestic market for long-term treasury or corporate bonds. This means that, on the one hand, it is difficult to fund public infrastructure investment and major private modernization projects. And, on the other, it becomes impossible for firms to hedge against exchange rate changes, further destabilizing foreign currency markets; and monetary intervention in order to counteract external shocks becomes very difficult. Financial liberalization has not led to this important outcome, for at least two reasons. First, fiscal reform has been geared to reducing budget deficits, and to avoiding monetization (that is, inflation targeting) by issuance of short-term treasury bills, rather than developing a long bond market. Second, the absence of institutional market-makers in these securities persists if no special facilities (such as rediscount facilities or tax incentives) are extended to pension and insurance funds to encourage demand for these assets.

With the deregulation of interest rates, banks gamble for higher profit by lending to the booming sector, such as real estate. This leads to an asset price boom that 'can exacerbate the adverse incentive on banks to take risk, increased interest rates, increased macroeconomic instability and, if banks' portfolios are concentrated on particular sectors, increased covariance in the returns to banks' borrowers' (Brownbridge and Kirkpatrick, 1999). The booms and slumps in the asset prices – where banks play a crucial role by credit expansion during upswings in the business cycle, thus raising the value of collateral, stimulating more borrowing, leading to over-indebtedness, and making borrowers vulnerable to any macroeconomic changes (for example, interest rate increases) and ultimately rendering them insolvent – frequently result in banking crises. Moreover, personnel in the banking sector in the developing countries often lack the skill required to evaluate risky investment projects and monitor borrowers. Indeed, the liberalized environment itself causes a moral hazard problem and induces the banks to take on risks.

Financial liberalization is usually associated with integration to the global capital market. In principle, this should make an international pool of liquidity available to the domestic financial system, which should then be more stable. However, in practice, the high degree of volatility of international capital inflows, combined with the thin and narrow nature of host markets subjects the recipient countries to shocks and crises, which can be both large and frequent. The quantity effect of the flows is exacerbated by the fact that arbitrage leads to the domestic interest rate being set by the world interest rate, plus expected devaluation, plus the perceived default risk premium. This uncovered interest rate parity principle leads to very high real rates of interest in emerging markets and asymmetric responses in terms of investment and output because of the impact on firms' balance sheets; the volatility of expected profits resulting from this has a strong depressive effect on private investment (FitzGerald, 2001). The orthodox policy response to these crises can further worsen the situation, as firms are forced into bankruptcy by credit restrictions and large devaluations, with asymmetric effects on balance sheets.

Domestic investment financed by foreign savings leads to a temporary increase in real income and perceived wealth, and a relaxation of lending standards by banks, as current trends are expected to continue (Reisen, 1999). With the increase in both consumption and investment, balance of payment deteriorates, which initially remains unnoticed. Overvaluation of the exchange rate can sustain this sense of optimism – and thus exacerbate the asset bubble. Hence, for most of the developing countries, the question of exchange rate policy is also crucial to the success of financial liberalization. Indeed, from the point of view of firms faced with irreversible investment decisions, macroeconomic stability and credit availability are more important than low interest rates or tax incentives (Pindyck and Solimano, 1993).

In sum, the *process*, rather than the *objectives* of financial liberalization in developing countries has emerged as the central problem. The original 'big bang' approach is clearly dangerous; but Clarke (1996) suggests that even the concept of an 'equilibrium' interest rate may be undefined, or at least unobtainable through the process of competition, since the rate required to balance financial markets differs from that required to equilibrate savings and investment. Specifically, Stiglitz *et al.*(2006) argue that a delay in capital market liberalization, despite a degree of continued financial repression, can be beneficial in developing countries. Further, an *increase* in repression (or control) in some areas of financial markets may be essential to ensure that the whole process does not get out of hand during the transitional period (Fanelli and Medhora, 1998).

Conclusions: policy lessons and epistemic implications

There are four main conclusions from this chapter. First, that financial depth ratios fluctuate widely over time for individual countries, while financial structures differ considerably between industrialized economies: so neither of these are reliable guides to desirable financial development in industrializing countries. Second, that, despite the assurances in the canonical literature, there is no simple relationship between financial development in terms of both depth (increased asset/income ratio) and structure (increased non-bank asset share) and economic growth, particularly in developing countries. Third, that financial liberalization cannot be demonstrated to raise overall savings or investment rates, or to increase corporate efficiency; although it does ensure bank solvency, albeit at the expense of small firms and long-term investment lending. And fourth, that too rapid a pace of financial reform and opening to global capital markets can create considerable instability despite efficiency gains, leading to a net reduction of investment and growth.

Two further questions arise logically from these conclusions. What are their implications for the design of future financial reform strategies in developing countries? And why does the orthodox model persist in the face of the evidence? I can do no more than sketch a response to these two questions here.

On the policy issues, a useful initial step would be to reappraise the role of commercial banks in developing countries, the traditional intermediaries between saving households and investing firms. Their move into asset management and consumer credit, and away from the financing of productive investment in general and SMEs in particular, has been encouraged by regulators concerned about bank liquidity. Similarly, the closure of public-sector development banks was justified by their heavy losses and vulnerability to political pressure, but the financing gap for long-term investment in key sectors such as exports and infrastructure remains. Public intervention is still needed to correct this market failure – although this could take the form of risk insurance, rediscount facilities, support for debt securitization and market-making, rather than traditional development banking. By extension, the relaxation of regulatory restrictions should avoid asset booms and systemic risk, rather than aim for banking efficiency alone.

Further, monetary policy should encompass exchange rates and be geared towards providing a credible and stable environment for firms rather than simply inflation targeting: specifically by providing a low real interest rate and a competitive real exchange rate, supported by appropriate tax incentives for long-term productive investment. The development of a long-term bond market should be a priority, as this would not only provide long-term capital for growth at reasonable real cost but also stabilize exchange rate expectations and enable the monetary authorities to intervene effectively to damp macroeconomic cycles caused by external shocks – as had been the case in OECD countries until recently.

On the epistemic issue of the persistence of a flawed paradigm of financial development in the face of the evidence, there are two obvious yet unsatisfactory answers. On the one hand, some would say that the previous model had simply failed, so that financial liberalization was the only option available. In consequence, the existence of a coherent analytical and empirical justification is irrelevant, or at best a post hoc rationalization.

On the other hand, others would say that financial liberalization simply reflects the interests of international banks, who form alliances with relevant fractions of domestic finance capital and determine the policies of international financial institutions. The orthodox model is then little more than propaganda, however sophisticated, or at best a case of interested parties taking advantage of misguided theorists.

A more insightful approach might be that of theorists of the diffusion of economic ideas, who identify three drivers of change in economic policy adoption.[9] These are: first, the role of internal political actors (including not only politicians and academics but also finance and banking officials) to whom decision-makers listen; second, external pressures from the international community, market actors such as banks and governments with strategic interests; and third, and possibly most important, the influence of 'epistemic communities', or key intellectual elites within a particular discipline, in this case not only economics but also finance and management. The epistemic community not only influences policy-makers directly by presenting dominant ideas as the only valid ones, but also has a deep influence on local and international officials (for example, in the World Bank and the International Monetary Fund – IMF) through their training at leading universities in the US and, to a lesser extent in the UK.

The epistemic community does not rely on economics journals to provide the latest research results or analytical models. These are available far more rapidly through policy conferences, consultancy missions and even academic working papers. Rather, academic journals, and to a lesser extent academic book publishers, act as arbiters of what is considered sound research. In the case of the literature on the effect of financial development on economic growth, and the benefits of specific institutional forms in particular, at least, it seems that the profession has failed in its proper duty.

Notes

1. As a young economics lecturer in Cambridge in the 1970s, I was fortunately encouraged by Ajit to work on development finance – an unfashionable research topic at that time.
2. I would like to thank Jahir Islam and Juan Yermo for valuable assistance with bibliographical sources. This chapter is a revised version of a working paper input to the UN *World Economic and Social Survey.*
3. Levine *et al.* (2000) also correct some methodological problems in Levine and Zervos (1998). The latter analysis does not account for potential simultaneity bias, nor does it control explicitly for country fixed effects. Levine *et al.* (2000) use the La Porta *et al.* (1998) measures of legal origin as instrumental variables to demonstrate causality.
4. This point on regional differences in financial structure is taken up again below.
5. Indeed, even at the theoretical level, the net effect of interest rates on saving is ambiguous because the wealth effect and the relative price effect have negative and positive effects, respectively; see FitzGerald (2006).
6. The financial dependence of each industrial sector is assumed to be the same as that for the US in all countries. This assumption begs the central question to be investigated and undoubtedly undermines the reliability of the results.
7. That is, they assume that the value of the external financing ratio for a specific industrial branch in the US can be applied automatically to the same branch in (say) India. No justification is given for this major assumption, which largely begs the question that this chapter sets out to answer.
8. Specifically, Rajan and Zingales (1998) give the following index values for accounting standards (implicitly set for US = 100), among others: Austria (54), Mexico (60), Germany (62), Netherlands (64), Philippines (65), New Zealand (70), Malaysia (76), UK (78). It is difficult to understand how research of this calibre is acceptable to leading journals and their referees.
9. This paragraph is based on the editors' introduction to FitzGerald and Thorp (2005).

References

Aivazian, V. A. (1998) 'Microeconomic Elements and Perspectives from Finance Theory', in J. M. Fanelli and R. Medhora (eds), *Financial Reform in Developing Countries*, Basingstoke: Macmillan for International Development Research Centre, Canada.

Allen, F. and D. Gale (1997) 'Financial Markets, Intermediaries and Intertemporal Smoothing', *Journal of Political Economy* 105: 523–46.

Andrés, J., I. Hernando and J. D. Lópes-Salido (1999) 'The Role of the Financial System in the Growth Inflation Link: The OECD Experience', Banco de España Working Paper, Banco de España, Madrid, October.

Arestis, P. and P. Demetriades (1997) "Financial Development and Economic Growth: Assessing the Evidence", *Economic Journal* 107 (442): 783–99.

Bailliu, Jeanine and Helmut Reisen (1997) 'Do Funded Pensions Contribute to Higher Aggregate Savings? A Cross Country Analysis', OECD Development Centre Working Paper No. 130, Organisation for Economic Co-operation and Development, Paris.

Beck, Thorsten, Asli Demirgüç-Kunt and Ross Levine (2004) 'Finance, Inequality and Poverty: Cross-country Evidence', NBER Working Paper No. 10979, National Bureau of Economic Research, Cambridge, Mass.

Brownbridge, M. and C. Kirkpatrick (1999) 'Financial Regulation in Developing Countries: A Critical Survey', Paper presented at the Finance and Development Research Programme Workshop, 9–10 July, Manchester.

Calderon, A. and V. FitzGerald (1997) 'Incomplete Adjustment: Fiscal Policy, Private Savings and Current Account Deficits in Mexico since 1982', in K. Jansen and R. Vos (eds), *External Finance and Adjustment: Failure and Success in the Developing World*, Basingstoke: Macmillan, pp. 121–56.

Clarke, R. (1996) 'Equilibrium Exchange Rates and Financial Liberalization in Developing Countries', *Journal of Development Studies* 32 (3): 391–413

Corbett, J. and T. Jenkinson (1997) 'How Is Investment Financed? A Study of Germany, Japan, the United Kingdom and the United States', *The Manchester School* 63 (Supplement): 69–93.

Demirgüç-Kunt, A. and V. Maksimovic (1996) 'Stock Market Development and Firm Financing Choices', *World Bank Economic Review* 10: 341–70.

Fanelli, J. M. and R. Medhora (1998) 'Financial Reform in Developing Countries: An Overview', in J. M. Fanelli and R. Medhora (eds), *Financial Reform in Developing Countries*, Basingstoke: Macmillan for International Development Research Centre, Canada.

Fanelli, J. M. G. Rozenwurcel and L. M. Simpson (1998) 'Country Case Studies: Argentina', in J. M. Fanelli and R. Medhora (eds), *Financial Reform in Developing Countries*, Basingstoke: Macmillan for International Development Research Centre, Canada.

FitzGerald, V. (2001) 'Short-term Capital Flows, the Real Economy and Income Distribution in Developing Countries', in S. Griffith-Jones, M. Montes and A. Nasution (eds), *Short-term Capital Flows and Economic Crises*, Oxford: Oxford University Press, pp. 29–51

FitzGerald, V. (2006) 'Models of Saving, Income and the Macroeconomics of Developing Countries in the Post-Keynesian Tradition', in P. Arestis, J. McCombie and R. Vickerman (eds), *Growth and Economic Development: Essays in Honour of AP Thirlwall*, Cheltenham: Edward Elgar, pp. 247–62.

FitzGerald, V. and R. Thorp (2005) *The Transmission of Economic Ideas in Latin America*, Basingstoke: Palgrave Macmillan.

Fry, M. J. (1988) *Money, Interest and Banking in Economic Development* (2nd edn 1995), Baltimore, Md.: Johns Hopkins University Press.

Fry, M. J. (1997) 'In Favour of Financial Liberalization', *The Economic Journal* 107 (May): 754–70.

Galbis, V. (1977) 'Financial Intermediation and Economic Growth in Less-developed Countries: A Theoretical Approach', *Journal of Development Studies* 13 (2): 58–72.

Ghani, E. (1992) 'How Financial Markets Affect Long-run Growth: A Cross-country Study', PR Working Paper No. WPS 843, January, Country Economic Operations, World Bank, Washington, DC.

Gibson, H. D. and E. Tsakalotos (1994) 'The Scope and Limits of Financial Liberalization in Developing Countries: A Critical Survey', *Journal of Development Studies* 30 (3), April: 578–628.

Günçavdi, O., M. Bleaney and A. McKay (1998) 'Financial Liberalization and Private Investment: Evidence from Turkey', *Journal of Development Economics* 57 (2): 443–55.

IMF (various years) *International Financial Statistics*, Washington, DC: International Monetary Fund.

IMF (2005) *Financial Stability Report 2005*, Washington, DC: International Monetary Fund.

Kapur, B. K. (1976) 'Alternative Stabilization Policies for Less-developed Economies', *Journal of Political Economy* 84 (4), August: 777–95.

King, R. G. and R. Levine (1993a) 'Finance and Growth: Schumpeter Might Be Right', *Quarterly Journal of Economics* 108 (3): 717–37.

King, R. G. and R. Levine (1993b) 'Finance, Entrepreneurship, and Growth: Theory and Evidence', *Journal of Monetary Economics* 32: 513–42.

La Porta, R., F. Lopez-de-Silanes, A. Shleifer and R. W. Vishny (1998) 'Law and Finance', *Journal of Political Economy* 106 (6): 1113–55.

Leahy, M., S. Schich, G. Wehinger, F. Pelgrin, T. Thorgeirsson (2001) 'Contributions of Financial Systems to Growth in OECD Countries', OECD Economics Department Working Paper No. 280, Organisation for Economic Co-operation and Development, Paris.

Levine, R. (2000) 'Bank-based or Market-based Financial Systems: Which Is Better?', Mimeo, University of Minnesota, Department of Economics, January.

Levine, R. and S. Zervos (1998) 'Stock Markets, Banks, and Economic Growth', *American Economic Review* 88 (3), June: 537–58.

Levine, R. N. Loayza and T. Beck (2000) 'Financial Intermediation and Growth: Causality and Causes', *Journal of Monetary Economics* 46 (1): 31–77.

Mankiw, N. G. (1986) 'The Allocation of Credit and Financial Collapse', *Quarterly Journal of Economics* 101 (3): 455–70.

Mathieson, R. J. (1980) 'Financial Reform and Stabilization Policy in a Developing Economy', *Journal of Development Economics* 7 (3), September: 359–95.

Mayer, C. (1990) 'Financial Systems, Corporate Finance and Economic Development', in G. Hubbard (ed.), *Information, Capital Markets and Investment*, Cambridge, Mass.: National Bureau for Economic Research.

McKinnon, R. I. (1973) *Money and Capital in Economic Development*, Washington, DC: Brookings.

McKinnon, R. I. (1989) 'Financial Liberalization and Economic Development: A Reassessment of Interest Rate Policies in Asia and Latin America', *Oxford Review of Economic Policy* 5 (4): 29–54.

Mosley, P. (1999) 'Micro–Macro Linkages in Financial Markets: The Impact of Financial Liberalization on Access to Rural Credit in Four African Countries', Finance and Development Research Programme Working Paper Series No. 4. Institute for Development Policy and Management, University of Manchester.

Noya, N., C. Casacuberta and F. Lorenzo (1998) 'Country Case Studies: Uruguay', in J. M. Fanelli and R. Medhora (eds), *Financial Reform in Developing Countries*, Basingstoke: Macmillan for International Development Research Centre, Canada.

Obstfeld, M. and K. Rogoff (1996) *Foundation of International Macroeconomics*, Cambridge Mass.: MIT Press.

Pindyck, R S. and A. Solimano (1993) 'Economic Stability and Aggregate Investment', NBER Working Paper No. 4380, National Bureau of Economic Research, Cambridge, Mass.
Rajan, R. G. and L. Zingales (1998) 'Financial Dependence and Growth', *American Economic Review* 88 (3): 559–86.
Reisen, H. (1999) 'Domestic Causes of Currency Crises: Policy Lessons for Crisis Avoidance', *IDS Bulletin* 30 (1): 120–33.
Sikorski, M. T. (1996) *Financial Liberalization in Developing Countries*, Cheltenham: Edward Elgar.
Singh, A. (2001) 'Financial Liberalisation and Globalisation: Implications for Industrial and Industrialising Economies', in K. S. Jomo and S. Nagraj (eds), *Globalisation versus Development*, Basingstoke: Palgrave, pp. 161–87.
Singh, A. (2003) 'The New International Financial Architecture, Corporate Governance and Competition in Emerging Markets: New Issues for Developing Economies', in Ha-Joon Chang (ed.), *Rethinking Development Economics*, London: Anthem Press, pp. 377–403.
Singh, A. (2007) 'Capital Account Liberalization, Free Long-term Capital Flows, Financial Crises and Economic Development', in Anwar Shaikh, (ed.), *Globalization and the Myths of Free Trade*, Oxford: Routledge, pp. 259–87.
Singh, A. and B. Weisse (1998) 'Emerging Stock Markets, Portfolio Capital Flows and Long Term Economic Growth, Micro and Macroeconomic Perspectives', *World Development* 26 (4): 607–22.
Stiglitz, J., J. A. Ocampo, S. Speigel, R. Ffrench-Davis and D. Nayyar (2006) *Stability with Growth: Macroeconomics, Liberalization and Development*, New York: Oxford University Press.
Stiglitz, J. and A. Weiss (1981) 'Credit rationing in markets with imperfect information', *American Economic Review*, 71 (3): 393–410.
Taylor, L. (1983) *Structuralist Macroeconomics: Applicable Models for the Third World*, New York: Basic Books.
Villanueva, D. and A. Mirakhor (1990) 'Strategies for Financial Reforms', IMF Staff Papers. 37.
Warman, F. and A. P. Thirlwall (1994) 'Interest Rates, Savings, Investment and Growth in Mexico, 1960–90: Tests of the Financial Liberalization Hypothesis', *Journal of Development Studies* 30 (3): 629–49.
Watson, C. M. (1993) 'Financial Liberalization and the Economic Adjustment Process', Development Studies Working Papers, No. 61, Queen Elizabeth House, University of Oxford.
van Wijnbergen, S. (1983) 'Interest Rate Management in LDCs', *Journal of Monetary Economics* 12 (3): 433–52.
Williamson, J. and M. Mahar (1998) 'A Survey of Financial Liberalization', *Essays in International Finance*, No. 211 Princeton, NJ: Princeton University.
World Bank (1989) *World Development Report 1989*, New York: Oxford University Press for the World Bank.
World Bank (2001) *Finance for Growth: Policy Choices in a Volatile World* New York: Oxford University Press for the World Bank.
World Bank (2005) *World Development Indicators*, Washington, DC: World Bank.

4
Micro-Finance, Macro-Finance and Egalitarian Development

Robert Pollin

Introduction[1]

The award of the 2006 Nobel Peace Prize to Muhammad Yunus, founder of the Grameen Bank in Bangladesh, and a former professor of economics at Chittagong University, Bangladesh, has brought increased attention to the role of micro-finance institutions as a tool for promoting economic development, and in particular as a means of creating viable employment opportunities for the very poor.

There is no question that Yunus and the Grameen Bank have made important contributions to fighting mass poverty. Indeed, as I discuss below, one major purpose of this chapter is to propose policies that learn from and build on these achievements. At the same time, the real accomplishments of micro-finance are being oversold in many circles. In particular, it has been promoted widely as an effective alternative to what Armendáriz de Aghion and Morduch (2005) describe as the 'failures of state-owned development banks' and similar large-scale public policy interventions to allocate credit on a subsidized basis. This view of macro-level development banking and subsidized credit allocation programmes stands in stark contrast to the perspective of Amsden (2001) on the effectiveness of such measures in the developing countries, which she terms the 'the rest.' Amsden writes:

> From the viewpoint of long-term capital supply for public *and* private investment, development banks throughout 'the rest' were of overwhelming importance... The government's role in long-run credit allocation was substantial even in parts of 'the rest' where development banks were of relatively minor importance. (2001, pp. 127–9)

More generally, Grameen-type micro-finance institutions are often characterized as being consonant with, and operating effectively within, an overall neoliberal development model that enshrines free-market solutions for promoting widespread prosperity in developing countries. This poses a severe problem for micro-finance as a policy tool. Of course, Ajit Singh has long been among both the most forceful critics of neoliberalism as well as the most creative expositors of viable egalitarian policy alternatives. As Singh wrote in 1997:

> There is considerable evidence that the liberal economy has not delivered, and that unless the current strategy is fundamentally altered the prospects for the world economy, for the people in the North as well as the South, are bleak. (1997a, pp. 12–13)

Within Professor Singh's broad analytic framework, the specific role of financial markets and institutions in development has long been one of his principal concerns. In this research on financial questions, Singh has shown, among other things, that liberalized financial markets typically promote persistent financial instability in developing countries, with few, if any, counteracting pay-offs via accelerated long-run growth. Moreover, as with Amsden, Singh has shown that, for the most part, state-guided, regulated financial systems in developing countries have been much more effective than unregulated markets in promoting long-term, sustainable development.[2]

This chapter has a twofold purpose. The first is to offer a balanced appraisal of micro-finance that acknowledges both its strengths and its weaknesses, especially in relation to a macro-finance framework that relies on development banks and subsidized credit allocation programmes. The second purpose is more positive. This is to construct a financial market policy framework that incorporates features of both micro-finance and a state-directed credit allocation model. My colleagues and I have been developing such a policy framework, as part of larger projects on pro-poor, employment-targeted economic programmes for both South Africa and Kenya.[3] In this chapter, I discuss our approach as we have developed it for Kenya. Kenya already operates with the most extensive set of micro-finance institutions in Sub-Saharan Africa, and therefore offers an excellent case study for observing both the limits of Grameen-style micro-finance and the potential for incorporating features of that model within an overall framework that builds on the achievements of large-scale subsidized credit programmes.

Micro-finance and macro development finance

Is unsubsidized micro-finance profitable? Should it be?

Muhammad Yunus launched the Grameen Bank in Bangladesh in 1976, and the industry's growth has been explosive since it opened its doors. As of 2002, there were roughly 2,600 micro-finance institutions worldwide, serving about 68 million clients.[4] These institutions have made important advances relative to the array of moneylenders and pawnbrokers that had previously controlled the provisioning of banking services to the world's poor. The first contribution of Yunus and the Grameen Bank model is simply to have recognized that credit and related services – including bank accounts and insurance policies – can be important resources for advancing the well-being of the poor, just as they are with everyone else. The second is in targeting women as loan recipients, empowering the women within their families and helping them to sustain their home-based micro-enterprises.

The most important advance is in developing an alternative to traditional collateral as a basis for lending to the poor. Under a traditional system, people obtain loans only if they have sufficient assets to surrender to the bank, moneylender or pawnbroker in the event of default. But poor people, by definition, have few assets to pledge – perhaps a few livestock animals, a small plot of land, or jewellery – and losing these few assets to a creditor is likely to bring destitution. Grameen's innovation was to create borrowing groups, typically of five women. Each group member could receive loans only as long as everyone made payments. This promotes both mutual support among group members as well as peer pressure to keep up with payments. It also created opportunities for large numbers of poor people to become creditworthy for the first time.

Counteracting these positive innovations, lending rates charged by Grameen and other micro-finance institutions far exceed standard measures of affordability. Nimal Fernando, of the Asian Development Bank, arguing in defence of high interest rates on micro-credit, nevertheless acknowledges that:

> The nominal interest rates charged by most MFI [micro-finance institutions] in the region range from 30–70 percent a year (on a reducing balance basis). The effective interest rates are even higher because of commissions and fees charged by the MFIs. Other factors – such as the compulsory deposits for obtaining a loan, frequency of repayments and the systems adopted to collect repayments, also raise the effective interest rates. (2006, p. 1)

These rates are lower than those moneylenders typically charge, but nevertheless remain punishingly high. Defenders of such arrangements contend that, accounting for the risks to the lender, these rates are appropriate; and that anything less will not attract profit-seeking bankers into this market. They also claim that subsidized rates will invite rent-seeking, such that those favoured with political connections, rather than those in need, will be the actual recipients of the subsidized credit.[5]

Despite charging such high rates, the Grameen Bank, among others, has long prided itself on maintaining repayment rates as high as 95 per cent. However, these figures have been disputed, including in a careful *Wall Street Journal* investigative report in 2001.[6] The report found that, in fact, Grameen allows distressed borrowers to roll over or stretch out their repayments rather than declaring them in default. This may well be the most effective and humane approach under the circumstances. But it is clearly inconsistent with a hard-nosed business model supported by a large proportion of micro-finance enthusiasts.

Moreover, interest rates and other financing charges for the poor – and correspondingly, default rates – would be higher still if micro-finance institutions did not themselves operate with subsidies. As Armendáriz de Aghion and Morduch write:

> The reality is that much of the microfinance movement continues to take advantage of subsidies – some from donors, some from governments, and some from charities and concerned individuals. *The Microbanking Bulletin*, for example, shows that sixty-six out of 124 microlenders surveyed were financially sustainable, a rate just over 50 percent. For microlenders focusing on the 'low-end', just 18 of 49 were financially sustainable as of the July 2003 accounting, a 37 percent rate. (2005, p. 232)

Morduch's own research finds that the Grameen Bank would have needed to increase its lending rates by about 75 per cent between 1985 and 1995 in order to break even without subsidies (Agihion and Morduch, 2005, p. 237).

Of course, it makes sense that micro-credit loans to the poor can be made profitable – truly profitable, without benefit of subsidies, hidden or open – only if the poor pay extremely high interest rates and other charges. Even when micro-finance institutions utilize creative systems of collateral, such as those developed by the Grameen Bank, the information costs, transaction costs and risks of such loans remain very high. Considered strictly as a profit-seeking activity, the repayment rates for borrowers of such loans would have to fully reflect these costs and risks to lenders. At the same time, borrowing rates that fully reflect these costs are likely to be overwhelming burdens to the poor. Putting such heavy financial burdens on the poor in turn defeats the purpose of the enterprise.

But this doesn't mean that micro-finance is not a viable tool for fighting poverty. It rather means that, given that it is indeed a viable tool, as the Grameen Bank and allied institutions have demonstrated, that government policy should openly subsidize these activities. The real question therefore becomes how best to establish such subsidy programmes – how large the subsidies should be, what the subsidized interest rates should be, and who should bear the costs of the subsidies. These are among the questions I address below in the context of Kenya.

Micro-finance requires a supportive policy environment

But whether the credit terms are low or high, micro-enterprises run by poor people cannot broadly be successful simply because they have increased opportunities to borrow money. For large numbers of micro-enterprises to be successful, they also need access to decent roads and affordable means of moving their products to markets. They need marketing support to reach customers, and they need a vibrant, well-functioning domestic market itself – that is, enough people with enough money to buy what these enterprises have to sell. Finally, micro businesses benefit greatly from an expanding supply of decent wage-paying jobs in their local economies. This is the best way of maintaining a vibrant domestic market. In addition, when the wage-paying job market is strong, it means that the number of people trying to survive as micro entrepreneurs falls. This reduces competition among micro businesses and thereby improves the chances that any given micro-enterprise will succeed.

These additional measures for supporting micro-enterprises – a decent transportation infrastructure, support in marketing the products of micro-enterprises, a high level of domestic demand, and an abundance of decent wage-earning jobs – were, in various forms, all closely associated with what used to be termed the 'developmental state' economic model. Different versions of the developmental state model – including state socialism, import-substituting industrialization, and the East Asian state-directed economies – prevailed in developing countries for the first thirty years after the Second World War, before these models were overtaken by neoliberalism. Each of these developmental state models encountered serious problems, but on balance they all achieved success in promoting economic growth and greater equality. This is in contrast with the neoliberal record of declining average growth rates and rising inequality.[7]

We can observe the relative achievements of a micro-finance model operating within a broadly neoliberal policy framework as opposed to a developmental state framework by comparing the experiences of a few Asian countries. In pointing out the gains achieved through micro-finance in developing countries, a recent article by Sam Daley-Harris (2007), director of the US Microcredit Summit Campaign, focuses on the case of Bangladesh. Of course, Bangladesh is where the micro-finance movement began in the mid-1970s, under Professor Yunus. At present, according to Daley-Harris, Bangladesh is 'the world's most saturated microfinance market.' Daley-Harris argues that Bangladesh has made dramatic advances in poverty reduction since the micro-finance movement began there, though he recognizes that factors in addition to micro-finance itself have also made contributions. Daley-Harris cites the following indicators of success in Bangladesh:

- By 2004, according to UNICEF, Bangladesh had already achieved the Millennium Development Goal on gender parity at the primary and secondary educational levels; the fertility rate in Bangladesh has fallen from 6.4 in 1970 to 3.2 in 2004; and the number of deaths of children under five per 1,000 live births has fallen from 239 per thousand in 1970 to 77 in 2004.
- More than 13,000 women have been elected to local government positions.
- Bangladesh has overtaken India in reducing its child mortality rate.

While these accomplishments are real, it is also helpful to consider these simple comparisons. In 1965, the average per capita income in Bangladesh was US$269 (in inflation-adjusted 2000 dollars).[8] In that same year, per capita income in Indonesia was US$195, 28 per cent lower than that in Bangladesh. As of 2004, Bangladesh's per capita income had risen to US$402 while that in Indonesia was at US$906. In other words, Bangladesh's per capita income had risen by 50 per cent between 1965 and 2004, while Indonesia's had risen by 365 per cent. But more to the point regarding poverty reduction: in the most recent years for which the World Bank reports figures, in Bangladesh the US$1 dollar a day poverty rate was 36 per cent (2000) while in Indonesia (in 2002) it was 7.5 per cent. Indonesia, moreover, is by no means a star in the firmament of the East Asian Tigers. If we consider Thailand, for example, in 1965 its per capita income was about 50 per cent higher than that in Bangladesh. By 2004, it had risen to almost 600 per cent higher than in Bangladesh. More importantly, as of 2002, Thailand had pushed the US$1 dollar/day poverty rate down to only 2 per cent.

What is responsible for the far greater economic achievements of Indonesia, and especially Thailand, relative to Bangladesh since the 1960s? Without pursuing an extended debate here about developmental strategies, we can at least say that Indonesia and Thailand achieved their successes despite the far less extensive role for Grameen-style micro-finance institutions serving their countries' poor. This does not mean that we should gainsay the real contributions of the Grameen Bank. But it does mean that our attention should focus to a far greater degree on the overall development strategy in which micro-finance institutions operate, and less on micro-finance *per se* as a tool of poverty reduction.

Learning from state-directed credit subsidy programmes

As I stated at the outset, one of the key institutions of the developmental state model that was largely dismantled under neoliberalism is the state-directed development bank. State-directed development banks provided cheap long-term credit for domestic businesses that enabled these businesses to expand their productive and marketing capabilities at a sustainable pace. This is the policy approach that Amsden describes as having been of 'overwhelming importance' to the development path both of countries that relied on development banks for allocating credit, as well as those where development banks per se were of minor importance. In this latter set of countries, Amsden writes that 'when necessary, the whole banking sector in these countries was mobilized to steer long-term credit to targeted industries, acting as a surrogate development bank', (2001, p. 129). Amsden describes Indonesia as being among the countries that made effective use of its state-led development bank, the Indonesian Development Bank, along with the cases of Mexico, Chile, South Korea and Brazil. Amsden also includes Thailand among the countries that did not rely on a state-led development bank per se, but rather deployed 'the whole banking system' to channel subsidized credit for development purposes. The other cases in this category cited by Amsden include Malaysia, Taiwan and Turkey.

It is true, as Amsden's discussion makes clear, that this macro development finance approach in 'the rest' was targeted primarily at promoting manufacturing capacity and exports, as opposed to being aimed directly at reducing mass unemployment and poverty. This is a crucial point, because what Amsden emphasizes as being key to the success of these models is that they operated under what she terms a 'reciprocal control mechanism', whereby 'subsidies were conditional on the fulfillment of performance standards, which were widespread both by industry and country' (2001, p. 160). It is when such control mechanisms and performance standards were not established or did not function effectively that subsidized credit allocation policies in developing countries failed. Amsden cites Argentina as a case where effective measures were never developed; and India, where they operated to an excessive, stifling extent.

Following Amsden's discussion, it seems reasonable to conclude that establishing reciprocal control mechanisms and performance standards as a precondition for obtaining subsidized credit can be relatively straightforward when the performance standard is itself straightforward – such as achieving a well-defined level of success in selling to export markets. But can such control mechanisms be made workable when the purpose of the policy is less well targeted – specifically, when the aim of credit subsidies is to promote poverty reduction and the expansion of decent employment?

This is the most basic question that needs to be explored if large-scale subsidized credit allocation programmes are to be made workable on behalf of micro-finance programmes focused on employment expansion and poverty reduction. We turn to a consideration of this and related questions in the next section of the chapter, which describes our approach to subsidized credit allocation in Kenya.

A credit allocation programme for Kenya

Brief profile of the Kenyan economy

The economy of Kenya, similar to that of most other low-income countries, is dominated by small-scale agriculture and its informal sector. Total employment in the country, as of the most recent 2005/6 survey, is 12.1 million, with another 1.4 million openly unemployed. Of those that are employed, 50 per cent are engaged in agricultural self-employment, 36 per cent are in the informal sector, and only 14 per cent are in the formal sector.

In terms of employment and poverty, the fundamental problem in Kenya is not unemployment per se or even low hours of employment. It is rather that the majority participating in the labour force is indeed working – most for more than 40 hours per week – but their income from work is very low. Of all Kenyans outside of agricultural self-employment who are participating in the labour force but are unemployed, roughly 65 per cent live in poverty. However, the proportions living in poverty are basically the same if a Kenyan is employed and working up to 39 hours per week. Specifically, for those working 1–27 hours per week, nearly 70 per cent live in poverty, and among those working 28–39 hours per week, about 66 per cent live in poverty.[9]

Among the labour force participants working 40 hours or more per week, the percentage living in poverty does go down – to 46.1 per cent, but still this percentage is very high. It is also important to recognize here, however, that a large majority of Kenyans do work 40 hours or more per week. This means, in turn, that even though the chances of living in poverty in Kenya do go down somewhat if one works 40 hours or more per week, it is still the case that the overwhelming proportion of labour force participants in Kenya who live in poverty are also working a full week.[10]

It will also be informative to examine a profile of household enterprises in Kenya, which are the dominant form of business enterprise outside agriculture. Household enterprises can either be informal or formal, and they do sometimes operate outside the home and with several employees. But about 90 per cent of household enterprises are informal. More than 80 per cent of all household enterprises provide some kind of service, mainly retail sales. Total employment in these enterprises is 5.2 million, of whom 80 per cent work in informal businesses. On average, earnings for these activities are very low. The median level of earnings, at Ksh2,370 per month, is at a level between the poverty line figures for Kenya's urban and rural regions. And this level of income typically will be used to support more than one person, often an unpaid family member also working in the business.

Especially pertinent for our discussion are the figures in Table 4.1. This shows the sources of start-up credit for household enterprises. As we can see, 80 per cent of household enterprises depend almost entirely on their own savings, gifts, or sales of existing assets to start their businesses. Only 3 per cent receive funds from Savings and Credit Cooperative Societies (SACCOs), which, as we shall discuss further below, are the predominant form of micro-finance enterprise in Kenya. Credit from banks or other formal financial institutions is almost non-existent.

This is the background in which my colleagues and I have developed an employment-targeted economic programme for Kenya. Our proposal has a range of components, including large-scale investments in roads and water infrastructure, much higher levels of support for agricultural extension services and marketing co-operatives, more expansionary monetary

Table 4.1 Sources of start-up credit for Kenyan household enterprises (percentages)

Own savings	Family loan or gift	Sale of existing asset	SACCO	Bank, financial institution	Money lender	Other
52.3	21.8	6.1	3.2	0.7	0.4	15.5

Source: 2005/6 Kenya Integrated Household Budget Survey (KIIHBS).

policy, inflation control interventions through food buffer stocks and incomes policies, and a crawling peg exchange rate regime to promote exports, especially within Sub-Saharan Africa itself.

Our proposal for subsidized credit is thus only one component of an overall approach, but it is nevertheless a central feature of the overall strategy. It is the most effective means of expanding opportunities for small-scale enterprises, which would in turn allow for productivity gains through economies of scale. It would also bring an increase in the formalization of these enterprises, since, with the opportunity to receive credit subsidies, businesses would have an incentive to pay taxes and become registered. The increased tax revenues could then be used to finance the subsidies, as well as the other measures we are proposing. If the average size of these firms is able to increase, it would also mean an expansion in higher-productivity wage employment, which would mean a contraction in the number of people trying to earn a living through small-scale enterprises, and this in turn would reduce competition among the now 2 million such firms.

Whether all this is viable depends on establishing a system of subsidized credit allocation that builds on the positive features of both the Grameen-type micro-finance model and the large-scale development banking model with reciprocal controls and performance standards. How we propose that this be accomplished is thus the next question to answer.

Kenya's financial system

Kenya's financial system already has some important positive features. These include:

(i) Kenya's commercial banking system is generally well-developed, and by some standard performance measures is more focused on lending to the private sector than is the case in other Sub-Saharan countries.

(ii) Kenya is developing as a regional financial centre, with emerging securities markets.

(iii) Kenya has a widespread system of micro-finance institutions (MFIs) already in place and operating. SACCOs are the most important of these, but there are others, both formal and informal, both client- and member-based. These include institutions such as the KREP bank (formal, client-based) and ROSCAs – Rotating Savings and Credit Associations (informal, member-based).

Despite these positive features, the contributions of the financial system to promoting economic growth, employment expansion and poverty reduction are inadequate. The main reasons for this inadequate performance are as follows:

(i) The commercial banking system lends more than one-third of its deposit base to the government. This, of course, reduces the availability of funds for businesses, especially small and medium-sized enterprises (SMEs) and small farmers.

(ii) More generally, the farming, SME and informal sectors are starved of credit. This is because (a) commercial banks do not generally lend to these sectors; and (b) the SACCOs and other MFIs do not have sufficient resources to provide large-scale funds. Moreover, the largest share of the lending done by the MFIs is for personal household purposes or family emergencies.

Given this combination of positive and negative features of the Kenyan financial system, the solution to the problem, at a fundamental level, seems straightforward: in some way to bring into much closer alliance the formal commercial banking system and the MFIs. In fact, proposals along these lines have been suggested by, among others, the World Bank, specifically in a 1994 study on Kenya, and the International Monetary Fund (IMF) in a more general 2005 study on Sub-Saharan African finance. This idea has also been raised in some previous research papers by Kenyan scholars (for example, Atieno, 2001). What remains is to flesh out a large-scale programme that could realistically be implemented on a short-term basis, but that is also capable of enabling a longer-term transformation of the Kenyan financial system. The proposal we present here will create a pool of subsidized credit at a level equal to roughly 20 per cent of the current level of private investment in Kenya, with a cost to the government of about 5 per cent of the fiscal budget.

Clearly, this would be a large-scale public subsidy programme. At the same time, as I describe below, the programme retains a system of market incentives and risks. Indeed – keeping Amsden's imperatives for successful credit allocation programmes in mind – the primarily reciprocal system and performance standard will be the market risks and rewards themselves. However, these risks and rewards will be established within a socialized market setting. As we shall see, the loan guarantee programme will lower dramatically the level of risk for commercial banks and MFIs who participate in the programme. The interest rates charged to borrowers will therefore have to fall commensurately. Beyond this, I also present an incentive-based system for minimizing opportunities to defraud the system profitably.

Basic features of the loan guarantee proposal

The proposal is for a large-scale policy intervention to link the formal commercial banking system with the SACCOs and other micro-finance entities. The MFIs are much more capable of making loans to small businesses, farmers and the informal sector – and can utilize more flexible systems of collateral for such loans.

As we noted above, something along these lines has been proposed in at least some documents of both the IMF and World Bank (see Sacerdoti (2005) on Sub-Saharan African finance in general; and Fafchamps *et al.* (1994, p. 88)). This point is also the main policy conclusion of the excellent 2001 paper by Atieno on Kenya's financial system. Atieno also reports, intriguingly, that loan guarantee programmes are already being implemented in Kenya, though she does not supply sufficient detail. For example, she writes about a Barclays Bank programme that offers loans for women entrepreneurs both as individuals and as groups.

Key details of proposal

We propose a loan guarantee fund similar to the one that Atieno reports Barclays Bank was operating on a small scale. That is, we propose a loan guarantee system in which the government offers commercial banks something in the order of a 75 per cent guarantee on loans that they make to SACCOs and other micro-finance entities. The commercial banks would have to demonstrate that the SACCOs are capable of making business loans, rather than simply emergency loans and personal loans.

For a programme of this sort to be successful at promoting decent employment and reducing poverty, it needs to operate on a large scale. Of course, any such programme will need to be phased-in gradually. But, as a matter of principle, it is important to show that it could operate on a large scale without placing excessive strains either on the government budget or on the capacities of the financial system.

Scale of operation

Consider a programme of roughly the following scale when fully operational. Private investment in Kenya in 2004 (the most recent year with non-provisional GDP data) was roughly 15 per cent of gross domestic product (GDP):

2004 GDP in market prices = Ksh1.3 trillion
2004 gross private domestic investment (GPDI) = Ksh200 billion

Let us assume that the loan guarantee programme is roughly equal to 20 per cent of 2004 GPDI of Ksh200 billion. Thus,

Total loans being guaranteed = Ksh40 billion (at 2004 prices)

Following the model from Barclays Bank (as reported by Atieno, 2001), let us assume that loans are guaranteed at a 75 per cent rate. This means that the government is guaranteeing Ksh30 billion in loans.

Let us also assume a default rate on these loans of 30 per cent. This is a very high rate, roughly equal, in fact to the actual 'alarming' rate reported for 2004 in what had been a confidential memo prepared by former Central Bank Governor, Andrew Mullei, to former finance minister, David Mwiraria.[11] According to the official District Annual Reports, the default rates on SACCOs between 2001 and 2005 ranged between 2.8 and 7.5 per cent. For the purposes of our exercise, we deliberately assume a very high default rate. This establishes a plausible upper limit of the costs of the loan guarantee programme.

Working with an assumption of a high default rate also underscores a key point of this proposal: that for commercial banks to make loans to micro-finance entities will entail real risks. Indeed, that the initiative will not be useful unless the commercial banks are willing to accept greater risks, and thus the reality that defaults will occur. At the same time, precisely because the banks will have a large share of their own funds committed to the guaranteed loans, they will operate with care when entering into agreements with micro-finance enterprises, even though 75 per cent of their loans would be guaranteed by the government.

The cost to the government of a 75 per cent guarantee with 30 per cent default rate on 40 billion in guaranteed loans can be calculated as follows:

$$\text{Ksh40 billion} \times 0.75 \times 0.3 = \text{Ksh9 billion}$$

Thus the direct annual expense of the guarantee programme of this magnitude, and building in the assumptions we have, would amount to Ksh9 billion per year. The total government budget for 2004 was Ksh188.9 billion at 2004 prices. Thus, at the 2004 level of economic activity and government spending, the loan guarantee programme, at full operation, would be equal to somewhat less than 5 per cent of the Kenyan general government budget. If we allow for a lower default rate, at, say, 15 per cent, then the costs of the loan guarantee programme fall correspondingly, to Ksh4.5 billion.

Extent of credit subsidy

The terms of the subsidy must meet four criteria:

1. Subsidies must be large enough such that the programme will succeed in building the necessary links between the commercial banks and the SACCOs and other micro-finance institutions;
2. The programme must still be seen as providing potential profit opportunities for both commercial banks and the micro-lenders;
3. The loan terms must be broadly consistent with the structure of interest rates, rewards, and risks within the Kenyan financial market as it currently operates; and
4. The terms must be understood easily by participants in the financial system.

A logical starting point for establishing an appropriate interest rate on subsidized loans is the government bond rate. With respect to default risk, government bonds are the least risky asset within the Kenyan financial system. At the same time, the Kenyan government bond rate reflects everything about the general level of risk in Kenya, including both inflation risk and country risk.

A subsidized loan from a commercial bank to a micro-credit lender would also incorporate general levels of country risk and inflation risk. The default risk on a subsidized loan would then depend on (i) the credit profile of the individual borrower; and (ii) the extent of the loan guarantee. Based on this, the rate on concessionary loans should be set at an increment above the government bond rate. How large an increment above the government bond rate would depend on the borrowers' profile and the extent of the government guarantee on loans.

To make this clearer, we can stipulate that a government bond issue in Ksh faces virtually zero default risk. Thus the interest rate on a private loan with a 100 per cent guarantee should be set at exactly the government bond rate. In contrast, the appropriate rate on a loan with no guarantee is, by definition, the market interest rate on that loan. As such, the government bond rate and the market interest rate define the range within which concessionary rates should be set.

The appropriate concessionary rate can therefore be derived simply as follows:

$$I^{lg} = i^{m} - LC,$$

where

$$LC = C(i^{m} - i^{b}),$$

and I^{lg} is the rate on loan guarantees, i^{m} is the market interest rate for a loan of a given risk class and maturity, C is the percentage of a loan that the government is guaranteeing, and i^{b} is the government bond rate for a given maturity.

To illustrate this calculation with an example, consider a case, which closely approximates actual Kenyan financial market conditions in July 2007, in which the government 3-year bond rate is 8 per cent, and the commercial bank rate is 13 per cent. In such a case, and assuming a 75 per cent loan guarantee programme, the concessionary loan rate I^{lg} would be 9.25 per cent.

Of course, the concessionary loan rate would rise if the government guarantee was less. Thus, if we assume that the loan guarantee is 50 per cent rather than 75 per cent, then the concessionary loan rate rises to 10.50 per cent.

For the programme to operate successfully, the subsidized lending rate that commercial banks make to SACCOs and other micro-finance institutions would also have to be incorporated into the rate at which the SACCOs themselves make retail loans to small businesses and farmers. Establishing the details of this retail lending rate would have to take into account the specific operations of the micro-credit units, including the means through which they establish collateral. Given the large number of micro-credit units operating in Kenya, it may be possible that establishing appropriate spreads for subsidized retail lending rates could result through market competition alone. This is a matter to consider in detail later. For now, it is sufficient to recognize the basic principles presented here on which subsidized lending – at both wholesale and retail levels – should be established.

Creating disincentives for fraud

The obvious way to defraud the system of loan guarantees is for borrowers and lenders to collude in obtaining guaranteed loans from the government, then deliberately defaulting on these loans to collect the government guarantee. As colluders in such an enterprise, the borrower and lender would then share the government guarantee payment.

As a simple example, consider a case in which a commercial bank makes a Ksh1,000 loan to a SACCO, which will then purportedly lend the money to small business owners, but in fact the commercial bank and SACCO are colluding to collect funds from the SACCO defaulting on the loan. Once the default is accepted as legitimate by the government, the government is then obligated to pay the commercial bank Ksh750, assuming a 75 per cent guarantee on the loan. The borrower and lender can then split these funds. Of course, the commercial bank and SACCO would have earlier worked out an arrangement for sharing the Ksh1000 in fraudulent 'loan funds'.

A loan guarantee system can be designed to minimize such opportunities for fraud. The first type of disincentive would entail creating an escrow account on the loan, to be held by the government. Once establishing such an escrow fund, this fund can be used to minimize the incentives for fraud. Thus, if the loan does not go into default, then the escrow funds are released to the borrower when the loan matures. But if the loan *does* go into default, the government only releases the escrow account funds back to the commercial bank after the conditions of the loan default have been investigated. In addition, this set of incentives can be combined with strict penalties for fraud as well as rewards for people who discover and report on such schemes. We now illustrate these considerations through the following example, and present the details in Table 4.2.

As the table shows, the main parameters of this case are as follows:

1. Amount of loan: Ksh1,000.
2. Terms of loan: 5 years at 5 per cent annual simple interest.
3. Government guarantee: 75 per cent of the principal on loan.
4. Escrow account: SACCO contributes Ksh100; commercial bank contributes 200Ksh.
5. Amount of funds for SACCO expenditure: Ksh800.

Table 4.2 Numerical example on collateral and escrow fund

	Case 1	**Case 2**
Guarantee	750	500
Total escrow	300	300
Borrower contribution	100	100
Lender contribution	200	200
If default, govt pays	750	500
Net gains from fraud:		
Borrower gain	275 (=375 – 100)	150 (=250 – 100)
Lender gain	175 (=375 – 200)	50 (=250 – 200)

Notes: Amounts are in Ksh – Kenyan shillings; Loan terms: Ksh1,000, 5 years at 5 per cent; Government guarantee: Varies, 75 per cent versus 50 per cent;
Escrow contributions: Constant at 10 per cent borrower; 20 per cent lender.

No default case

With this loan, if there is no default, the SACCO pays Ksh50 per year in interest plus repaying the principal. At the end of 5 years, the SACCO also receives the Ksh300 (plus accrued interest) on the escrow account.

Default case

SACCO is out Ksh100 of own money, plus the opportunity to receive the Ksh200 additional money in the escrow funds. The commercial bank is out Ksh250, receiving Ksh750 in government guarantees.

Incentive to defraud the system

Assume the SACCO and the commercial bank are in a conspiracy to defraud the government of the Kksh750 of the loan guarantee. Their arrangement is that each will receive half of the money coming from the government guarantee – that is, each will receive Ksh 375 from loan guarantee.

The net outcomes are as follows:

SACCO: Gains Ksh275 (=Ksh375 from guarantee – Ksh100 contribution to escrow).

Commercial bank: Gains Ksh175 (=Ksh375 from guarantee – Ksh200 to escrow).

This incentive to defraud the system could be large enough to encourage this type of fraudulent operation. If so, apart from the punishments to be faced if the fraud was discovered (more on this below), the way to weaken such incentives would, straightforwardly, entail some combination of either (i) reducing the level of the guarantee; or (ii) increasing the escrow fund obligations for both borrower and lender.

If we assume that the guarantee is only 50 per cent of the loan, but the escrow commitment remains the same, the incentives reduce to the following:

Borrower: Gains Ksh150 (=Ksh250 from guarantee – Ksh100 contribution to escrow).
Lender: Gains Ksh50 (= Ksh250 from guarantee – Ksh200 contribution to escrow).

From these examples, we can see that, by reducing the size of the guarantees or increasing the amount of the escrow commitments, incentives for fraud are diminished. But by pursuing such measures, one also obviously weakens the benefits to be accrued from the loan guarantee programme, and thereby the prospect that the programme could be used as a major financing tool contributing to economic growth and employment expansion.

Incentive-based monitoring

The way to sustain a more expansionary loan guarantee programme – that is, including a higher guarantee ratio and lower escrow contribution ratios – is to create severe penalties for fraud along with strong incentives for 'whistleblowers' to report abuses of the system. This means mobilizing incentives to monitor the system rather than relying primarily on government investigators to prevent fraud. This approach to monitoring financial market regulations was developed by Dean Baker (2003) with respect to the so-called Tobin tax – a tax on speculative transactions in global currency markets. A variation on Baker's idea could be applicable here. For example:

In the case of a Ksh1,000 loan with a 75 per cent guarantee:

1. Minimum penalty to commercial bank for gaming the system: 'treble damages' – that is, Ksh2,250.
2. Reward for whistleblowing: Full amount of guarantee – that is, Ksh750.

In addition, both the commercial bank and SACCO would lose their licences to operate.

Through combining the escrow system with the incentive-based monitoring approach, it should be possible to put a workable set of incentives in place to operate the loan guarantee programme.[12]

Additional financial market reform initiatives

A loan guarantee programme of this sort is both feasible and highly desirable for Kenya, and indeed can serve as the foundation to link Kenya's well-developed commercial banking system with its similarly well-developed micro-lending institutions. But operating on its own, this measure will not be sufficient to move Kenya's financial system on to a sustainable developmental path. Other initiatives will also provide important support. Among those that we discuss in Pollin *et al.* (2007) are establishing reliable private credit-rating operations and revitalizing public investment banks. The approach we take with the public investment banks here is in parallel with the loan guarantee programmes operating through the commercial banks and MFIs: that is, we propose that the public investment banks operate as public/private partnerships, to maintain both a large subsidized component as well as private initiative and risk-taking.

Summary and conclusions

The achievements of the micro-finance movement pioneered by Muhammad Yunus and the Grameen Bank are real and significant. The Grameen model has brought new opportunities for poor women to enjoy independent livelihoods, and has initiated new thinking on how to establish collateral among the world's poor. It has also emphasized the role of finance more generally in advancing the well-being of the poor. At the same time, considered on an economy-wide basis, the achievements of micro-finance institutions appear to be modest, especially in comparison with the macro-finance developmental policies that were implemented successfully in the countries that Amsden has termed 'the rest'.

This chapter has explored the relative contributions of micro- and macro-finance institutions as policy approaches for fighting mass poverty by promoting decent employment. Drawing on this discussion, the chapter then focused on conditions in Kenya, one of the poorest countries in the world, but one that already has both the most extensive system of micro-finance institutions in Sub-Saharan Africa as well as a sophisticated commercial banking system. The chapter has explored ways in which these existing micro-finance and commercial banking institutions in Kenya might be integrated more successfully and mobilized to promote decent employment creation and poverty reduction. The key idea is to synthesize features of micro-finance along with a large-scale subsidized credit allocation programme. The credit allocation programme would utilize market incentives in establishing effective control mechanisms and performance standards for subsidy recipients. This discussion of Kenya's situation can perhaps encourage further thinking beyond this particular case on ways to make large-scale subsidized micro-finance a more effective tool for fighting mass poverty in developing countries.

Notes

1. I benefited substantially from discussions with other participants at the September 2007 Festschrift conference in honour of Professor Ajit Singh.
2. See, among Professor Singh's prodigious writings on this broad theme, Singh, 1993, 1997b, 1998 and 2004.
3. See Pollin *et al.* (2006) and Pollin *et al.* (2007). We have done this work under the auspices of the International Poverty Centre of the United Nations Development Programme.
4. See the survey feature 'The Hidden Wealth of the Poor', *The Economist,* 3 November 2005.
5. See, among others, von Pischke *et al.* (1983); and *The Economist* survey, 3 November 2005. Armendáriz de Aghion and Morduch (2005) also summarize this perspective.
6. Pearl and Phillips (2001). Rahman (1999) reaches a different conclusion regarding high repayment rates at the Grameen Bank – that the borrowers face intense pressure to maintain regular repayment schedules. Rahman concludes that pressure such as this 'increases the debt-liability on the individual households, increases tension and frustration among household members, produces new forms of dominance over women and increases violence in society.' Establishing which perspective is more generally accurate remains an important task for future researchers.
7. Some basic figures and references on this, as well as further references, are provided in Pollin (2003, ch. 5).
8. All data in this and the following paragraphs come from the World Bank's *World Development Indicators*, 2006.
9. The poverty thresholds on which my colleagues and I based these calculations are from the 2005/6 Kenya Integrated Household Budget Survey (KIHBS). This study measures *consumption* poverty, while the figures we are relying on are employment income figures only. Thus people could have higher levels of consumption than income through non-labour sources of income and receipt of in-kind consumption goods. Thus these calculations should be seen as only broadly indicative, and not as precise calculations of Kenyan poverty rates.

10. Our approach to studying the Kenyan labour market proceeds very much in the tradition advanced by Professor Hans Singer and his collaborators in their classic 1972 work for the ILO, *Employment, Incomes, and Equality: A Strategy for Increasing Productive Employment in Kenya.*
11. 'Three Out of 10 Debts Gone Bad as "Serial Defaulters" Run Amok in Kenya's Banks', http:/allafrica.com.stories/200607040023.html, 8 March 2006.
12. These views are consistent with the concern expressed by the World Bank that credit guarantee systems also maintain workable methods of contract enforcement.

References

Amsden, Alice (2001) *The Rise of 'The Rest': Challenges to the West from Late-industrializing Economies*, Oxford: Oxford University Press.

Armendáriz de Aghion, Beatriz and Jonathan Morduch (2005) *The Economics of Microfinance*, Cambridge, Mass.: MIT Press.

Atieno, Rosemary (2001) 'Formal and Informal Institutions' Lending Policies and Access to Credit by Small-Scale Enterprises in Kenya: An Empirical Assessment', AERC Research Paper 111, African Economic Research Consortium, November.

Baker, Dean (2003) 'Tobin Taxes: Are They Enforceable?', in James Weaver, Randall Dodd and Jamie Baker (eds), *Debating the Tobin Tax: New Rules for Global Finance*, Washington, DC: New Rules for Global Finance Coalition, pp. 101–8.

Daley-Harris, Sam (2007) 'Debate on Microcredit', *Foreign Policy in Focus*, 21 June 2007; http://fpif.org/fpiftxt/4324.

Fafchamps, Marcel, Tyler Biggs, Jonathan Conning, and Pradeep Srivastava (1994) 'Enterprise Finance in Kenya', Draft document, Regional Program on Enterprise Development, Africa Region, The World Bank, June.

Fernando, Nimal A. (2006) 'Understanding and Dealing with High Interest Rates on Microcredit: A Note to Policy Makers in the Asia and Pacific Region', Asian Development Bank.

International Labour Organization (1972) *Employment, Incomes and Equality: A Strategy for Increasing Productive Employment in Kenya*, Geneva: ILO.

Pearl, Daniel and Michael M. Phillips (2001) 'Grameen Bank, Which Pioneered Loans for the Poor, Has Hit a Repayment Snag', *Wall Street Journal*, 27 November, p. A1.

Pollin, Robert (2003) *Contours of Descent: U.S. Economic Fractures and the Landscape of Global Austerity*, New York/London: Verso.

Pollin, Robert, Gerald Epstein, James Heintz and Léonce Ndikumana (2006) *An Employment-Targeted Economic Program for South Africa*, Brasilia: International Poverty Centre of the United Nations Development Program and Northampton, Mass.: Edward Elgar.

Pollin, Robert, Mwangi wa Githnji, and James Heintz (2007) *An Employment-Targeted Economic Program for South Africa*, Brasilia: International Poverty Centre of the United Nations Development Program and Northampton, Mass.: Edward Elgar.

Rahman, Aminur (1999) 'Micro-credit Initiatives for Equitable and Sustainable Development: Who Pays?', *World Development*, 27 (1): 67–82.

Sacerdoti, Emilio (2005) 'Access to Bank Credit in Sub-Saharan Africa: Key Issues and Reform Strategies', IMF Working Paper WP/05/166, International Monetary Fund.

Singh, Ajit (1993) 'The Stock Market and Economic Development: Should Developing Countries Encourage Stock Markets?', *UNCTAD Review*, 4: 1–28.

Singh, Ajit (1997a) 'Liberalization and Globalization: An Unhealthy Euphoria', in Jonathan Michie and John Grieve Smith (eds), *Employment and Economic Performance: Jobs, Inflation and Growth*, London: Oxford University Press.

Singh, Ajit (1997b) 'Financial Liberalisation, Stock Markets and Economic Development', *The Economic Journal*, 107 (442), May: 771–82.

Singh, Ajit (1998) "'Asian Capitalism" and the Financial Crisis', CEPA Working Paper Series III, No.10, Center for Economic Policy Analysis, New School for Social Research; http://www.newschool.edu/cepa/papers/archive/cepa0310.pdf.

Singh, Ajit (2004) 'Capital Account Liberalization, Free Long-Term Capital Flows, Financial Crises and Economic Development', Working Paper No. 245, Centre for Business Research, University of Cambridge.

The Economist (2005) 'The Hidden Wealth of the Poor: A Survey of Microfinance', 3 November.

Von Pischke, J. D., Dale Adams and Gordon Donald, (eds), (1983) *Rural Financial Markets in Developing Countries: Their Use and Abuse*, Baltimore, Md.: World Bank/Johns Hopkins University Press.

5

Financial Liberalization: The Current State of Play

Philip Arestis and Malcolm Sawyer

Introduction

The purpose of this chapter is to review some of the problematic issues that have come to the fore in debates over the 'financial liberalization' thesis. In doing so, this chapter seeks to indicate 'the current state of play' of the thesis and also to attempt to discover what we have learnt from the work undertaken on the issue of financial liberalization and its relevance to the finance–growth nexus. We begin with a brief examination of the experience with financial liberalization policies, followed by an examination of the main problems; we also add to the list of problems by looking more closely into the role of institutions, a problem that seems to have been played down by the proponents. A final section summarizes the argument and concludes by attempting to take a position on what the current state of play is with respect to the thesis in question. Ajit Singh has contributed substantially to this area, and we hope that this chapter follows the tradition he has established to view both the thesis of financial liberalization and the policies that emanate from it as problematic. We concur with this view, as we hope to show in what follows.

Experience with financial liberalization policies

The general idea of financial liberalization appeared from the 1970s onwards to overcome the perceived problems and difficulties arising from what was later termed 'financial repression' (McKinnon, 1973; Shaw, 1973). The latter referred to a high degree of regulation of the banking and financial system in many countries, and specifically control by the Central Bank and government of the level of interest rates and allocation of credit. These were usually perceived to involve the enforcement of interest rates on loans below the 'market level', and the associated direction of loans towards those sectors given preferential treatment in the allocation of credit (and away from the sectors without such treatment). These policies involved financial regulations and state-owned or state-directed banks, all of which were used for a range of economic and social purposes – for example, subsidizing housing, supporting financial infrastructure, development and industrial policy in more general terms, as well as promoting exports and small businesses (Grabel, 1997). Central banks in both developing and developed countries supported these policies and activities via a variety of tools and mechanisms, most importantly through subsidizing credit and regulating financial institutions to direct credit to specific sectors and for specific purposes (Epstein, 2006).

The recommendation of the financial liberalization proponents was the removal of ceilings on interest rates and the scrapping of credit allocation policies. The effects of financial liberalization were argued to be an increase in the quantity and the quality of investment through a more efficient allocation of credit. In the case of liberalization of international capital flows, there are added benefits: both the private and the public sectors have access to capital and other resources, such as technology, which are not available domestically as a result of low income, savings and growth, as well as capital flight. An increase in private capital flows would raise capital stock, productivity and investment, along with economic growth and employment. All these increase efficiency and policy discipline. Consequently, liberalization of capital flows is paramount to promote sound economic performance, particularly investment and growth.

The early experience of countries undergoing financial liberalization has been reviewed in a number of studies (see, for example, World Bank, 1993; Demetriades and Luintel, 1996; Arestis and Demetriades, 1997, 1998; Arestis, 2004, 2005). This experience led to the conclusion that financial liberalization had limited success but also suffered numerous and unambiguous failures. Financial liberalization enhanced the integration of developing and other countries into global markets, thus enabling governments and large firms to enjoy more finance from access to international credit markets. Typically, though, the early financial liberalization experience unleashed a massive demand for credit by households and by firms, which was met by banks providing the loans but was not matched by a comparable increase in the saving rate.[1]

Interest rates on loans rose as households demanded more credit to finance purchases of consumer durables, and firms plunged into speculative investments. Banks were eager to meet the increased demand for loans, even though many were high-risk, in the belief that government bail-outs would prevent bank failures. In terms of bank behaviour, banks increased deposit and lending rates to compensate for losses attributable to loan defaults. A widespread finding was that higher real interest rates failed to increase savings (Bandiera *et al.*, 2000, in a sample of eight developing countries), failed to increase bank lending (Jayaratne and Strahan, 1996, in the case of US interstate bank branch deregulation), and failed to boost investment, which often fell as a proportion of GNP over the period (see, for example, Arestis and Demetriades, 1997; Zhu *et al.*, 2004). Loans often financed the acquisition of existing assets with an inflation of asset prices. The only type of savings that *did* increase was the use of foreign savings – that is, external debt. This, however, made the 'liberalized' economies more vulnerable to oscillations in the international economy, increasing the debt/asset ratio, and thus service obligations, and promoting the debt crises experienced in the recent past. Financial liberalization thus managed to displace domestic markets by international markets. Increases in long-term productive investment never materialized either. Instead, short-term speculative activities flourished, whereby firms adopted risky financial strategies, thereby causing banking crises and economic collapse.

In spite of the early troublesome attempts at financial liberalization, and the increasing problems and scepticism surrounding the financial liberalization thesis, it had an early and continuing impact on development policy through the promotion of financial and other liberalization by the IMF and the World Bank. These two institutions, perhaps in their traditional role as promoters of what were claimed to be free market conditions, were keen to encourage financial liberalization policies in developing countries as part of more general reforms or stabilization programmes. When events following the implementation of financial liberalization prescriptions did not confirm their theoretical premises, revisions were made to the main tenets of the thesis. It was postulated that it was a 'big bang' approach to financial liberalization, in which regulations and constraints on bank behaviour that had generated problems were sudden withdrawn, notably those of large increases in bank lending and consequent financial crises. Gradual financial liberalization and a 'sequencing of financial liberalization' (for example, Edwards, 1989; McKinnon, 1991) is recommended. Employing credibility arguments, Rodrik (1987) and Calvo (1988) suggest a narrow focus of reforms with financial liberalization left to last. Financial liberalization, in this view, is the last step in an overall liberalization process.

A further response by the proponents of the financial liberalization thesis has been to argue that, where liberalization failed it was because of the existence of implicit or explicit deposit insurance coupled with inadequate banking supervision and macroeconomic instability (for example, McKinnon, 1988a, 1988b; 1991; World Bank, 1989; Villanueva and Mirakhor, 1990). These conditions were conducive to excessive risk-taking by the banks, a form of moral hazard, which can lead to 'too high' real interest rates in view of the higher risk, bankruptcies of firms and bank failures. This experience led to the introduction of new elements into the analysis of the financial liberalization thesis, in the form of preconditions, which should be satisfied before reforms are contemplated and implemented. These are caused by problems emanating from differential speeds of adjustment in different types of markets. This analysis leads to recommendations including 'adequate banking supervision', aiming to ensure that banks have a well-diversified loan portfolio; 'macroeconomic stability', which refers to low and stable inflation and a sustainable fiscal deficit; and the sequencing of financial reforms.

Differential speeds of adjustment were argued to be possible causes of serious problems affecting attempts at financial liberalization (McKinnon, 1991), with labour and then goods markets becoming more sluggish to adjust to changes than financial markets. Thus financial markets could not be reformed in the same manner as other markets without creating awkward difficulties. Recognition of these problems has led the proponents of the financial liberalization thesis to suggest the desirability of sequencing of reforms with reform (liberalization) of the real sector, which has come to be seen as a prerequisite to financial reform. Thus financial repression would have to be maintained during the first stage of economic liberalization. Furthermore, there is the possibility that different aspects of reform programmes may work at cross-purposes, disrupting the real sector in the process. This is what Sachs (1988) labelled as 'competition of instruments'. A crucial example of this arose when unexpected increases in domestic interest rates lead to a large appreciation of the exchange rate, thereby damaging exports and stimulating imports, and more generally damaging the real sector and employment. Sequencing becomes important again. It is thus suggested that liberalization of foreign trade and international capital transactions should take place after liberalization of domestic financial markets. In this context, proponents suggest caution in 'sequencing' in the sense of gradual financial liberalization emphasizing the achievement of macroeconomic stability and adequate bank supervision as preconditions for successful financial reform (and Sachs, 1988; McKinnon, 1988b; Villanueva and Mirakhor, 1990). It is also argued by the proponents that the authorities should move more aggressively on financial reform in good times and more slowly when borrowers' net worth is reduced by negative shocks, such as recessions and losses resulting from terms of trade (see also World Bank, 1989). Caprio *et al.* (1994) reviewed the financial reforms in a number of primarily developing countries, with the experience of six countries studied at some depth and length. They conclude that managing the reform process rather than adopting a *laissez-faire* approach is important, and that sequencing, along with the initial conditions in finance and macroeconomic stability, are critical elements in implementing financial reforms successfully.

These post hoc theoretical revisions were thought to be sufficient to defend the original thesis of a disappointing record with the predictions of financial liberalization thesis of positive effects on savings and investment not being validated, and some ensuring problems of financial crises. Despite all these modifications, however, the proponents of the financial liberalization thesis do not even contemplate abandoning it. No amount of revision has changed the objective of the thesis, which is to pursue the *optimal* path to financial liberalization, leaving the financial sector free from any political (that is, state) intervention. Sequencing does not salvage the financial liberalization thesis, for the simple reason that it depends on the assumption that financial markets clear in a Walrasian manner while the goods markets do not. In a neoclassical approach this is a strange assumption, since the well-known Walras's law, in which excess demand in markets sum to zero, suggests that, if financial markets clear, then so too will the goods market. Further, it is widely recognized that information in an uncertain world is necessarily asymmetric – that is, different people have varying amounts of information, and specifically the information and knowledge of a potential borrower clearly differ from the information and knowledge of a potential lender. It is then inevitable that financial markets will involve what are often termed imperfections: there will be credit rationing, and differential interest rates reflecting differences in risk assessment.

Even where the 'correct' sequencing took place (for example, in Chile), with trade liberalization preceding financial liberalization, not much success can be reported (Lal, 1987). The opposite is also the case where financial liberalization preceded trade liberalization – such as in Uruguay, where the experience was very much the same as in Chile (Grabel, 1995).

Stiglitz (2000) highlights the difficulties with the sequencing literature in explaining the South-East Asian crisis, where strong macroeconomic fundamentals, accompanied by sound systems of banking regulation and supervision, and reasonable economic policies along with sound financial institutions were in place. But still the South-East Asian financial crisis of 1997–8 was not prevented. Kaminsky and Schmuckler (2003) conclude that 'the ordering of liberalization does not matter in general. Opening the capital account or the stock market first does not have a different effect than opening the domestic financial sector first' (p. 31).

Arestis and Glickman (2002) argue that 'sequenced' programmes of 'free' market reforms favoured by the proponents of financial liberalization raises the feeling of invulnerability, weakening inhibitions against speculation and reinforcing the tendency towards euphoria (Minsky, 1986). In an open economy, this mood will spread rapidly beyond the confines of the country concerned. In the absence of capital controls, speculators will turn their attention to the domestic economy, especially so since the higher interest rate differentials might be in their favour. Capital flows will offset any tendency for the domestic upswing to push interest rates higher. The exchange rate may be pegged without much difficulty, or allowed to appreciate. In either case, the external position is interpreted as evidence of 'economic' health, fuelling optimism further. Success is an endogenous factor driving financial innovation forward, and openness extends the scope of achievable success. Sooner or later the economy can be led to one of the following: a crisis that is domestic in origin but impacts on its external situation; a crisis that is external in origin but impacts on its domestic situation; or to a crisis that is a combination of these two factors. Under these conditions, the exchange rate becomes a source of further uncertainty. Speculators begin to doubt the ability of the state to support its currency, and they may very well move against the currency concerned, possibly on a massive scale, as in the case of the 1997 South-East Asian crisis. This analysis clearly suggests that financial liberalization should be expected to lead to crisis. The experience of countries with financial liberalization discussed above and in Arestis and Glickman (2002), clearly testify to this real possibility. Consequently, Minsky's (1986) view that the instability of the financial system threatens high growth rates and low unemployment is validated by these experiences. Financial liberalization, as a key euphoria-inducing factor, 'intensifies this threat by adding further major stresses to the financial infrastructure' (Arestis and Glickman, 2002, p. 258).

It would not be an exaggeration to suggest, in fact, that the upheavals of the South-East Asian crisis are still evident in terms of the persistent and growing imbalances between the US and Asia, which are still being experienced at the time of writing; imbalances thought to have their roots in the financial South-East Asian crisis of 1997 (Asian Development Bank, 2007).[2] In this respect, the countries involved may very well be vulnerable to a new financial calamity, which could be triggered by a hard landing in the US that is almost certain to cause a painful slowdown in Asia. The Asian Development Bank (2007) study recommends more effective regulation and governance along with improved financial systems in Asia as a prelude to avoiding such calamity.

We argue in the rest of this chapter that there are a number of issues in these propositions, critical in the development of the financial liberalization thesis, but not problem-free. They are, in fact, so problematic that they leave the thesis without serious theoretical and empirical foundations.

Critical issues of the financial liberalization thesis

This section deals with the critical issues of the financial liberalization thesis, in an attempt to draw conclusions on both its theoretical and empirical importance. We summarize briefly some 'old' issues, with which we have dealt previously, followed by an attempt to deal with a 'new' issue: that of the importance of institutional factors.

Old issues

Arestis and Demetriades (1998) and Arestis (2004, 2005) suggest and discuss a number of problematic issues, as follows:

- the relationship between financial liberalization and economic development: the difficulty lies in establishing the cause and effect between financial development and economic growth. For as Arestis and Demetriades (1997) show, once the contemporaneous correlation between the two variables has been accounted for, there is no longer any evidence to suggest that financial development helps to predict future growth. This reinforces the difficulty of establishing the link between financial development and economic growth that was first identified by Patrick (1966) and further developed by McKinnon (1988a), who argued that: 'Although a higher rate of financial growth is positively correlated with successful real growth, Patrick's (1966) problem remains unresolved: What is the cause and what is the effect? Is finance a leading sector in economic development, or does it simply follow growth in real output that is generated elsewhere?' (p. 390);[3]

- the relationship between savings and investment: in the financial liberalization thesis it is postulated that savings precedes investment in the sense that the available savings provide funding for investment, and that savings flow into investment. But savings cannot finance capital accumulation; this is done by the banking sector. With a credit-creating financial system, it is banks, and not savers, that finance investment. It is rather that, when investment is financed and occurs, then corresponding savings are generated, and hence it is investment that precedes savings;
- hedge and curb market effects: this provides an interesting critique of the financial liberalization thesis, which emanates from the structuralist theory (Taylor, 1983; Van Wijnbergen, 1983). It suggests that higher interest rates from financial liberalization might leave unchanged or, indeed, decrease the total supply of funds. This is because of hedge effects, which may not materialize – in which case the total supply of funds may not be affected; or to curb effects, which may reduce it. Hedge effects are a result of substitution of hedge assets – gold and land are the most obvious examples – for bank deposits, caused by higher interest rates. However, it should readily be conceded that both the hedge and curb effects have not been unambiguously validated empirically (Ghate, 1992).
- the role of sequencing: in addition to the problems identified above, we may note the conclusions of Kaminsky and Schmuckler (2003), who discuss the relevant findings to conclude that 'the ordering of liberalization does not matter in general. Opening the capital account or the stock market first does not have a different effect than opening the domestic financial sector first' (p. 31).
- free banking and the stability of the financial system: the underlying assumption of the thesis is that market forces do produce stability in the banking and financial systems. Arestis and Demetriades (1998) suggest that, even in the most frequently discussed cases of free banking, the system may either have worked because of support emanating from outside the system itself, or it was simply marred by serious problems. The upshot is that banking systems need to be regulated (Dow, 1996). Further serious theoretical drawbacks spring from two sources, *asymmetric information* (producing moral hazard and adverse selection) and *uncertainty*, which are particularly acute in a free banking system.
- the role of financial policies: Arestis *et al.* (2003) provide an assessment of the effects of several types of financial policies on the average productivity of capital in fourteen countries, including both developed

and developing countries. Their findings suggest that the effects of these policies vary considerably across countries, probably reflecting institutional differences. These results are very much within the spirit of Stiglitz's (1998) proposition that 'there are a host of regulations, including restrictions on interest rates or lending to certain sectors (such as speculative real estate), that may enhance the stability of the financial system and thereby increase the efficiency of the economy. Although there may be a trade off between short-run efficiency and this stability, the costs of instability are so great that long run gains to the economy more than offset any short term losses' (p. 33).

- the role of stock markets and speculation: speculation is particularly acute in the case of stock markets (though property markets are also often damaged by speculative bubbles). Stock market financial assets are highly liquid and volatile, thus making the financial system more fragile rather than less (Arestis *et al.*, 2001), thereby encouraging short-termism at the cost of long-term growth. Financial liberalization, therefore, is less likely to enhance long-term growth prospects.
- the magnitude of distributional effects of interest rate changes: there are distributional effects that are ignored by the financial liberalization thesis. The distinction between 'demand determined' and 'cost-determined' price sectors is relevant. In the 'demand determined' sector, prices are determined by supply and demand, while in the 'cost-determined' price sector prices are administered. High interest rates hit the small firms harshly, but leave the big firms fairly unscathed. The weak, therefore, are victimized. Further distributional effects are discussed by Milanovic (2005), who concludes that major increases in domestic and in global inequality have occurred over the period during which extensive financial liberalization policies were pursued.
- related to the distributional aspect is the question of the relationship between financial liberalization and poverty. The key message that emerges is that, in the literature on financial liberalization, there is still no clear understanding of how the mechanisms involved in moving from financial repression to a liberalized regime influence different segments of the population and, in particular, the poor. It appears that a straightforward application of the standard liberalization policies without taking any precautions to protect the initially disadvantaged groups of the population from potential losses can worsen the living conditions of these groups (Arestis and Caner, 2005). Financial liberalization can worsen the situation of the poor by increasing income and wealth inequality as well by shifting political

and economic power from non-financial to financial actors, with the latter becoming the dominant group (Grabel, 2003). In this context, Cornia (2003) provides evidence that shows that capital account liberalization has the strongest impact on widening inequality within the country concerned; domestic financial liberalization has the next most important negative effect on the poor.

The conclusion from these contributions is that there are numerous problems connected with financial liberalization. This conclusion is strengthened further by Arestis and Sawyer (2005), where adding the following items expands the list of problematic cases for the thesis under scrutiny:

- the relationship between financial liberalization and crises: the analysis by Arestis and Glickman (2002) clarifies the point in the argument that 'financial liberalization produces an upward step-change in the intensity of the domestic drive towards financial innovation .... It thereby speeds up the process by which debt ratios of commercial concerns and financial institutions rise, escalating financial fragility, and it hastens the day when banking and financial crises loom' (Arestis and Glickman, 2002, pp. 244–5).
- the relevance of privatizing state banks to financial development and growth: Demetriades and Andrianova (2004) summarize the results relating to this proposition to conclude that 'the privatization of state banks is, at best, unnecessary, since it is better to build institutions that foster the development of private banks and remove subsidies from state banks. At worse it is detrimental, since when institutions are weak it will almost certainly lead to financial disintermediation' (p. 57).
- the role of legal and political factors: political factors linked with the establishment and maintenance of the rule of law with an efficient and effective legal system involving respect for property rights, contract laws, bankruptcy laws and so on is important in promoting financial development and growth. The difficulty, with this relationship is, however, that there is little variation in legal origins, which makes it very difficult to establish a convincing relevant relationship.
- the importance of capital account liberalization to macroeconomic policies: the financial liberalization thesis suggests that freeing up the capital account has positive effects on economic growth, through rising global linkages via cross-border financial flows. The financial crisis in South-East Asia showed that where it is possible to invest short-term

capital inflows in productive activities, an asset price bubble could be created.

- impact of financial liberalization at the corporate level: financial liberalization is assumed to have positive effects on corporations in that it exposes cronyism and enhances market discipline. However, Stiglitz (2004) argues that to the extent that capital-market liberalization causes greater consumption and output instability, it then 'increases the risk premium firms require for investment, thereby discouraging investment' (p. 63).

In all these cases examined, however relevant they might be, an important factor is missing. This is the role of institutions, which, while in the 'role of legal and political factors', referred to above, begins to appear as a possible missing factor, it does not exhaust the list. In what follows we propose to deal with the role of institutional factors more extensively.

New issue: institutional factors

In the original contributions to the financial liberalization debate, indeed to the whole debate of the finance–growth nexus, institutional factors did not play a crucial role. Subsequently, though, an interesting discussion emerged on the question of whether financial structure matters or not. The focus of the discussion was on the relative importance of bank-based and market-based financial systems (Gerschenkron, 1962; Stiglitz, 1985; Singh, 1997; Allen and Gale, 1999). More recently, empirical evidence has also been produced on the issue (see, for example, Arestis *et al.*, 2001; Demirgüç-Kunt and Levine, 2001; Levine, 2002, 2003). In view of the enormous growth of stock markets, particularly in 'emergent markets', since the 1980s, a lively debate emerged on whether well-developed stock markets may be able to offer different kinds of financial services compared to banking systems (Arestis and Demetriades, 1997; Singh, 1997). As such, stock markets may provide a different kind of impetus to investment and growth than the development of the banking system. Atje and Jovanovic (1993), Levine and Zevros (1995, 1996) and Levine (1996), provide empirical evidence of a strong, and positive, relationship between stock market developments and economic growth. They argue that stock markets may affect growth through liquidity, which makes investment less risky. Companies enjoy permanent access to capital through liquid equity issues. This argument leads to the conclusion that 'stock market development explains future economic growth' (Levine, 1996, p. 8). The studies by Atje and Jovanovic (1993) and Levine and Zervos (1995, 1996) differ in two respects: Levine and Zervos use indexes of stock market development as do Atje and Jovanovic, but, unlike the latter, their indexes combine a number of characteristics; and, unlike Atje and Jovanovic, Levine and Zervos control for initial conditions and other relevant factors that may influence economic growth. It is worth noting, however, that Zhu *et al.* (2004) demonstrate that the results arrived at by Levine and Zervos (1995, 1996) are not robust in that they are driven by their choice of outlier countries. Once more, appropriate outliers are utilized. It is no longer the case that a statistically significant relationship can be detected between economic growth and liquid stock markets. Furthermore, Arestis *et al.* (2001) offer a critique of the positive relationship between stock market development and economic growth; stock market volatility is an important variable, which should be considered carefully. Once this is properly undertaken, empirical evidence, which is not supportive of the 'stock market development explains future economic growth' thesis, is derived.

A broad literature has established that the financial sector in an economy can be important in determining the average productivity of capital. However, the causal nature of this relationship is now known to exhibit considerable variation across countries, which indicates that institutional factors or policies may play a critical role in determining how the process of financial development affects economic growth (Arestis and Demetriades, 1997). Arestis *et al.* (2002) demonstrate that the direct effects of financial repression in some developing countries are much larger than, and in some instances the reverse of, those emanating from changes in the real interest rate. Arestis *et al.* (2003) provide a further assessment of the effects of several types of financial policies on the average productivity of capital in fourteen countries, including both developed and developing countries. These findings suggest that the effects of the policies examined vary considerably across countries, probably reflecting institutional differences. They also demonstrate that the main predictions of the financial liberalization literature do not receive adequate empirical support. In contrast, their findings provide significant support for the thesis, currently gaining increasing support among international policy-makers, that some form of financial restraints may indeed have positive effects on economic efficiency.

The importance of institutional factors is also confirmed by Demirgüç-Kunt and Detragiache (2001), who demonstrate that institutional quality is inversely related to the incidence of financial fragility that usually follows episodes of financial liberalization. Further support is provided by the structuralist theory (Taylor, 1983; Van Wijnbergen, 1983). As noted above, hedge effects may leave unchanged, or indeed decrease, the total supply of funds following higher interest rates resulting from financial liberalization. Institutional factors are clearly present in this analysis and play a significant role in it.

La Porta *et al.* (1998) draw on the distinction between civil law and common law in their study of the significance of law factors to financial development and growth. Civil law has its origins in Roman law, and relies on formal rules, statutes and a comprehensive code in settling disputes. Three types of such law – French, German and Scandinavian – are based on the Roman law with varying degrees of dependence. Common law, which originates from the law of England, is based on precedents from judicial decisions and on the views of judges in resolving disputes. La Porta *et al.* (1998) find in their sample of forty-nine countries that civil-law countries have the weakest shareholder and creditor protection, while the common-law countries have the strongest. Legal origins also influence significantly legal enforcement, with the common-law countries (and Scandinavian civil-law countries) being endowed with the best quality of law enforcement, while the French civil-law countries have the worst. But the main determinant of legal enforcement is per capita GDP, so that rich countries with a civil-law tradition offer better law enforcement than poor common-law countries. In a different paper, but utilizing the same sample, La Porta *et al.* (1997) offer evidence suggesting that, while no significant difference can be established in terms of banking development, civil-law countries have lower levels of capital market development than common-law countries.

These findings can be compared to those of Rajan and Zingales (2003), who find that in civil-law countries of the French type, financial development was higher than in common-law countries in the pre-Second World War period. It was after the Second World War when civil-law countries began to lag behind common-law countries. Furthermore, legal origins 'may themselves be determined by historical, cultural, socio-economic and political factors' (Demetriades and Andrianova, 2004, p. 58), many of which influence financial development. Zingales (2003) adds to the difficulties by suggesting that legal origins are also correlated with a number of quality indicators, such as efficiency of the judiciary, bureaucratic quality, and many other factors. The upshot of the argument is that the purported link between all these factors and legal factors is very difficult, if not impossible, to gauge. A further difficulty with the relationship between legal origins and financial development and growth, is that there is little variation in legal origins, since most countries have a civil-law tradition, but a great deal of variation in financial development and growth. The example of Rajan and Zingales (2003), that in general terms financial development peaked before the First World War, declined in the inter-war period and well after the Second World War, before growing to a new peak at the end of the twentieth century, is relevant to the argument. This U-shaped pattern suggests that other, more important, variables besides legal origins affect financial development and growth. The same authors stress political factors. But whether it is legal or political factors, the point remains that institutional factors play an important part in the process.

The discussion of legal and political factors is closely related to the role of institutions in the finance–growth nexus. It is the case that little is known about how institutions interact with each other, and their path of development and transformation. Indeed, the relevant literature is not very helpful to policy-making, since it does not provide much guidance on what institutions to transform, how to transform them, or what form they should take. The real challenge, then, is the design and transformation of institutions to provide high-quality services. In this context, the study by Arestis *et al.* (2005) is important in that it offers a holistic approach to viewing factors that should be taken into account when considering accessibility to international financial flows. They suggest that norms, incentives, regulations, capacities and organizations are crucial elements in the design of institutions that would promote robust economic growth.

The analysis so far clearly implies that institutions matter in the financial liberalization debate. However, a further stage has emerged, which suggests that financial structure does not matter. Panel and cross-section studies both at cross-country level (Demirgüç-Kunt and Levine, 1996; Levine, 2002, 2003; Beck and Levine, 2004) and at industry and firm level (Demirgüç-Kunt and Levine, 2001; Beck and Levine, 2002; Demirgüç-Kunt and Maksimovic, 2002) conclude that financial structure is irrelevant to economic growth. Neither the bank-based nor the market-based financial system can explain economic growth, but rather it is the overall provision of financial services that is important.

Arestis *et al.* (2004), however, take on board the possibility of cross-country heterogeneity, and ask whether financial structure appears to be significant in explaining economic development when cross-country heterogeneity is fully accounted for in econometric investigations. Time series data on financial structure are utilized and formally test whether the data of the sample countries can be pooled. Applying both time series and dynamic heterogeneous panel methods, which do not impose any cross-country restrictions on parameters and adjustment dynamics, long-run relationship between financial structure and economic growth are estimated. Significant heterogeneity in cross-country parameters and adjustment dynamics are found. Tests show that data cannot be pooled for the countries utilized for the purposes of the exercise, nor do panel parameters correspond to country-specific estimates. These results clearly show that panel regressions hide important cross-country differences. Overall, these results clearly demonstrate that institutional factors are very important to the financial liberalization thesis. Such factors are not always accounted for in both theory and policy analyses.

Summary and conclusions

We have identified a further aspect of some importance to financial liberalization. We suggest that this critical issue of the thesis is marred by serious difficulties. We looked at the available evidence and found that it is not of much help to the thesis either. It is clear from this excursion into the literature that no convincing evidence has been provided in support of the propositions of the financial liberalization hypothesis. On the contrary, the available evidence can be interpreted as indicating that the theoretical propositions of the thesis are at best weak, and as such they ought to be abandoned. We may therefore conclude by agreeing with Stiglitz (1998), that the financial liberalization thesis is 'based on an ideological commitment to an idealized conception of markets that is grounded neither in fact nor in economic theory' (p. 20). The current structure is in some way a 'natural' phenomenon, rather than the direct result of specific laws, institutions and policies of government. Therefore, the debate begins with assumptions regarding institutional structure that are in fact policy options subject to review.

The current state of play for the financial liberalization thesis is, we suggest, that the predictions and prospects for development promised by financial liberalization have not materialized, and instead a degree of financial instability has been generated.

Notes

1. For a recent study that supports the argument that financial liberalization has had 'little empirical support', see Townsend and Ueda (2007). The same study, though, argues that there are sizeable welfare gains from financial liberalization. The period covered by the study is, though, 1976–96 for Thailand. The more interesting and relevant period of post-1997, the South-East Asian crisis, is not covered, which tends to lead to doubts about the validity of the empirical arguments of the study on the size of the welfare gains. A relevant

and more encompassing study is that by the Asian Development Bank (2007), which paints a different picture once the entire period is included.

2. Asia, in an attempt not to allow vulnerability to capital outflows, pursued policies of low exchange rates and trade surpluses (China, for example, accumulated foreign exchange reserves of more than US$120bn). The US promptly obliged, thereby becoming 'consumer of last resort' through low interest rates and government deficits; and creating in the process balance-of-payments current account deficits. The result has been an unbalanced global economy, which has continued for some time, increasingly posing a serious threat of a potentially more damaging financial crisis than the 1997 South-East Asian turmoil.
3. A recent European Central Bank working paper (Papaioannou, 2007) reviews the finance/growth literature and pays attention to causality. It concludes that while strong correlation between finance and growth has been established, still more work is needed on the causality between the two variables, and on the channels through which finance and growth are linked.

References

Allen, F. and D. Gale (1999) 'Bubbles, Crises, and Policy', *Oxford Review of Economic Policy*, 15 (3): 9–18.

Arestis, P. (2004) 'Washington Consensus and Financial Liberalisation', *Journal of Post Keynesian Economics*, 27 (2): 251–71.

Arestis, P. (2005) 'Financial Liberalisation and the Relationship Between Finance and Growth', in P. Arestis and M. Sawyer (eds), *Handbook of Alternative Monetary Economics*, Cheltenham: Edward Elgar.

Arestis, P. and A. Caner (2005) Financial Liberalization and Poverty: Channels of Influence, in P. Arestis and M. Sawyer (eds), *Financial Liberalization: Beyond Orthodox Concerns*, Basingstoke: Palgrave Macmillan.

Arestis, P. and P. O. Demetriades (1997) 'Financial Development and Economic Growth: Assessing the Evidence', *Economic Journal*, 107 (442): 783–99.

Arestis, P. and P. O. Demetriades (1998) 'Financial Liberalization: Myth or Reality?', in P. Arestis (ed.), *Method, Theory and Policy in Keynes: Essays in Honour of Paul Davidson, Vol. 3*, Cheltenham: Edward Elgar.

Arestis, P., P. O. Demetriades and B. Fattouh (2003) 'Financial Policies and the Aggregate Productivity of the Capital Stock', *Eastern Economic Journal*, 29 (2): 217–42.

Arestis, P., P. O. Demetriades, B. Fattouh and K. Mouratidis (2002) 'The Impact of Financial Liberalization Policies on Financial Development: Evidence from Developing Economies', *International Journal of Economics and Finance*, 7 (2): 109–21.

Arestis, P., P. O. Demetriades and K. B. Luintel, (2001) 'Financial Development and Economic Growth: The Role of Stock Markets', *Journal of Money, Credit and Banking*, 33 (1): 16–41.

Arestis, P. and M. Glickman (2002) 'Financial Crisis in South East Asia: Dispelling Illusion the Minskyan Way', *Cambridge Journal of Economics*, 26 (2): 237–60. Reprinted in R. E. Allen (ed.), *The International Library of Writings*

on the New Global Economy: The Political Economy of Financial Crises (2004), Cheltenham/Northampton, Mass.: Edward Elgar.
Arestis, P., A. D. Luintel and K. B. Luintel (2004) 'Financial Structure and Economic Growth: Evidence from Time Series Analyses', *mimeo*, Cambridge Centre for Economic and Public Policy, Department of Land Economy: University of Cambridge.
Arestis, P., A. D. Luintel and K. B. Luintel (2007) 'Financial Structure and Economic Growth: Accounting for Cross-country Heterogeneity', Mimeo, Cambridge Centre for Economic and Public Policy, Department of Land Economy, University of Cambridge.
Arestis, P., M. Nissanke and H. Stein (2005) 'Finance and Development: Institutional and Policy Alternatives to Financial Repression Theory', *Eastern Economic Journal*, 31 (2): 245–63.
Arestis, P. and M. Sawyer (2005) 'Financial Liberalization and the Finance–Growth Nexus: What Have We Learned?', in P. Arestis and M. Sawyer (eds), *Financial Liberalization: Beyond Orthodox Concerns, International Papers in Political Economy Series*, Basingstoke: Palgrave Macmillan.
Asian Development Bank (2007) *Beyond the Crisis: Emerging Trends and Challenges*, The Philippines: Asian Development Bank.
Atje, R. and B. Jovanovic (1993) 'Stock Markets and Development', *European Economic Review*, 37 (2–3): 632–40.
Bandiera, O., R. Caprio, P. Hanohan and F. Schiantarelli (2000) 'Does Financial Reform Raise or Reduce Saving?', *Review of Economics and Statistics*, 82 (2) – 239–63.
Beck, T. and R. Levine (2002) 'Industry Growth and Capital Accumulation: Does Having a Market- or Bank-Based System Matter?', *Journal of Financial Economics*, 64: 147–80.
Beck, T. and R. Levine (2004) 'Stock Markets, Banks and Growth: Panel Evidence', *Journal of Banking and Finance*, 28: 423–42.
Calvo, G. (1988) 'Servicing the Public Debt: the Role of Expectations', *American Economic Review*, 78: 647–61.
Caprio, G. Jr., I. Atiyas and J. A. Hanson. (eds) (1994) *Financial Reform: Theory and Experience*, Cambridge: Cambridge University Press.
Cho, Y.-J. and D. Khatkhate (1989) 'Lessons of Financial Liberalisation in Asia: a Comparative Study', World Bank Discussion Papers, No. 50.
Cornia, G. A. (2003) 'Globalization and the Distribution of Income Between and Within Countries', in H.-J. Chang (ed.), *Rethinking Economic Development*, London: Anthem Press, pp. 325–45.
Demetriades, P. O. and S. Andrianova (2004) 'Finance and Growth: What We Know and What We Need to Know', in C. A. E. Goodhart (ed.), *Financial Development and Economic Growth: Explaining the Links*, Basingstoke: Palgrave Macmillan.
Demetriades, P. O. and K. B. Luintel (1996) 'Financial Restraints in the South Korean Miracle', *Journal of Development Economics*, 64 (2), 459–79.
Demirgüç-Kunt, A. and E. Detragiache (2001) 'Financial Liberalization and Financial Fragility', in G. Caprio, P. Honohan and J.E. Stiglitz (eds), *Financial Liberalization: How Far, How Fast?*, Cambridge: Cambridge University Press, pp. 96–122.
Demirgüç-Kunt, A. and R. Levine (1996) 'Stock Markets, Corporate Finance and Economic Growth: An Overview', *World Bank Economic Review*, 10 (2): 223–39.

Demirgüç-Kunt, A. and R. Levine (2001) *Financial Structures and Economic Growth: A Cross-Country Comparison of Banks,* Markets and Development, Cambridge, Mass.: MIT Press.
Demirgüç-Kunt, A. and V. Maksimovic (2002) 'Funding Growth in Bank-Based and Market-Based Financial System: Evidence from Firm Level Data', *Journal of Financial Economics*, 65: 337–63.
Dow, C. S. (1996) 'Why the Banking System Should Be Regulated', *Economic Journal*, 106 (436): 698–707.
Edwards, S. (1989) 'On the Sequencing of Structural Reforms', Working Paper, No. 70, OECD Department of Economics and Statistics.
Epstein, G. (2006) 'Central Banks as Agents of Economic Development', UNU-Wider and PERI; www.umass.edu/peri.
Gerschenkron, A. (1962) *Economic Backwardness in Historical Perspective: A Book of Essays*, Cambridge, Mass.: Harvard University Press.
Ghate, P. (1992) 'Interaction Between the Formal and Informal Financial Sectors', *World Development*, 20 (6): 859–72.
Grabel, I. (1995) 'Speculation-Led Economic Development: A Post-Keynesian Interpretation of Financial Liberalization Programs', *International Review of Applied Economics*, 9 (2): 127–49.
Grabel, I. (1997) 'Savings, Investment and Functional Efficiency: A Comparative Examination of National Financial Complexes', in B. Pollin (ed.), *The Macroeconomics of Saving, Finance and Investment*, Ann Arbor: University of Michigan Press, pp. 251–98.
Grabel, I. (2003) 'Ideology, Power and the Rise of Independent Monetary Institutions in Emerging Economies', in J. Kirshner (ed.), *Monetary Orders: Ambiguous Economics, Ambiguous Politics, The Macroeconomics of Saving, Finance and Investment*, Ithaca, NY: Cornell University Press, pp. 25–52.
Jayaratne, J. and P. E. Strahan (1996) 'The Finance–Growth Nexus: Evidence from Bank Branch Deregulation', *Quarterly Journal of Economics*, 111 (3): 63970.
Kaminsky, G. L. and S. L. Schmuckler (2003) 'Short-Run Pain, Log-Run Gain: The Effects of Financial Liberalization', IMF Working Paper WP/03/34, Washington, DC: International Monetary Fund.
Lal, D. (1987) 'The Political Economy of Economic Liberalization', *World Bank Economic Review*, 1 (2): 273–99.
La Porta, R., F. Lopez-de-Silanes, A. Shleifer and R. W. Vishny (1997) 'Legal Determinants of External Finance', *Journal of Finance*, 52 (3): 1131–50.
La Porta, R., F. Lopez-de-Silanes, A. Shleifer and R. W. Vishny (1998) 'Law and Finance', *Journal of Political Economy*, 106 (6): 1113–55.
Levine, R (1996) 'Stock Markets: A Spur to Economic Growth', *Finance and Development*, 33 (1): 7–10.
Levine, R. (1997) 'Financial Development and Economic Growth: Views and Agenda', *Journal of Economic Literature*, 35 (2), 688–726.
Levine, R. (2002) 'Bank-based or Market-based Financial Systems: Which Is Better?', *Journal of Financial Intermediation*, 11 (4), 398–428.
Levine, R (2003) 'More on Finance and Growth: More Finance, More Growth?', *Federal Reserve Bank of St. Louis Review*, 85 (4): 31–46.
Levine, R. and S. Zervos (1995) 'Stock Market Development and Long-run Growth', *World Bank Economic Review*, 82 (4): 942–63.

Levine, R. and S. Zervos (1996) 'Stock Markets, Banks and Economic Growth', World Bank Policy Research Paper No. 1690, Washington, DC: World Bank.

McKinnon, R. I. (1973) *Money and Capital in Economic Development*, Washington, DC: Brookings Institution.

McKinnon, R. I. (1988a) 'Financial Liberalisation in Retrospect: Interest Rate Policies in LDCs', in G. Ranis and T. P. Schultz (eds), *The State of Development Economics*, Oxford: Basil Blackwell.

McKinnon, R. I. (1988b) 'Financial Liberalisation and Economic Development: A Reassessment of Interest-rate Policies in Asia and Latin America', Occasional Papers, No. 6, International Centre for Economic Growth.

McKinnon, R. I. (1991) *The Order of Economic Liberalization: Financial Control in the Transition to a Market Economy*, Baltimore, Md.: Johns Hopkins University Press.

Milanovic, B. (2005) *Worlds Apart: Global and International Inequality, 1959–2000*, Princeton. |NJ: Princeton University Press.

Minsky, H. P. (1986) *Stabilizing an Unstable Economy*, New Haven, Conn.: Yale University Press.

Papaioannou, E. (2007) 'Finance and Growth: A Macroeconomic Assessment of the Evidence from a European Angle', European Central Bank Working Paper Series, No. 787/July, Frankfurt am Main, Germany: European Central Bank.

Patrick, H. (1996) 'Financial Development and Economic Growth in Underdeveloped Countries', *Economic Development and Cultural Change*, 14 (2): 174–89.

Rajan, R. and L. Zingales (2003) 'The Great Reversals: The Politics of Financial Development in the 20th Century', *Journal of Financial Economics*, 69 (1): 5–50.

Rodrick, D. (1987) 'Trade and Capital Account Liberalization in a Keynesian Economy', *Journal of International Economics*, 23 (1/2): 113–29.

Sachs, J. (1988) 'Conditionality, Debt Relief and the Developing Countries' Debt Crisis', in J. Sachs (ed.), *Developing Country Debt and Economic Performance*, Chicago: University of Chicago Press.

Shaw, E. S. (1973) *Financial Deepening in Economic Development*, New York: Oxford University Press.

Singh, A. (1997) 'Stock Markets, Financial Liberalisation and Economic Development', *Economic Journal*, 107 (442): 771–82.

Stiglitz, J. E. (1985) 'Credit Markets and the Control of Capital', *Journal of Money, Credit, and Banking*, 17 (1): 133–52.

Stiglitz, J. E. (1998) 'The Role of the State in Financial Markets', in M. Bruno and B. Pleskovic (eds), *Proceedings of the World Bank Annual Conference on Development Economics*, Washington, DC: World Bank, pp. 19–52.

Stiglitz, J. E. (2000) 'Capital Market Liberalization, Economic Growth and Instability', *World Development*, 28 (6): 1075–86.

Stiglitz, J. E. (2004), 'Credit Market Liberalization, Globalization and the IMF', *Oxford Review of Economic Policy*, 20 (1): 57–71.

Taylor, L. (1983) *Structuralist Macroeconomics: Applicable Models for the Third World*, New York: Basic Books.

Townsend, R. M. and K. Ueda (2007) 'Welfare Gains from Financial Liberalization', IMF Working Papers, WP/07/154, Washington DC: International Monetary Fund.

Van Wijnbergen, S. (1983) 'Interest Rate Management in LDCs', *Journal of Monetary Economics*, 12 (2): 433–52.

Villanueva, D. and A. Mirakhor (1990) 'Interest Rate Policies, Stabilisation and Bank Supervision in Developing Countries: Strategies for Financial Reform', IMF Working Papers, WP/90/8, Washington DC: International Monetary Fund.
World Bank (1989) *World Development Report*, Oxford: Oxford University Press.
World Bank (1993) *The East Asian Miracle: Economic Growth and Public Policy*, Oxford: Oxford University Press.
Zhu, A., M. Ash and R. Pollin (2004) 'Stock Market Liquidity and Economic Growth: A Critical Appraisal of the Levine/Zervos Model', *International Review of Applied Economics*, 18 (1): 63–72.
Zingales, L. (2003) 'The Weak Links', *Federal Reserve Bank of St. Louis Review*, 85 (4): 47–52.

6

Global Financial Regulation versus the Engines of Financial Instability

Robert H. Wade[1]

Introduction

The sheer frequency of financial crises since the mid-1980s, compared to 1945–70, suggests that the post-Bretton Woods system is prone to inherent instability. Over this recent period, financial crises have occurred in the Atlantic economy and Japan with a frequency of one every three to four years. Out in the periphery, ninety-four countries experienced at least one severe currency crash in the period 1990–2003 (ILO, 2004, p. 40). These frequencies are of an order of magnitude higher than during the Bretton-Woods period 1945–70. A 'system' that permits this much instability is not much of a system.

However, according to Kenneth Rogoff, chief economist at the International Monetary Fund (IMF) during 2001–3, 'the policy community has developed a smug belief that enhanced macroeconomic stability at the national level combined with continuing financial innovation at the international level have obviated any need to tinker with the [international financial] system' (Rogoff, 2007).

This 'smug belief' in the soundness of the international financial system is seen in retrospective interpretations of the Asian crisis. Mainstream interpreters continue to put the blame on mistakes or defects in the crisis-affected countries. Here is IMF deputy managing director Anne Krueger's explanation of the Asian crisis, written in 2006:

> At first it was assumed in some quarters that these crises reflected capricious shifts in investor sentiment; that national economies were now subject to the whims of speculators... But it became clear that

> painful though these crises were, they had their origin in underlying weaknesses in the economies affected – weaknesses to which investors had reacted. In some cases, governments had accumulated debts that were unsustainable. In others, rapid private sector credit growth had led to a sharp deterioration in the quality of lending with a rise in the number of bad loans.[2]

IMF deputy managing director, Stanley Fischer, writing in 2001, identified the central problem as the crisis-affected countries' fixed exchange rates (as distinct from the intrinsic risks of unrestricted international capital flows or poor regulation in the lending countries), and identified the solution as free-floating exchange rates: 'Had exchange rates been flexible, the six crises ... would either not have happened, or would not have taken the form they did. That is why the shift to flexible rates among the emerging market countries is the most important change in the international financial architecture during the past decade'.

In 2003, Fischer reiterated his belief: 'I believe that the move to flexible exchange rates has made more of a difference to the international financial system than any other change. That change takes away a major risk factor'.

Conversely, many in the policy community believe that the IMF's interventions in the Asian crisis worked well. Krueger wrote in 2006: 'The Fund was heavily involved in the resolution of these crises ... [I]t is clear that with hindsight the adjustment programs put in place with Fund support were far more successful than most observers believed possible at the time'.

Michel Camdessus, IMF managing director during the Asian crisis (infamously photographed in the pose of a domineering headmaster towering over then-president Soeharto of Indonesia as he signed on the IMF's dotted line), said on a return visit to Indonesia in 2006 that Indonesia's recovery showed that the Fund's prescriptions had been right.

These powerful opinion-shapers – who form part of what could be called the High Command of world finance – consider that the current international financial system is basically sound: floating exchange rates adjust imbalances, capital flows to where it is most productive, and Fund prescriptions are effective in avoiding crises and containing them when they occur. Hence there is no case for more-than-tinkering with the international financial system.

Given that international financial markets are at the time of writing vastly bigger and more complex than at the time of the Asian crisis, and given that the world is probably (as of September 2007) in the early stages of a Great Unwind from what has been described as the first Truly Global Bubble, this chapter addresses five questions:

1. What is the current system of global financial regulation?
2. Why is it not more effective in reducing the frequency and severity of financial crises?
3. What are the causes of the current regulatory system?
4. What is driving the high frequency of crisis?
5. What are promising directions of policy reform?

Global financial regulation today: the standards–surveillance–compliance (SSC) system

In the wake of the financial crises in Mexico (1994–5) and East Asia/Brazil/Russia (1997–8) came an upsurge of discussions about the need for a 'new international financial architecture' (NIFA). The discussion included proposals for a number of new organizations, such as a global financial regulator, a sovereign bankruptcy court, an international deposit insurance corporation, and the like; and for expanded powers for the IMF, including to support standstills and even capital controls, so as to give countries better protection against creditor panics (see further, Wade, 2007).

But, after 2000, as the 'emerging markets' crisis remained as just that and did not spread to the heartlands, discussions petered out. On the face of it, nothing major has been done to strengthen international financial regulation since the mid-1990s.

However, this is misleading, because the High Command has put an enormous amount of effort into formulating standards of best practice. The premise is that the Asian and other emerging markets crises occurred because, in the words of a World Bank report published in 2001, 'these [crisis-affected] countries did not follow International Accounting Standards and ... this likely triggered the financial crisis. Users of the accounting information were *misled* and were not able to take precautions in a timely fashion' (Vishwanath and Kaufman, 2001, p. 44, emphasis added).

Compliance with standards of best practice by governments and firms around the world will, said the IMF, 'help mitigate the impact of an external crisis by supporting continued access to external borrowing' and 'help *prevent* crises [by reducing the cost of foreign capital and thereby help a government] remain solvent in cases it otherwise might not have remained solvent' (IMF, 2003, p. 26, emphasis in original).

The standards of best practice cover the domains of (a) data dissemination (especially macroeconomic data); (b) banking regulation; (c) corporate governance; and (d) financial accounting. The participating entities include official ones such as the Bank for International Settlements (BIS), IMF, World Bank, US Treasury and Federal Reserve; hybrid ones such as the Financial Stability Forum (established in 1999 in response to the Asian crisis); and unofficial ones such as the Institute for International Finance, International Accounting Standards Board, International Association of Insurance Supervisors, International Organization of Securities Commissions, and International Federation of Stock Exchanges.

Standards do not enforce themselves. To improve the observance of the new standards, the IMF has taken on a much wider role than in the past in mounting systematic surveillance of national economies to gauge the degree of compliance; and so too will the BIS in overseeing compliance with the new Basel II standards of capital adequacy, being rolled out in 2008.

In 1999, the IMF (supplemented by the World Bank) set about producing Reports on the Observance of Standards and Codes (ROSCs). Between 1999 and the end of 2006 the IMF produced 502 ROSCs and the World Bank 92, a total of almost 600; 130 countries had at least one ROSC.

These ROSCs fed into a larger exercise called the Financial Sector Assessment Program (FSAP). This comprised three main assessments: (i) compliance with standards (based on the ROSC); (ii) stability of the financial system; and (iii) the financial sector's needed reforms. Operationally, the FSAP exercise may entail, for a large country, a sizeable team of people from the IMF, the World Bank and outside consultants having a sustained dialogue with a country's financial authorities on critical matters such as, for example, payments systems, and feeding back their findings to the authorities.

At much the same time on a separate but parallel track, the Basel Committee on Banking Supervision, under the umbrella of the Bank for International Settlements (the club for rich world central banks), was developing a new set of standards for bank capital and bank supervision. The impetus came from the bank regulators' feeling overwhelmed by financial innovations in the 1990s, coupled with the prevailing norm that 'markets (as distinct from regulators) know best'. Formulating the new set of standards came to be known as the Basel II process, the successor of Basel I, whose standards were by then considered to be out of date. The initial Basel II proposals from the Basel Committee were published in 1999, the Asian crisis having given the project added urgency.

The expectation was that the 'high quality information' resulting from these surveillance exercises would, directly or indirectly, come into the hands of market participants, who would reward entities in high compliance economies with cheaper finance and punish those in low compliance economies with more expensive finance. This incentive mechanism would shift the world's financial system towards uniform and comprehensive standards of best practice, and as a result become more stable – and, it was hoped, also more expansionary. (Initially, the IMF pressed for more direct enforcement powers, through conditionality; but was rebuffed by the corporate segment of the High Command.)

I call this the standards–surveillance–compliance (SSC) system of international financial regulation.

One of its central objectives is to strengthen developing countries' ability to sustain high integration into the world financial system. Conversely, the objective is to further constrain policy-making and institutional arrangements in developing countries in order to ensure they fit the preferences of international investors for full openness, arms-length relations between firms, banks, financial markets and government, and free capital mobility.

Effects of the SSC system

At first glance, transparency and universal standards of best practice are as desirable as motherhood and apple pie. But things are not so simple. I am sure that the SSC system has brought some systemic benefits, but here I emphasize the disadvantages.

Effects on behaviour of financial market participants

It seems that financial operators pay little attention to the data provided through 'transparency' exercises – even though then they would presumably no longer be 'misled'. A recent independent evaluation of the IMF's Financial Sector Assessment Program (FSAP) concluded that 'while many authorities identified the '"signalling role" to markets as one of their motivations for participating in the FSAP exercise, the impact of FSSAs [Financial Sector Stability Assessments] on the views of financial market participants appears modest'.[3] Again, 'Our interviews with a wide range of market participants indicate that most have limited knowledge of the contents of FSSAs'.[4]

Financial operators pay more attention to 'traditional' macroeconomic indicators like inflation than compliance with standards of good financial practice. Studies of the link between compliance with standards and cost of foreign capital have found no significant impact of the former on the latter (IEO, 2006a). Yet, as noted, the Fund's approach to enforcement of compliance with standards of best practice relies on indirect enforcement through financial markets rewarding high-compliance countries and punishing low-compliance countries. If financial markets do not pay much attention to the data released from surveillance exercises, the enforcement mechanism is hobbled.

To the extent that markets *do* pay attention to the information made available through transparency exercises, the effects may be to make financial markets less stable and more prone to crisis, because of what could be called the 'homogenization' effect. The transparency exercises, by homogenizing the data about economies and reducing the diversity of opinion on the near future, may accentuate the tendency to pro-cyclical herding behaviour – bankers and investors buying what others are buying, selling what others are selling, and owning what others are owning.

If the impacts of IMF surveillance on the behaviour of financial market participants is either modest or pro-cyclical, what about the likely impact of the Basel II standards? It is likely that Basel II standards will also generate pro-cyclical tendencies and raise the volatility of borrowers' access to bank finance. Avinash Persaud, former head of research at State Street Bank, argues that Basel II's move towards more quantitative, market-sensitive risk management practices will reinforce herding behaviour and market volatility in a vicious circle (Persaud, 2001, p. 61). Two other analysts make a similar point:

> [T]he application of models-based risk management may result in the creation of second-order dangers [which] raises questions about the recent move of financial regulators worldwide toward an integration of mathematical risk assessment tools in the regulatory framework. (Holzer and Millo, 2004, p. 17)

One reason is that the Basel II standards encourage the more sophisticated banks – those based in developed countries – to adopt a single type of internal-ratings-based (IRB) model, a model that relies on current asset prices (which tend to be pro-cyclical), and raises the capital requirements at times of downturns when banks are less able to meet the requirements. A second reason is that banks will tend to react similarly to similar signals – because they are using the same type of risk assessment model, which leads them to downgrade or upgrade clients *en masse* (Claessens *et al.* 2003, p. 6). So Basel II standards, like IMF standards, may well make market participants behave in ways that increase rather than decrease market volatility.

The other big problem with Basel II – and other international financial regulations – is that since banking is all about transforming the maturity of debt between the shorter term and the longer term, adequate 'liquidity' is essential for stable banking; yet the international regime addresses the adequacy of capital but not the adequacy of liquidity. And for good reason: rules for liquidity adequacy are inherently more difficult to devise. While amounts of capital can be prescribed, amounts of liquidity cannot be prescribed – by definition, since, if prescribed, liquidity vanishes. Adequate bank liquidity can only be governed by principles rather than by regulation, with a financial supervisor checking that the principles are being followed. There is no international mechanism for doing this.

Effects on surveillance of the world economy

The SSC system continues to encourage a focus on the national level, and to eclipse the surveillance and governance of the world economy as a whole. As Rachel Lomax, deputy governor of the Bank of England, said recently, 'The Fund does not devote enough time and effort to overseeing the system as a whole, through assessing global economic prospects and analysing international economic linkages and policy spillovers (so-called multilateral surveillance) ... The Fund needs to be better focussed on the big global issues, including financial issues and on the interactions between different regions and countries' (Lomax, 2006, p.8).

Moreover, the IMF's Independent Evaluation Office finds that the Fund's operational staff tend not even to *read* the IMF's global stability reports, let alone integrate findings into their bilateral work. Only 14 per cent of senior staff said that the IMF's findings from its 'multilateral surveillance' were discussed with national authorities (IEO, 2006b). Conversely, bilateral surveillance reports show little discussion of policy spillovers, even from systemically important countries such as Germany, Russia and the US.

It is a disquietening thought that our 'international' governance organizations such as the World Bank and the IMF are not really 'world' organizations at all in terms of what they look at and what they govern. Operationally, they treat the global, for the most part, as the sum of the national. It is as though we still have not made the paradigm shift in global economic governance that Keynes made in national economic governance when he showed that the national economy does not function like households and firms writ large.

Effects on developing countries' access to finance and competitiveness of developing country banks[5]

Standards of best practice are rarely distributionally neutral: they benefit some participants more than others. The standards coming out from the Basel Committee, the IMF, the FSF and so on – and surveillance in line with the standards – may be having at least two far-reaching impacts that are disadvantageous for developing countries and advantageous for developed ones, especially those with an Anglo-American type of political economy.

First, Basel II, as compared to Basel I (or as compared to a 'first-best' solution), will shift competitive advantage even further towards developed country banks and against developing country banks, by raising the cost of finance to developing countries; and will probably hurt development prospects more broadly by making developing countries' access to finance more pro-cyclical.

Basel II requires banks with less sophisticated risk management systems – which tend to be based in developing countries – to carry relatively more supervisory capital than banks with more sophisticated systems. Therefore it raises their costs of lending relative to those with more sophisticated risk management systems, which tend to be based in developed countries. The latter are allowed to establish their credit risks and capital adequacy themselves ('self-supervise'), subject to the financial supervisor approving their model. Also, Basel II requires bigger differential risk weighting to lower-rated borrowers than Basel I, who are disproportionately in developing countries. And its standards insufficiently recognize the risk diversification benefits of lending to clients in developing countries.

The Basel Committee's own recent quantitative impact study reveals a large variance in the amount of capital required for banks using the different Basel II-based risk assessment methodologies. For example, some banks using the advanced 'internal-ratings-based' (IRB) approach – coming predominantly from developed countries – are expected to have large *reductions* of their capital requirements of the order of 30 per cent, compared to Basel I. Banks using the simpler 'foundational' approach – predominantly from developing countries – are expected to experience an *increase* in their capital requirements of over 38 per cent (Basel Committee on Banking Supervision, 2006, p. 2). The Basel II standards thus give structural advantage to large developed country banks, and a structural disadvantage to developing country banks – and to the regional, national and local economies in which they are established.

The upshot is that developing countries under Basel II could face a higher cost of capital and a lower volume of lending than under Basel I, with more pro-cyclical volatility, and with their banks having less chance of establishing international operations and more likely to be taken over by developed country banks (Claessens *et al.*, 2003, p. 17).

The pull towards norms of Anglo-American capitalism

Another far-reaching impact of the SSC system is the way that the new standards and surveillance mechanisms tend to frame a global 'attractor' point, in that they take the liberal market economy or Anglo-American type as the 'normal' or 'proper' type of capitalism (Vestergaard, 2007). The liberal or Anglo-American type is characterized by:

(i) short-term and arm's-length relations between banks, non-financial companies, and the state;
(ii) non-discretionary regulation which is delegated to 'independent' agencies, such as the Financial Services Agency in the UK;
(iii) banks orientated towards maximizing profits; and
(iv) free capital mobility.

The key feature is the last, because in the absence of restrictions on capital mobility, the preferences of international financiers tend to push governments to move towards the other features. So the IMF has been a leading proponent of unrestricted capital movements. It asserted in September 1996 that, 'international capital markets appear to have become more resilient and are less likely to be a source of disturbances' (IMF, 1996, p. 294.)

In May 1997 the IMF announced that it intended to revise its Articles of Agreement (for only the third time), 'to make the promotion of capital account liberalization a specific purpose of the IMF and to give it jurisdiction over capital movements' (IMF, 1997a, pp. 131–2).

And in case anyone did not get the message, the IMF said, 'unrestricted capital flows [is intended to be] a condition of membership in the global economy'(IMF, 1997b, 131–2).

The IMF and other norm-making bodies have subsequently gone quieter about the imperative of unrestricted capital flows, but the financial constituency in the US, UK and France continues to give it high priority.

A contrasting type of political economy has prevailed in East Asia, at least until quite recently, based on (a) longer-term and more 'multiplex' relations between companies, financiers, and the state; (b) discretionary regulation; (c) some banks invested with social purposes beyond profit maximizing (including development banks); and (d) restrictions (some overt, others covert) on capital mobility. I have argued elsewhere that this system was an important driver of the very high rates of investment and diversification in capitalist East Asia from the 1950s to the 1980s, particularly because it enabled large firms to carry high levels of debt to equity compared to counterparts operating in an Anglo-American type of capitalism. High debt/equity ratios supported high rates of investment.[6]

As long as a national or regional economy operates on the basis of long-term relationships, patient capital and government guarantees, Anglo-American capital is at a disadvantage in these markets. On the other hand, US and UK financial firms know they can beat all comers in an institutional context of arm's-length relations, stock markets, free capital mobility, and new financial instruments. Therefore – they say – the co-ordinated market economy must be changed towards 'ours', the 'normal' type of capitalism, to prevent 'unfair' competition.

In this spirit, the US Senate passed a bill in September 1998 stating that no US funds may be available to the IMF until the Treasury Secretary certifies that all the G7 governments agree publicly that they will expect the IMF to require of its borrowers, (a) liberalization of trade and investment and (b) elimination of 'government directed lending on non-commercial terms or provision of market distorting subsidies to favoured industries, enterprises, parties or institutions' (for example, elimination of sectoral industrial policy).

The Basel Committee's rules illustrate the mechanism by which the SSC system pulls towards the Anglo-American model. The rules have as their ostensible purpose the enforcement of a uniform level of prudence sufficient to make bank failure and contagion unlikely. The High Command – taking as 'normal' the Anglo-American system of arm's-length relations between banks, firms and government, and banks orientated solely towards maximizing profits – has defined the level of prudence in terms of the level of the bank's assets, liabilities and core capital. Hence the Basel Committee's rules of prudence translate into rules about capital adequacy. But in a national economy where banks receive government guarantees they have to mobilize less capital for their operations. This has been the case with Japanese banks, other East Asian banks, the German *Lande* banks, and developing-country development banks. These are different kinds of banks from those assumed in the Basel rules, and are not devoted solely to maximizing profits for their shareholders. Their government guarantees allow them to support a cross-subsidizing mixture of public and private purposes, and to operate with a trading ethic that does not force them to drop unprofitable borrowers overnight. The High Command, however, considers that such banks have an unfair competitive advantage, and wants them to behave like 'normal' banks without government guarantees – which means giving up their mix of public and private purposes.

In other words, the High Command translates justifiable concerns about prudence into rules of capital adequacy which tend to move a key feature of political economies towards the Anglo-American model.

Moreover, financial systems are subsystems within a larger institutional complex. Changes in financial systems spill over into changes in related institutional areas, including corporate governance, product markets, labour markets, and further on into the welfare state and education. By making it more difficult for developing countries to reform their financial systems in the direction of the East Asian type, the SSC system also makes it more difficult for developing countries to adopt other features of a 'co-ordinated market economy', as distinct from a 'liberal market economy' (Hall and Soskice, 2001; Vestergaard, 2007).

So, to the extent that the High Command is able to get its standards of best practices accepted as 'normal' and non-compliance as 'deviant', it imparts a 'global warming' type of change in the international political economy away from co-ordinated market economies towards the attractor point, the liberal market economy of the Anglo-American type. Therefore the High Command's efforts at surveillance should not be understood as just an add-on to previous efforts at market liberalization. The drive for 'transparency' involves not so much 'removing the veil' as a massive programme of *standardizing,* using standards derived from best practice in the liberal market economy type of capitalism rather than from good practice in more co-ordinated forms of capitalism. This is why the change is big enough to warrant the label Post-Washington Consensus: it is a change in mindset from 'liberalize the market' globally to 'standardize the market' globally.[7]

Reasons behind the SSC system

How did this agenda of transparency, standards, and surveillance crystallize? Whose preferences counted? The short answer is that representatives of developing countries and their financial organizations had virtually no place in formulating the agenda or the implementation. The G7 finance ministers led the debate. Of the bodies which did the further decision-making and implementation – the Financial Stability Forum, the Basel Committee, and the OECD – include virtually no developing-country members, while the IMF and the World Bank are dominated by the G7 states.[8] The G7 states are highly responsive to the preferences of private financial organizations based in their states. The large array of international standard-setting unofficial bodies of the kind mentioned earlier have almost no representation from developing countries.

The big international banks have an especially effective spokesperson for the industry in the form of the Institute for International Finance (IIF), based in Washington, DC, which does research and lobbying on their behalf. When the Basel Committee on Banking Supervision came under pressure from its member states (developed countries) to consult with 'the industry' about improving the working of Basel I in the mid 1990s, the Basel Committee turned to the IIF as its principal interlocutor. When formulating Basel II, the Basel Committee relied even more on the IIF. But the IIF has the reputation of being the voice of the international – mainly developed country – banks, and of taking little notice of the preferences of less international banks, including most developing country banks.[9]

In short, the SSC and related agendas emerged because they reflect the interests of developed-country financial firms,[10] and representatives of these firms and developed-country states were largely responsible for formulating the standards. Having said that, it is misleading to say that the spread of Anglo-American norms occurs only because of 'supply' push, as distinct from 'demand' pull. The diffusion mechanism involves two steps. First, supply push from the IMF, the Financial Stability Forum, the G20 and so on, especially in the wake of the Asian crisis, for developing countries to adopt best-practice standards, which turn out to be derived from Anglo-American as distinct from, say, Japanese or Scandinavian practice. But these best-practice standards are for the most part fairly general. At the second, demand pull step, developing country governments, once they begin to adopt the standards formally, turn for models to more specific regulations on the books in Western countries, and in particular to the regulations of the Anglo-American countries.

The perverse interaction between financial markets and trade imbalances

I have argued that the current system of global financial regulation is not effective at curbing financial instability, as judged not just by the outcomes (high frequency of crisis) but also by the inputs (the SSC system). Fischer might have been right up to a point when he said the move to flexible exchange rates 'takes away a major risk factor'; but it also opens other sources of vulnerability. On the other hand, the current system may well be effective in reaching the bigger prize, the shift of the centre of gravity of global political economy towards the Anglo-American type and the marginalizing of alternatives, including developmental capitalist states, as in the Senate bill of 1998.

Whatever the specific causes or inner wheels of specific crises, what features of the financial architecture in place since the end of Bretton Woods are generating a continuing high frequency of financial instability at the global level? Here, I draw attention to just one of the causal mechanisms, which is both important and neglected. As a result of this mechanism, imbalances in the form of large current account surpluses and deficits persist, and can then adjust suddenly in the form of painful contraction in deficit countries and disruption in surplus countries – rather like an earthquake after a build-up of tectonic tension. Given the trade imbalances, even small events in specific markets, such as the market for 'sub-prime' mortgages, can trigger the panic that is often the immediate precursor of abrupt changes in financial variables, which then knock-on into the 'real' economy.

The global financial architecture characterized by the combination of (i) the Dollar Standard (use of the US dollar as a national currency and international currency); (ii) floating exchange rates between the OECD economies; and (iii) free capital mobility generates a tendency towards macro imbalance and financial fragility, via perverse interaction between financial markets and trade imbalances.

Consider the relationship between trade imbalances and the exchange rate. If the theory on which the High Command bases its prescription of floating currencies and free capital mobility is correct, we can expect to see countries with large current-account deficits showing a tendency towards exchange rate depreciation (falls in both the nominal exchange rate and the real effective exchange rate [REER], which is the most comprehensive measure of the overall competitiveness of countries). The fall in the value of their currencies translates into a fall in the prices of their products on the world market, and an increase in their competitiveness; and it induces an expenditure switch from foreign to domestic goods. On the other hand, when countries are running large current-account surpluses, we expect appreciation.

Instead, we often see the opposite: countries with large current account deficits experience appreciation, countries with large surpluses experience depreciation. These trends move the world economy even further from 'equilibrium', and generate even further potential for disruptive adjustment. Of the seventeen non-minnow countries with the *biggest* current account deficits between 1996 and 2006, fourteen experienced appreciation of the real effective exchange rate (REER) in that period, three had no change, and none had the depreciation predicted by standard theory. Of the seven countries with the *biggest* surpluses, five experienced a depreciation. Japan, Germany and Switzerland, all with big surpluses and adhering to 'floating' exchange rate regimes, experienced falls in the real value of their currencies, further lowering the price of their exports on world markets and increasing their surpluses.[11]

The underlying mechanism can be illustrated with reference to Iceland (though Iceland, being a minnow, is not included in the above figures). For several years prior to 2008 Iceland ran a current account deficit to GDP of close to or above 20 per cent, which must be a world record for a 'developed' economy. In the face of this world-record current-account deficit, what has happened to the krona? The theory of flexible exchange rates would predict depreciation. But the krona has been appreciating – showing sustained periods of appreciation and capital inflows, disrupted by short, panicky devaluations in 2005, 2006 and 2007 as carry traders unwound their positions, followed by resurgent appreciation.

Thanks to free capital movements and government monetary policy targeted only at the domestic price level (and not also the exchange rate), Iceland is receiving a vast speculative capital inflow in search of the big interest rate differential between Iceland and other economies such as Japan and Switzerland. Inflation is running at around 6 per cent. The central bank lending rate is 13 per cent; consumer credit is about 17 per cent, and overdrafts 23 per cent. Icelanders are borrowing as though there is no tomorrow. Brokers cruise the country to persuade people to switch existing loans in krona into loans denominated in Japanese yen and Swiss francs, cutting their interest rate on consumer credit from 17 per cent to 6 pr cent, and on mortgages from 11 per cent to 4 per cent. The narrow streets of Reykjavik are choked with giant SUVs, typically bought on credit, much of it denominated in Japanese yen and Swiss francs. Monetary policy – the central bank's use of the short-term interest rate – has lost its effectiveness.

Similarly, New Zealand's current-account deficit rose from 3 per cent of GDP to 9 per cent between 2001 and 2006, while the NZ dollar appreciated. South Africa's current account went from a surplus of 0.1 per cent of GDP to a deficit of 7 per cent in the same period, while the rand appreciated. As the earlier figures suggest, Iceland, New Zealand and South Africa are not anomalies.

This is a topsy-turvy world, in which international financial markets – configured in this particular way – push exchange rates in the wrong direction, amplifying rather than reducing current account imbalances. Financial operators are acting like drunken airline pilots, or so it would seem. But in fact, they are acting quite rationally; it is the theory of exchange rate adjustment to trade imbalances that is wrong, because of what it leaves out. Where capital flows are unrestricted, and where some governments are inflation-phobic and others are trying to stimulate, both using monetary policy, interest rates in the first set of countries are likely to rise to levels which attract large capital inflows to capture the interest rate differentials. The capital inflows countervail the mechanism of depreciation in the presence of a current-account deficit.

For international financial operators, the nominal interest rate rather than the real interest rate is what counts (because they do not depend on the purchase of domestic products). Hence unrestricted capital movements and monetary policy focused on inflation alone generate wonderful arbitrage opportunities for international financial operators – and dangerous levels of debt.

This mechanism is not new; it has been in place ever since the move to free capital mobility in the late 1970s. What makes the current disequilibria so large is that hedge funds, private equity funds and now sovereign wealth funds have boosted flows to a whole new level. Being largely unregulated, they are able to mobilize such large amounts of capital from banks, pension funds and proliferating billionaires that their investment in a country with a higher interest rate than the countries from which they are borrowing can itself trigger long-lasting appreciation of the exchange rate – and hence almost guarantee them very high returns on equity. Not surprisingly, they strongly defend the system that allows them to generate high returns by their own actions and continues to increase the share of capital income in world income.

In response to these opportunities, financial operators have long since marginalized their former role of creating credit money for the 'real' economy. They create credit money above all for operations within the financial sector itself, for the purpose of arbitraging between asset categories and between national economies. In conditions of bubbles, they can generate large profits by (i) borrowing heavily against a small proportion of their own equity; and (ii) using borrowed money to arbitrage across perhaps quite small price differentials, quickly going in, waiting for appreciation, then quickly going out again, taking profits, then repeating. While the word 'bubble' carries a negative connotation in everyday speech, financial operators have a strong collective interest in generating bubbles and lobbying central banks accordingly.

Summary and conclusions

In the contest between our current system of global financial regulation (the SSC system) and the 'finance–trade' engine of instability, the latter is winning. The engine continues to drive many countries' exchange rates in the wrong direction, amplifying trade imbalances and providing an impetus for micro crises to become macro crises. It will go on winning as long as we stick with the combination of Dollar Standard, floating exchange rates and free capital mobility, on the specious grounds that floating exchange rates are a good protection against volatile capital flows. The truth is closer to the opposite: capital is volatile because the exchange rate is unanchored, and the exchange rate is unanchored because capital is volatile.

The current financial market instability in the US and Europe, and the historically high frequency of financial crises in both the core and the semi-periphery of the world economy during the post-Bretton Woods era, underlines the need for tighter financial regulation, nationally, regionally and globally. There is a remarkable asymmetry in the regulation of the market for food and drugs and the regulation of the market for finance: the sale of food and drugs is covered by regulations on health and safety, while the sale of financial products – which can be very dangerous in a different way, and which, via the exchange rate, affect the whole level of prices in a small, open economy – is more lightly regulated, in particular the sale of non-bank financial products. But the 'market' will not undertake self-regulation; the public authorities must do it. The need is greater today than ever before, because of the exceptional size of financial markets relative to GDP and unprecedentedly low transaction costs; and because of the recent proliferation of arrangements for splitting, spreading and hiding risk, to the point where no one is able to assess or take responsibility for it – and where the sellers of financial services consequently produce 'too much', because they bear too few of the costs of free capital mobility to society.

To shift the international financial system towards more stable arrangements we need a change in international norms, to sanction three national-level changes in particular. One is to re-introduce capital controls as acceptable instruments of national economic management, whether on inflows or outflows. Recent institutional innovations in payments systems – notably the Continuous Linked Settlement (CLS) Bank for wholesale interbank payments – should facilitate this. A national monetary authority wishing to curb excessive inflows or outflows could – provided the relevant agency, such as the CLS Bank, had constitutional authority – instruct the agency to levy a variable fee on transactions involving its currency (over and above the agency's normal fee), the additional fee being set at the necessary disincentive level. Of course, the major financial centres would have to co-operate to close down alternative 'offshore' payments channels.

The second national-level change is that central banks should set interest rates with both the general domestic price level *and* the exchange rate in mind – and hence adopt a managed exchange rate rather than either a fixed rate or a free floating one. This means making sure that uncovered interest rate differentials do not become too large; which in practice may mean tolerating higher inflation so as to curb exchange rate appreciation resulting from the carry trade (assuming that capital controls are not completely effective). Other instruments, including incomes policies, should also be deployed to curb inflation.

The third national-level change is the regular use of GDP-linked, domestic-currency-denominated bonds as the vehicle of foreign borrowing. Repayment would be linked to GDP, which in turn is linked to tax revenue, which is linked to ability to repay. In good times, repayments would be higher than with non-GDP, foreign-currency-denominated bonds; and in bad times, the opposite would apply. The aim is to have repayments correlated positively with ability to repay, and not, as at present, correlated negatively.

At the global level, no doubt a code of conduct for exchange rate management would be a good thing in principle, including rules about which objective gives when low inflation and competitive exchange rate conflict. Such a code would complement the existing WTO rules on tariffs and export subsidies – removing the present imbalance in rule-boundedness between trade and exchange rates. It is an 'imbalance' because changes in the nominal exchange rate that deviate from inflation differentials affect international trade in the same way as tariffs and export subsidies, and should therefore be equally subject to multilateral oversight. To move in this direction would require changes in multilateral governance. The present G7 finance ministers would have to give way to the G4, comprising the US, the eurozone, Japan and China. The G4 would undertake outreach to non-eurozone Britain on an ad hoc basis, as the G7 have been undertaking outreach to China.

But the practicalities of overseeing economies and enforcing actions to avoid exchange rate changes costly to the world economy are probably too daunting on a global scale. For several reasons, the IMF has lost credibility for undertaking such a role. One of them is that the US government likes to undermine it when it says something about the US with which the government disagrees, as illustrated by what happened in August 2007. In the words of a newspaper report:

> The U.S. Treasury took two years to persuade the International Monetary Fund to police global currency markets – and just two months to trash the initiative once the IMF adopted it.
>
> Treasury officials recruited the fund to be a currency regulator as China and other countries tried to gain a trade advantage with exchange rates. Instead, the fund took aim at the dollar, calling it overvalued in an Aug. 1 report. The Treasury objected, and on Aug. 2 an aide to Treasury Secretary Henry Paulson Jr told Congress that it was impossible to measure a currency's fair value.
>
> 'The U.S. Treasury has cut the legs from under the IMF before it even started the race', said Michael Mussa, chief economist at the fund from 1991 to 2001 ... 'This was foolish and unnecessary when they could have just said nothing'. (Swann, 2007)

Regional monetary co-ordination is a direction of travel to be encouraged, as a substitute for a global monetary system that has failed to protect developing-country interests. The ten member states of the Association of Southeast Asian Nations, plus Japan, China and South Korea, have been exploring the creation of an Asian Currency Unit, or ACU, based on a weighted average of key regional currencies. The ACU is intended to be a benchmark independent of the US dollar, around which Asian countries co-ordinate their exchange-rate policies. They would denominate their export prices, loans and bond issuance in ACUs. China and Japan, despite all their other disagreements, are interested in this proposal (Wade 2006). Of course, there are doubts about whether countries as diverse as Japan and Indonesia could operate with a common currency.

J. M. Keynes is a source of inspiration on how to reduce instability and expand the room for national or regional policy choice (weaken the gravitational pull of the Anglo-American type of capitalism). Not the brilliant and opaque *General Theory* but 'The end of *laissez-faire*' (1926) and 'Poverty in plenty: is the economic system self-adjusting?' (1934) (Kirshner, 1999). Here Keynes not only campaigned against unregulated capitalism but also set out the logic of the 'middle way', a type of market capitalism where some markets are managed and subject to limits determined through a political process – his middle way being a lot more substantive than the later Third Way of Anthony Giddens, Tony Blair and Bill Clinton.

Middleware is another source of inspiration. Middleware refers to a type of software that functions as a translator or communicator between different software programs, by taking existing programs and putting 'glue' between them. More generally, it refers to an approach to information systems that values decentralization and diversity. It is the opposite of the monolithic approach of 'enterprise resource planning' systems (for example SAP – Systems, Applications and Products in Data Processing), which starts by throwing out existing programs. Only since the early 1990s has middleware come to be developed as a legitimate approach. We might use ideas from middleware to inform the development of rules of trade and finance, which intermediate between different national or regional regimes, rather than attempt to get a single neoliberal model adopted universally.

Notes

1. Thanks to Jakob Vestergaard, Kevin Young, Jane D'Arista, Charles Goodhart, Howard Davies, Adrian Wood, and John Williamson. My broad line of argument on the East Asian developmental state has been inspired by the writings of Ajit Singh going back to the early 1980s.
2. My own interpretation, emphasizing 'external' factors but recognizing the links between external and internal, is given in Wade, 1998a, 1998b, 2000; Wade and Veneroso, 1998. See also Duncan 2005.
3. IEO (Independent Evaluation Office), 2006, p. 13. In this section on the effects of the SSC system I am indebted to Jakob Vestergaard, 2007.
4. IEO, 2006a, p. 57. See also IMF, 2005. The latter reports that the use of Reports on Standards and Codes (ROSCs) by market participants is low and has not increased in recent years (as indicated by responses to the question, 'To what extent do you use ROSCs in your work?'). The most used information was about compliance with Basel Core Principles and Data Dissemination; but even these scored only in the low 3s on a scale of 1 (not at all) to 5 (a very great deal).
5. I am indebted to Kevin Young for points made in this section.
6. Wade, 2004 and see references in note 2. See also Zysman, 1983.
7. This is a central point of Vestergaard, 2007.
8. The Financial Stability Forum brings in a few developing countries, such as China, as auxiliary members of some of its subcommittees. The G20 grouping of developed- and developing-country finance ministers, formed in 1999 by the US Clinton Administration with membership chosen by the US Treasury and the German finance ministry, is less a forum of debate than an occasion

for Durkheimian effervescence of faith in free markets and the Washington Consensus. See Gruen *et al.*, 2002.

9. This, notwithstanding that about half of its membership comes from developing countries.
10. This point is central to Claessens *et al.*, 2003.
11. UNCTAD, 2007, table 1.6. Of the seven countries with the biggest surpluses, only China and Russia have experienced appreciations. The pattern is not particularly sensitive to the choice of starting year within the decade 1996–2006.

References

Basel Committee on Banking Supervision (2006) *Results of the Fifth Quantitative Impact Study*, Basel: Bank for International Settlements, 16 June.

Claessens, S., G. Underhill and X. Zhang (2003) 'Basel II Capital Requirements and Developing Countries: A Political Economy Perspective', Typescript, Center for Global Development, October.

Duncan, R. (2005) *The Dollar Crisis*, Singapore: Wiley.

Fischer, S. (2001) 'The International Financial System: Crises and Reform', The Robbins Lectures, London School of Economics, October.

Fischer, S. (2003) 'Globalization and Its Challenges', *American Economic Review*, 93: 1–29.

Gruen, D., T. O'Brien and J. Lawson (eds) (2002) *Globalisation, Living Standards and Inequality: Recent Progress and Continuing Challenges,* Reserve Bank of Australia.

Hall, P. and D. Soskice (2001) *Varieties of Capitalism: The Institutional Foundations of Comparative Advantage*, Oxford University Press.

Holzer, B. and Y. Millo (2004) 'From Risks to Second-order Dangers in Financial Markets', CARR Discussion Paper, London School of Economics.

IEO (2006a) 'Report on the Evaluation of the FSAP', IMF.

IEO (2006b) 'An evaluation of the IMF's multilateral surveillance', IMF, February, at www.imf.org/external/np/ieo/2006/ms/eng/pdf/report.pdf.

ILO (2004) *Economic Security for a Better World*, Geneva.

IMF (1996) *IMF Survey*, 23 September, Washington ,DC.

IMF (1997a) *IMF Survey*, 12 May, Washington, DC.

IMF (1997b) *IMF Survey*, 26 May, Washington, DC.

IMF (2003) *Review of Contingent Credit Lines*, Washington DC.

IMF (2005) 'The Standards and Codes Initiative – Is It Effective? And How Can It Be Improved?' Washington, DC.

Kirshner, J. (1999) 'Keynes, Capital Mobility and the Crisis of Embedded Capitalism', *Review of International Political Economy* 6 (3): 313–37.

Krueger, A. (2006) 'The New Economic Century: Experience and Opportunity in the Reform Process', Address to The Fraser Institute, Vancouver, 3 May.

Lomax, R. (2006) 'International Monetary Stability – Can the IMF Make a difference?', Lecture delivered at Somerset House, London, 1 November.

Persaud A. (2001) 'The Disturbing Interactions between the Madness of Crowds and the Risk Management of Banks in Developing Countries and the Global Financial System', in S. Griffith-Jones and A. Bhattacharaya (eds), *Developing Countries and the Global Financial System*, Commonwealth Secretariat.

Rogoff, K. (2007) 'No Grand Plans, but the Financial System Needs Fixing', *Financial Times*, 8 February.

Swann, C. (2007) 'U.S. Currency Push on IMF Backfires', *International Herald Tribune*, 24 August.

UNCTAD (2007) *Trade and Development Report 2007*, Geneva.

Vestergaard, J. (2007) 'More Heat than Light? A Critical Assessment of the New Regulation of International Finance', Discussion Paper, Center for the Analysis of Risk and Regulation (CARR), London School of Economics.

Vishwanath, T. and D. Kaufman (2001) 'Towards Transparency: New Approaches and Their Application to Financial Markets', *World Bank Research Observer*, 16: 1.

Wade, R. (1998a) 'The Asian Debt and Development crisis of 1997: Causes and consequences', *World Development*, 26: 8.

Wade, R. (1998b) 'From "Miracle" to "Cronyism": Explaining the Great Asian Slump', *Cambridge Journal of Economics*, 22: 6.

Wade, R. (2000) 'Wheels within Wheels: Rethinking the Asian Crisis and the Asian Model', *Annual Review of Political Science*, 3: 85–116.

Wade, R. (2004) *Governing the Market*, Princeton, NJ: Princeton University Press.

Wade, R. (2006) 'The Case for a Global Currency', *International Herald Tribune*, 4 August.

Wade, R. (2007) 'A New Global Financial Architecture?', *New Left Review*, 46, July/August: 113–29.

Wade, R. and F. Veneroso (1998) 'Two Views on Asia: The Resources Lie Within', By Invitation, *The Economist*, 7–13 November: 19–21.

Zysman, J. (1983) *Governments, Markets, and Growth: Financial Systems and the Politics of Industrial Change*, Ithaca, NY: Cornell University Press.

7

The Developmental Potential and Political Economy of Private Remittances: What Do We Know, and What Do We Need to Know?

Ilene Grabel

Introduction[1]

Development economics is perhaps more prone than other fields in economics to search for panaceas. It seems that private remittances are now occupying the space that has been vacated by other 'magic bullets' of the last few years – namely, foreign direct and portfolio investment, state governance, Anglo-American corporate governance, institutions, country 'ownership,' investment climate, property rights, transparency, micro-credit and social capital. Some of these fads have had a longer half-life than others. But the bloom is now off many of these roses, not least because of the profoundly important work of Ajit Singh.

In Singh's wide-ranging oeuvre, we have the best example of work in modern development economics that is theoretically rich while remaining grounded in the empirical, institutional, historical and political realities of the developing world. His work is also marked by a passion for improving the conditions of life for the majority of the world's population, and for pressing policy-makers to think creatively about enduring problems. In this scholar (and friend), we have a deep marriage of theoretical rigour and creative practice – it is therefore fitting that he has spent the majority of his professional career in Keynes's home city – Cambridge, UK.

In connection with this chapter on remittances, it is worth recalling three of the many strands of Singh's highly influential work. First is his challenge to conventional wisdom on portfolio investment, corporate finance and the role of banks in the provision of external finance to firms in developing countries (Singh and Weisse, 1998; Singh, 1999a, 2006). Second is his rejection of the idealization of the Anglo-American model of finance and corporate governance, coupled with his articulation of an alternative developmental approach (Singh, 2002; Singh and Zammit, 2006). And third is his intervention into the debate over the East Asian financial crisis of 1997–8, in which he rejects the common and simplistic view that the crisis was caused by crony capitalism, and the related view that developing countries seeking to avoid this fate would do well to become good students of the Bretton Woods institutions (Singh, 1999b; Glen and Singh, 2005).

Taking a page from Singh, I examine here private remittances, the latest facet of the global development landscape to be burdened with the weight of excessive exuberance. Remittance studies are still in their infancy, and so we might hope to find some circumspection among those in the field. Instead, we find among development economists and policy-makers alike a level of enthusiasm for this resource that far exceeds what is warranted by the evidence.[2]

To date, most studies of remittances tend to be microeconomic in scope. These narrow studies focus on the experience of a single country or sometimes a region. Few scholarly studies have attempted to understand remittances within a broader developmental and political economy context. This chapter will attempt such an examination. It draws together findings from the multidisciplinary literature on remittances with the goal of taking stock. What do we know, what don't we know and what do we still need to know about the economic, political and social consequences of remittances? We shall see that, even at this early stage of research, it is becoming clear that remittances play complex and contradictory roles in developing countries. From a policy perspective, this is certainly inconvenient. But, as Singh has taught us, we can't begin to sort out just what policy responses are appropriate by pretending that matters are simpler than they in fact are.

Empirical dimensions and lacunae

In what follows, I provide a brief survey of the chief empirical trends and characteristics of remittances.

Measurement

Remittances are the financial resource flows that arise from cross-border movements of people (Kapur, 2004). They have therefore grown alongside the growth in migration flows since the early 1980s.

The consensus among remittance researchers is that the most comprehensive measure of recorded remittances is the sum of the following three items that appear in the IMF's annual *Balance of Payments Yearbook*: (i) unrequited transfers/worker remittances refer to money sent by migrants (that is, those who work abroad for more than a year) to family and friends on which there are no claims by the sender; (ii) migrant transfers refer to the net worth of migrants moving from one country to another; and (iii) compensation of employees refer to funds sent abroad by temporary workers (that is, those who work abroad for less than a year). The data on recorded remittances that appear below utilize this measure.

Data problems

There are numerous, well-documented problems with the coverage, quality and comparability of recorded remittance data. In addition to problems with recorded remittance data, there is the more vexing issue of unrecorded remittances. Estimates place the true size of remittance flows at 50 per cent or more above reported levels (World Bank (WB), 2006).

It is hard to say exactly how the use of informal remittance channels has been affected by changes in banking, security and immigration regulations since 11 September 2001. On the one hand, tightened oversight over financial flows, the closure of some informal channels, and reductions in the cost of sending remittances via formal channels in wealthy countries may explain why recorded remittances to some countries have increased dramatically in recent years (World Bank, 2006). On the other hand, it is possible that migrant communities might be relying more on informal channels for sending remittances because of privacy concerns and the uncertain and hostile climate that they face in many countries.

Finally, it is worth noting that some flows that approximate remittances will never show up in the data as such. Examples of flows that function as a kind of remittance include in-kind transfers of consumer goods, direct payments on behalf of family members for insurance premiums and school fees, and non-resident bank deposits intended to be drawn on by family members (Ratha, 2003; Solimano, 2004).

Trends and characteristics

In 2006, recorded remittances to developing countries are estimated to have reached US$206 billion, more than six times the level in 1990 (see Table 7.1).

Region

As is clear from Table 7.1, remittance flows have grown in all regions of the developing world, but most rapidly in Europe and Central Asia

Table 7.1 Migrant remittances to developing countries (US$ billions, current dollars)*

Inflows	**1990**	**2000**	**2001**	**2002**	**2003**	**2004**	**2005**	**2006 (estimated)**
All developing countries	31	85	96	117	145	165	193	206
By country income group								
Low-income countries	8	22	26	32	40	42	48	55
Middle-income countries (MIC)	23	63	70	85	105	123	145	152
Lower MICs	14	43	48	61	75	86	98	102
Upper MICs	9	20	22	24	30	37	47	50
By region								
East Asia and the Pacific	3	17	20	29	35	39	45	47
Europe and Central Asia	3	13	13	14	17	23	31	32
Latin America & the Caribbean	6	20	24	28	35	41	48	53
Middle East & N. Africa	11	13	15	16	20	23	24	25
South Asia	6	17	19	24	31	31	36	41
Sub-Saharan Africa	2	5	5	5	6	8	9	9

Note: *Workers' remittances, migrant transfers and compensation of employees.
Source: World Bank DPG (2007), Remittances dataset; WB staff calculations based on *IMF Balance of Payments Statistics* 2007 *Yearbook*, available at:
http://siteresources.worldbank.org/EXTDECPROSPECTS/Resources/476882-1157133580628/RemittancesData_updated2007.xls.

and East Asia and the Pacific (World Bank, 2007). Latin America and the Caribbean remain the largest recipients of remittances. However, as a share of GDP, remittances are highest in the Middle East and North Africa (Mohapatra *et al.*, 2006).

Sub-Saharan Africa receives the smallest pool of remittances among regions of the developing world, and has experienced slower growth than the other regions listed here. However, the data for Africa are understood to be particularly inaccurate because of problems with reporting, because the formal banking system has low credibility and very limited reach (especially in rural areas), and because the costs of sending remittances through formal channels is extremely high (Julca, 2007; World Bank, 2007).

The World Bank (2007) notes that remittances to South Asia appear to be growing steadily because of strong demand for labour in Persian Gulf and European economies. It also notes that remittances to Latin America and the Caribbean appear to be slowing, probably because of slowdowns in the housing sector in the US. It is also likely that recent changes in US immigration policies and politics are impeding the flow of migrants and their ability to secure employment.

Income level

As we can see from Table 7.1, the majority of remittances do not flow to the poorest countries. Indeed, in 2006, low-income countries received only 27 per cent of remittances to the developing world. In the same year, nearly half of all remittances received by developing countries went to lower middle-income countries (US$102 billion), while the other half of them are divided almost equally between upper middle-income (US$50 billion) and low-income countries (US$55 billion).

In contrast, when compared to GDP, remittances are relatively far more important to low-income than to middle-income countries. For example, in 2005, remittances were equivalent to 3.5 per cent of GDP in low-income countries, compared to 1.5 per cent of GDP in middle-income countries (WB, 2007). The top recipients of remittances in nominal terms in 2006 were four large countries, namely India (US$27 billion), Mexico (US$24 billion), China (US$22 billion) and the Philippines (US$15 billion) (World Bank DPG, 2007). But as a share of GDP in 2006, the top recipients of remittances were small, low-income countries – namely, Moldova (where remittances were equivalent to 30 per cent of GDP), Tonga (27 per cent), Guyana (22 per cent) and Haiti (21 per cent) (Ratha, 2007).

Remittances in relation to other international capital flows and sources of foreign exchange

Recorded remittances are the second largest source of external finance to developing countries after FDI (WB, 2007). Indeed, in many developing countries, recorded remittances are the largest source of external finance (Mohapatra *et al.*, 2006).[3] Since the mid-1990s, remittances to developing countries have become an increasingly important source of foreign exchange and purchasing power. During this period, recorded remittances to developing countries have grown faster than other international private capital flows and official development assistance.

Moreover, remittances are far less concentrated in large developing economies than are foreign direct and portfolio investment.

Data from the World Bank (2006) further illustrate the growing importance of remittances to purchasing power in developing countries. The Bank reports that, in 2004, remittances were larger than public and private capital inflows in thirty-six developing countries, and larger than merchandise exports in Albania, Bosnia and Herzegovina, Cape Verde, Gaza, Haiti, Jamaica, Kiribati, Lebanon, Nepal, Samoa, Serbia and Montenegro, and Tonga. In another twenty-eight countries, they were larger than the earnings from the most important commodity export. And for many small countries, especially island economies, remittances (along with foreign aid and tourism) have become the main sources of income (Kapur, 2004).

Source countries

High-income countries are the dominant source of remittances. In 2005, the US was the largest source country, with nearly US$41 billion in outward remittances (World Bank DPG, 2007).

Outward remittances from developing countries are not inconsequential, however. In 2005, they amounted to US$38 billion (World Bank DPG, 2007). Ratha and Shaw (2007) estimate that between 9 per cent and 30 per cent of total remittance flows to developing countries originate in other developing countries, where at least half of all migrants from developing countries reside. Official data on South–South remittances are thought to capture a much smaller portion of these flows than do the data on North–South flows. One reason for this is that the cost of sending remittances through formal channels from developing countries is even higher than sending them from wealthy countries (Ratha and Shaw, 2007).

Stability, cyclicality and the insurance function

Remittances are less volatile than other international private capital flows, and they are counter-cyclical. Thus remittances do not induce or aggravate instability in developing countries, in contrast to other international private flows that tend to be strongly pro-cyclical.

Remittances are a form of self-insurance in developing countries. The insurance function is reflected in the tendency of migrants to send more remittances to their countries of origin following downturns in the economy, financial crises, natural disasters, and/or political/civil conflicts (Ratha, 2007).

There is also some evidence that remittances may remain stable when there is an economic downturn in the sending country (Ratha, 2003). This is probably because remittances are driven by familial bonds and social obligations. The motivations for sending remittances confound some analysts, who seem driven to feats of econometric and statistical gymnastics aimed at demonstrating that remittances are principally (or, at least, significantly) the outcome of rational, wealth-maximizing investment motives on the part of migrants rather than the outcome of familial obligations (Alper and Neyapti, 2006). This is very much a minority position in the literature. Most analysts suggest that remittances are driven by altruism or by implicit social contracts within families.

The state of knowledge: the economic, political and social effects of remittances

We now turn to the diverse and cross-cutting economic, political and social consequences of remittances. Here I draw together what we know about remittances, and what we do not know. Drawing on the most recent scholarship, I highlight areas of consensus among researchers and identify those areas where further investigation is warranted.

Poverty

There is a general consensus in the empirical literature that remittances reduce poverty. Remittances increase the income of recipients directly, but also reduce poverty indirectly through their effects on growth, access to capital, and the demand for labour in the countries that have sent migrants (World Bank, 2006).

A controversy exists, however, about the magnitude of the poverty reduction effect. Adams and Page (2005) is perhaps the most widely cited study to demonstrate a rather significant effect of remittances on poverty. Using data from seventy-one developing countries, they find that a 10 per cent increase in per capita remittances is associated with a 3.5 per cent decline in the share of people living in poverty. Perhaps more interesting is their finding that, dollar for dollar, the income remitted by migrants reduces poverty much more than does income generated by domestic economic activity. Other studies support a less powerful effect on poverty. For example, literature surveyed by López-Córdova and Olmedo (2006) suggests that remittances reduce poverty, but the effect may be small and is sensitive to the precise measure of poverty that is adopted.

Most studies of remittances and poverty do not distinguish between remittances' direct effect on transient poverty and their effect on structural poverty. It is clear that remittances have a direct effect on transient poverty via the provision of income (and, hence, support for consumption). This effect on transient poverty is particularly important following crises and conflicts, as we saw in the previous section.[4] Numerous studies support this finding; for example, Yang (2003) presents evidence that households in the Philippines with overseas migrants did substantially better following the Asian financial crisis than did those with no family members living abroad.

But the effect of remittances on structural poverty is far less clear, as Kapur (2004) rightly acknowledges. We would expect remittances to affect structural poverty through indirect channels, such as via its long-term effects on human capital formation and labour markets. However, the extent to which remittances reduce structural poverty depends very much on 'selection effects' – that is, on the income and skill attributes of the migrants themselves. Are migrants drawn from the poorest and lowest-skilled segments of the labour pool, and do those who migrate legally versus illegally have equivalent attributes? If, for example, migrants are drawn chiefly from the poorest members of society, then the receipt of remittances will raise the incomes of the poorest families. Similarly, if migrants are drawn chiefly from the lowest rungs of the labour market, then the reduced labour supply in the home country will cause wages to rise for lower-skilled workers at home. In this case, structural poverty will be reduced by the combined effects of the receipt of remittances and the higher wages available to the unskilled workers who are left behind.

There are good reasons, however, to believe that the significant upfront financial costs of migration mean that the poorest of the poor cannot afford to migrate. (Note that migration schemes involving some form of indentured servitude allow the costs of migration to be paid over time. Such arrangements might be seen as equalizing the opportunity to migrate at the cost of diminished freedom, but, especially in the case of illegal migration, they might also increase the total cost of migration so substantially that they greatly undermine its benefits.) There is also the broader matter of the capability to migrate, using the term in the sense of Sen (1992). It is reasonable to assume that those who are most likely to migrate, and hence to send remittances, possess a broad range of capabilities (such as the ability to function in a strange cultural environment away from the family) that make them less likely to come from the very bottom rungs of society. If this is correct, then remittances may have the undesirable effect of reinforcing existing disparities in capabilities.

Unfortunately, to date there has been little research on selection effects. The research that is available does not show unambiguously that migrants are drawn from the poorest or the lowest-skilled members of society. Indeed, some country-specific studies find evidence of an intermediate or positive selection effect such that migrants are more likely to be drawn from the intermediate- or higher-skilled segments of the labour market. If this is generally applicable, then the effects of remittances on structural poverty might be more limited than would otherwise be the case.

Inequality

In contrast to the strong link between remittances and transient poverty, there is simply no unambiguous evidence that they reduce inequality (Ratha, 2003; López-Córdova and Olmedo, 2006; World Bank, 2006;). Some studies have found that remittances widen inequality because they flow disproportionately to better-off households (because of the positive selection effects discussed above), while others find that they reduce inequality because they flow primarily to the very poor.

There is some evidence of a temporal dimension to the link between remittances and inequality (Stark and Taylor, 1986). Remittances may increase income inequality in a particular village or region at the start of migration from that area, but as migration from that location becomes well established, remittances may eventually reduce the degree of inequality in the area.

To date, the issue of regional inequality and remittances remains largely unexplored in the literature. If migration patterns are path-dependent, then remittances might induce or deepen regional inequality within a sending country. Path dependence in migration might occur because the establishment of a regular migration channel might increase the capability of others in the same region to migrate. This returns us to the issue of differing migration capabilities, a factor that future research may find is self-perpetuating and which may therefore reinforce existing inequalities.

Another factor that warrants future research is whether remittances reduce or aggravate racial or ethnic inequalities within a country. If certain racial or ethnic groups have a greater capacity to migrate (because of pre-existing migration channels, greater initial conditions of wealth, or a greater likelihood of acceptance abroad because of religion or race), then remittances may aggravate racial or ethnic inequalities within the country. The only mention of this issue in the literature concerns Cuba. Kapur (2004) notes that remittances to Cuba have a strong racial bias, since the Cuban diaspora is mostly white, while the island's population is mostly black. He also notes that remittances to the country have an urban bias: 20 per cent of the population lives in Havana, but the city receives about 60 per cent of the remittances to the country. Whether remittances aggravate racial, ethnic and/or regional inequalities in other countries are issues that deserve further investigation.

Consumption

Not surprisingly, there is a consensus among empirical researchers that remittances are used primarily to finance basic subsistence consumption of food, rent and health care for households that are below a threshold level of income (Kapur, 2004; World Bank, 2006). For example, Burgess (2007) reports that around 80 per cent of remittances in Mexico are used for basic needs; Solimano (2004) cites research on Ecuador that finds that 60 per cent of remittances are spent in this manner, and a household survey in Latin America reports that daily household expenses absorb 46 per cent and 84 per cent of remittances, respectively, in Brazil and El Salvador (López-Córdova and Olmedo, 2006). Support for subsistence consumption is critically important to sustaining poorer households because they lack access to insurance and credit, and are therefore immensely vulnerable to income shocks (World Bank, 2006).

The nature of the multiplier effects of remittance-financed consumption has received scant attention in the literature. Indeed, Julca (2007) is the only study that calls for the development of measures of the diverse multiplier effects of remittances – for example, on regions and sectors. One analyst suggests that multiplier effects will be induced to the extent that remittances stimulate consumption of domestically-produced goods (Kapur, 2004), but the degree to which this is the case has not yet been explored sufficiently. Moreover, the same study suggests that consumption financed by remittances will increase domestic tax receipts.

In my view, there are several factors that might mitigate or even negate these multiplier effects. In many developing countries, a large proportion of basic needs goods are imported. In this case, the multiplier effect of consumption financed by remittances will be limited, and such consumption might even aggravate trade deficits. Moreover, many goods in developing countries (especially in rural areas) are purchased through informal vendors who obviously do not collect consumption taxes at the point of sale. Future research should determine the precise nature of the leakages, multiplier and tax implications of remittances.

Savings, private investment and human capital

There is unambiguous evidence that once basic needs are met, remittances are used for savings, debt repayment, consumer durables, land and housing purchases, small enterprise development and small-scale agricultural production, and education and healthcare (Sander, 2003; Ratha, 2003, 2007). A household survey of Latin America provides some evidence of the diverse uses of remittances in the region (comparative studies for other regions are not available at this time). It reports that 2 per cent of remittance inflows are used for education in Ecuador, while 17 per cent are used for the same purpose in the Dominican Republic; 1 per cent of inflows are used for business in Mexico, while 10 per cent are similarly used in Brazil and Guatemala; 11 per cent of inflows are used for savings in Guatemala, and 7per cent of inflows are used for acquiring property in Brazil (López-Córdova and Olmedo, 2006).

Many studies find that remittances contribute to household savings (again, once basic needs are met). In Pakistan, for example, household surveys indicate that in the late 1980s and early 1990s, the marginal propensity to save was higher for income from international remittances than from either domestic remittances (from urban to rural areas within the same country) or from income on rental property (Ratha, 2003). Moreover, there is evidence that (holding constant for income) the propensity to save among households that receive remittances is higher than in non-recipient households (Kapur, 2004), and that households, in general, tend to save a larger proportion of remittance income than other sources of income.

There are numerous national studies that highlight the contribution of remittances to investment and entrepreneurship among small businesses and agriculturalists – for example, in South Africa, Mexico, China, Egypt, Pakistan, Turkey, and countries across the Caribbean (World Bank, 2006, ch. 5; Burgess, 2007, and citations therein). Based on these country experiences, there is speculation that remittances increase access to working capital through two channels: directly through the provision of resources; and indirectly, by increasing the pool of capital made available by formal financial institutions. The indirect effect is assumed to come about because a stable flow of remittances increases household creditworthiness by buttressing and stabilizing income (World Bank, 2006).

The importance of remittances as a source of working capital in Mexico has been widely studied. One analyst of the country states that 'remittances are an essential source of [working] capital for many small enterprises' (Papademetriou, cited in Burgess, 2007). Massey and Parrado (1998) found around 21 per cent of businesses in the six largest migrant-sending states in Mexico were initially financed from US earnings.

The role of remittances in supporting small enterprise development and entrepreneurship has also been demonstrated in a range of studies outside the Mexican context.[5] For example, Dustmann and Kirchkamp (2001) show that half of all returned immigrants to Turkey become entrepreneurs, and that the capital for starting these businesses stems from savings and capital acquired abroad. McCormick and Wahba (2001) find that total overseas savings and time spent overseas have a positive and significant effect on entrepreneurship in Egypt. Many studies find that remittances reduce credit constraints and stimulate entrepreneurship (Funkhouser, 1992; World Bank, 2006).

Remittances also facilitate investment in housing. For example, Parrado (2004) shows that being in the US during the previous year increased the likelihood of home acquisition by 1.2 times, and that every additional year of work experience in the US raised the likelihood of homeownership by another 2.8 per cent.

Remittances not only support savings and physical investment, but they also support investment in human capital (Ratha, 2007). Investment in human capital has potentially far-reaching and long-term economic and social benefits that may be difficult to quantify, but that are none the less critical.

Remittances are used to pay school fees, and hence enhance educational attainment. They have also been found to help families to keep children in school even following shocks that led to a decline in non-remittance income. For example, a study of El Salvador and Sri Lanka found that children in households that receive remittances have a lower school dropout rate, and that households that receive remittances spend more on private tuition (Ratha, 2007). A number of studies conclude that remittances improve educational attainment among children in recipient households. Cox Edwards and Ureta (2003) find that receipt of remittances lowers the probability that children leave school early in El Salvador; and Yang (2003) finds that remittances increase school enrolment rates for children in the Philippines. López-Córdova (2005) finds that illiteracy rates among children between 6 and 14 years old are lower, other things being constant, as the fraction of households that receive remittances rises in a given Mexican municipality. Kapur (2004) argues that in those cases where remittances flow to poorer families, they can enhance girls' educational attainments by cushioning household incomes after an income shock (since school attendance by girls is disproportionately affected by shocks to family income). There is also a compelling body of evidence linking the receipt of remittances to better health outcomes, particularly among children.

It is clearly important that remittances support some small enterprise and agricultural development and investments in human capital. But these achievements must be placed in a broader context. It is widely known that the formal financial system and the state in the developing world have long underserved small business and agriculture. This problem has become more severe in the neoliberal era as states have dismantled long-standing programmes that provided at least some assistance to small firms and agriculturalists, such as through protection from international competition, price and technical support, and the provision of working capital by the state or formal financial institutions at subsidized rates.[6]

At the same time, formal financial institutions in many developing countries have turned their limited attention away from small business and agriculture and towards the kinds of speculative activities that have flourished in the era of financial liberalization (Grabel, 1995). In this environment of 'speculation-led development' (Grabel, 1995), formal financial institutions have also been released of their (admittedly weak) state-mandated obligations to provide support to small business and agriculture. It may be that efforts to capture the booming remittance market will eventually cause formal financial institutions to respond to their smaller customers (see Grabel, 2007).

States in the developing world have also long underinvested in human capital. But this situation too has become far more severe in the neoliberal era, when state support for education and public health has been curtailed radically, and the privatization of many essential public services has placed them out of reach of large sections of the population. Remittances therefore play the role of *partially* filling growing, large shortfalls in resources available for working and human capital. Though the hard numbers have yet to be assembled, it is entirely reasonable to assume that these large shortfalls in support for small business, small agriculture and human capital could not possibly be filled by remittances. In this connection, it is worth recalling that the poorest countries do not receive the majority of these flows, and they remain rather concentrated in some parts of individual countries.

In this context, it is important to learn whether remittances create a form of 'public moral hazard' on the part of developing-country governments. That is, by partially resolving important bottlenecks, do remittances in fact encourage states in the developing world to ignore their traditional responsibilities because they perceive (or hope) that remittances will fill various voids? The possibility that remittances may induce or aggravate public moral hazard is a matter that deserves serious consideration.[7]

Long-term growth

The vast majority of studies on the subject find limited or mixed evidence of a link between remittances and growth (World Bank, 2006; Ratha, 2007).

A few studies have concluded that there is no evidence of a positive relationship. For example, one study using data from 101 developing countries from the period 1970–2003 found no significant link between remittances and per capita income growth (IMF, 2005). In contrast, several single-country studies claim unequivocally that remittances promote growth. For example, Adelman and Taylor (1990) found that every dollar Mexico received from migrants increased GNP by US$2.69 to US$3.17 (depending on whether remittances were received by urban or rural households).

It is not likely that further empirical research will generate a consensus on the link between remittances and growth. This is because research must first resolve a rather large number of empirical issues that do not lend themselves to certainty, such as how to measure the diverse multiplier effects and leakages associated with remittances, how migration affects labour markets and hence wages in sending countries, the characteristics of emigrants and of the households that receive remittances, and whether emigration is a temporary response to an economic shock or is instead a permanent response to opportunities and constraints. The answers to these questions condition the effects that remittances will have on growth. For example, if remittances go primarily to the poorest households, they will be used for subsistence consumption rather than investment. If emigrants are primarily drawn from the high-skill segment of the labour pool, then they may have a negative effect on growth (because output in the country of origin suffers) (Solimano, 2004). If emigration is temporary (or the commitment to send remittances only extends for a limited time), then remittances provide a transitory boost to consumption, investment and and/or growth (Solimano, 2004). But if commitments to send remittances are long-term, then the effect of remittances may be more sustained.

Further complicating research on the relationship between remittances and growth is the fact that the effects of remittance-financed investments on physical assets and human capital are necessarily indirect and long-term (Ratha, 2007). In addition, it is difficult to determine the true scale of South–South migration, since so much of it is undocumented. The scale of South–South migration matters because there is evidence that remittances stemming from this flow have smaller multiplier effects than do those associated with North–South migration (Ratha and Shaw, 2007).

Labour force participation and labour markets

A few studies find limited evidence that the receipt of remittances reduces labour force participation in recipient households. This phenomenon tends to be described in terms of moral hazard or a 'culture of dependence' that develops once households come to expect remittances.

Chami *et al.* (2005) is the most widely cited study to document this phenomenon. They found that remittances discourage work effort on the part of recipient households that chose 'leisure' (that is, remittances) over labour. They further find that the reduction in labour effort may translate into reduced economic growth. A few studies have found that the negative effect on labour force participation is greater for women than for men. For example, Funkhouser (1992) found evidence of a stronger negative effect on women's labour supply in Managua, Nicaragua.

The scant research on the issue of labour market participation renders these findings not terribly compelling on their own. Moreover, it is not clear that this phenomenon – were it generally found to hold – is either troubling or surprising. There may be good reason to celebrate a backward-bending supply of labour by at least some family members, particularly in the light of research showing that the incidence of infant mortality is reduced by declines in labour-force participation by mothers (Duryea *et al.*, 2005), and other research findings that in the Philippines remittances reduce labour force participation but increase schooling among children (Yang, 2003). Moreover, across the developing world, women face substantially greater work burdens than do men, once work in the informal sector is taken into consideration. We might therefore welcome the levelling effects of remittances on labour contributions.

Were it to be demonstrated broadly through research, a negative effect on labour force participation need not be surprising. Reduced labour force participation by some remaining family members (for example, children) may be at the heart of the bargain involved in the decision to send a family member abroad to work. It is also the case that a negative effect on labour supply among remaining family members may stem not from any induced moral hazard, but from the creation of 'employment deserts' in communities or regions that experience large-scale migration and are left with no viable local economy. Relatedly, Kapur (2004) suggests that remittances have created vast 'migra-villages', whose subsistence comes to depend on remittances.

Finally, the question as to whether wages rise or fall in the home economy as the labour force contracts has not been addressed to date by empirical researchers. It is difficult to predict any general effect on wages prior to resolving the issue of whether positive, intermediate or negative selection effects in migration are the norm. There is also the matter of whether the reservation wage of those remaining in the home country is increased by remittances.

Brain drain versus brain gain

To date, there has been limited examination of whether remittance inflows and the possible accretion of skills garnered by working abroad (that is, 'brain gain') ultimately offset the output and social losses associated with a reduction in a country's supply of skilled labour ('brain drain'). Ratha (2003) argues that brain drain is partially offset by brain gain. This is because skilled workers are likely to be afforded more opportunities to be productive in wealthy countries. In addition, the origin economies of these workers may benefit over time from the networks and knowledge that skilled workers develop abroad (Ratha, 2003).

This view is rejected by Kapur (2004) and Nayyar (2008), who argue that there are many reasons to expect that brain gain does not offset the long-term economic effects of the loss of human capital embodied in a country's most educated workers. This is because brain drain generally follows capital flight (Kapur, 2004). Thus a country loses not one, but two factors that are essential to development. In addition, the loss of a country's most educated workers is not a one-off loss, as it also reduces the productivity of those left behind (Nayyar, 2008). Moreover, I argue that the loss of a country's most educated or skilled citizens must have lasting social and political consequences for a country (which may also affect the quality of civic life and political 'voice' in the sense of Hirschman [1986]). Finally, it may be that more significant than any output losses associated with brain drain are the even larger opportunity costs associated with the unemployment or underemployment of the most educated segments of the population who remain behind in employment deserts created by migration.

At this point, there is obviously no clear consensus among the few analysts who have studied the relative costs of brain drain/brain gain. In my view, the long-term economic and social effects of brain drain are unlikely to be offset fully by any potential for brain gain. But this matter can only be adjudicated by careful empirical research.

Old and new 'Dutch diseases'

There is some evidence that remittance inflows induce a Dutch disease effect, though the issue has been far from widely studied, and some controversy exists about the phenomenon. The 'Dutch disease effect' refers to the currency appreciation that is caused by sudden, large inflows of capital (in the form, for example, of remittances, portfolio investment, direct foreign investment).

Some analysts argue that remittances have induced strong Dutch disease effects (López-Córdova and Olmedo, 2006). Others argue that the link between remittances and the Dutch disease is particularly important in small countries where remittances are very high (Kapur, 2004). Evidence in support of a remittance-induced Dutch disease appears, for example, in Ameudo-Dorantes and Pozo (2004), who find that a doubling of remittances resulted in a real exchange rate appreciation of about 22 per cent in thirteen Latin-American countries between 1979 and 1998.

Other studies take the view that any Dutch disease effect of remittances is a minor concern, because the flows tend to be stable, persistent and grow gradually over time (World Bank, 2006). Therefore, the effect on exchange rates is likely to be less significant than is the case for other types of capital inflows that are prone to windfall effects or are cyclical. One study dissents from the view that remittances induce any Dutch disease effect. Rajan and Subramanian (2005) did not find any evidence that remittance flows slow down growth by affecting competitiveness.

Other analysts use the term Dutch or 'remittance disease' to refer to other unintended negative consequences of remittances. For example, Banuri (1986) argues that countries receiving large remittances often have to abandon support for highly valued exchange rates and tariff barriers (despite any government preferences to the contrary). As a consequence, the economy's aggregate investment portfolio shifts towards agriculture and services and away from industry. Using the term 'remittance disease', Julca (2007) argues that the support for consumption provided by remittances allows developing-country governments to ignore changes in the composition of trade and production (for example, the shift to higher-priced imported corn in Mexico is made possible by the income support provided by remittances). This raises the more general issue of whether the income support and social insurance function of remittances allows governments to ignore the negative consequences of their policy decisions, and to shift the burden of adjustment to these policies on to the senders of remittances.

Summary and conclusions

There is more to be said about the effects of remittances, particularly with respect to their social and political dimensions, but space constraints prevent exploration of these matters here (but see Grabel (2008) for discussion). These include, for example, the impact of remittances on the financial services industry in remittance-sending and receiving countries; public sector borrowing costs and credit ratings; public investment and infrastructure, particularly as concerns whether remittances crowd-in or crowd-out public investment; family viability and the quality of childrearing for those left behind; domestic politics and internal political struggles, which may be affected by disparate access across groups to remittance income;[8] the long-term consequences for civic life in remittance-receiving countries where 'exit' in the form of migration is the only means of support for vast portions of the population; the ability of migrant-receiving countries to affect political processes and outcomes in the sending countries, not least by cutting off migration flows; the perceived aid obligations of wealthy countries to poorer countries (as some now claim that remittances are privatized international aid); the willingness of governments in remittance-receiving countries to shift the burden of adjustment to natural, economic and political shocks on to already vulnerable and geographically-dispersed households; and the degree to which governments in developing countries have (falsely) come to conflate the receipt of remittances with a development strategy.

A full assessment of the developmental implications of remittances would have to take into account all of these complexities. And this returns us to the theme with which we began. As we have learnt from Ajit Singh, there can be and will be no magic bullet that leads inexorably to development. Development is inherently complex and contradictory, involving transformations and disruptions, and new social, political and economic processes that must be discovered along the way rather than read off a blueprint. Students of Singh will therefore not be surprised by the status of remittance studies today, replete as they are with conflicting findings and ambiguity. How could it be otherwise, when the factors that induce migration and remittance flows are so many, so interdependent and so diverse?

In the face of recognition such as this, Ajit Singh has shown us how to retain a commitment to the interests of the dispossessed across the globe, without despair. He has shown us that giving up on the hunt for simplistic solutions need not entail giving up on the hunt for economic justice. Instead, it should drive us, as it has always driven him, to look carefully and patiently, to find the nuance, and to look for solutions that embrace rather than repress the inherent complexity of social existence. Remittance studies stands to benefit greatly from just these sensibilities. There is good work to be done here, and it is important that we get on doing it.

Notes

1. Maria Sperandei and Ania Jankowski provided excellent research assistance. I thank George DeMartino for critical reactions to this paper.
2. Fortunately, there are exceptions to the rule. For example, Kapur (2004), Burgess (2007) and Julca (2007) advance sceptical and original arguments about remittances, while Ratha has generated authoritative and wide-ranging empirical studies that are principally responsible for the explosion of interest in remittances.
3. If we adjust the data to include estimates of remittances sent through informal channels, total remittance inflows are larger than FDI and more than twice as large as official aid received by developing countries.
4. The reduction of transient poverty has important spillover effects for human capital investment, as we shall see below.
5. Citations in this and the following paragraph are drawn from the literature review in López-Córdova and Olmedo (2006).
6. Writing on Mexico, Burgess (2007:12) makes a point that has currency well beyond the country. She writes: 'in rural communities (in Mexico], migration and remittances have become critical alternatives to the withdrawal of the state from the agricultural sector, particularly in poor, southern states...Not only did many rural workers lose their jobs, but those who maintained small farms lost their sources of credit or investment.'
7. Relatedly, there is a need for empirical research that examines the effect of remittances on state behaviour concerning public investment. If remittances catalyse public investment that would not otherwise occur, then naturally the net effect is positive (and perhaps substantial). But if remittances crowd-out public investment by inducing a public moral hazard (as per the above), then their contribution may be marginal or even negative.
8. As the Cuban case referred to above suggests.

References

Adams, R. and J. Page (2005) 'Do International Migration and Remittances Reduce Poverty in Developing Countries?', *World Development*, 33 (10): 1645–69.

Adelman, I. and E. Taylor (1990) 'Is Structural Adjustment with a Human Face Still Possible? The Case of Mexico', *Journal of Development Studies*, 26: 387–407.

Alper, A. and B. Neyapti (2006) 'Determinants of Workers' Remittances: Turkish Evidence from High Frequency Data', *Eastern European Economics*, 44 (5): 91–100.

Ameudo-Dorantes, C. and S. Pozo (2004) 'Workers' Remittances and the Real Exchange Rate: A Paradox of Gifts,' *World Development*, 32 (8): 1407–17.

Banuri. T. (1986) 'Macroeconomic Effects of Worker Remittances', Ph.D. Dissertation, Harvard University.

Burgess, K. (2007) 'Neoliberal Reform and Migrant Remittances: Symptom or Solution?', Unpublished paper, Fletcher School, Tufts University, Medford, Mass., USA.

Chami, R., C. Fullenkamp and S. Jahjah (2005) 'Are Immigrant Remittance Flows a Source of Capital for Development?', IMF Staff Papers, 52 (1): 55–81.

Cox Edwards, A. and M. Ureta (2003) 'International Migration, Remittances and Schooling: Evidence from El Salvador', *Journal of Development Economics*, 68: 309–28.

Duryea, S., E. López-Córdova and A. Olmedo (2005) 'Migrant Remittances and Infant Mortality: Evidence from Mexico', Unpublished manuscript, Inter-American Development Bank.

Dustmann, C. and O. Kirchkamp (2001) 'The Optimal Migration Duration and Activity Choice After Re-migration', IZA Discussion Paper No. 266.

Funkhouser, E. (1992) 'Migration from Nicaragua: Some Recent Evidence', *World Development*, 20 (8): 1209–18.

Glen, J. and A. Singh (2005) 'Corporate Governance, Competition and Finance: Re-thinking Lessons from the Asian Crises', *Eastern Economic Journal*, 31 (2): 219–42.

Grabel, I. (1995) 'Speculation-led Economic Development: A Post-Keynesian Interpretation of Financial Liberalization in the Third World', *International Review of Applied Economics*, 9 (2): 127–49.

Grabel, I. (2008) 'Remittances: A Political-Economy Analysis', Unpublished paper, University of Denver; Graduate School of International Studies; Denver, Colorado USA.

Hirschman, A. (1986) *Rival Views of Market Society*, New York: Viking: 77–104.

IMF (2005) *World Economic Outlook: Globalization and External Imbalances*. Washington, DC, April, ch. 2.

Julca, A. (2007) 'New Approach to Remittances for Development: A Model for Mainstreaming Remittances in Poor Countries', Unpublished paper, United Nations, New York, USA.

Kapur, D. (2004) 'Remittances: The New Development Mantra?', G24 Discussion Paper No. 29.

López-Córdova, E. (2005) 'Globalization, Migration, and Development: The Role of Mexican Migrant Remittances', *Economía*, 6: 217–56.

López-Córdova, E. and A. Olmedo (2006 'International Remittances and Development: Existing Evidence, Policies, and Recommendations,' Institute for the Integration of Latin America and the Caribbean, Occasional Paper No. 41.
Massey, D. and E. Parrado (1998) 'International Migration and Business Formation in Mexico', *Social Science Quarterly*, March, 79 (1): 1–20.
McCormick, B. and J. Wahba (2001) 'Overseas Work Experience, Savings and Entrepreneurship Amongst Return Migrants to LDCs', *Scottish Journal of Political Economy*, 48 (2): 164–78.
Mohaptra, S., D. Ratha, Z. Xu and K. M. Vijayalaskmi. (2006 'Remittance Trends 2006', Migration and Development Brief 2, World Bank Development Prospects Group.
Nayyar, D. (2008) 'International Migration and Development', in J. Stiglitz and N. Serra (eds), *Towards a New Global Governance: The Washington Consensus Reconsidered*, Oxford: Oxford University Press.
Parrado, E. (2004) 'US Migration, Home Ownership, and Housing Quality', in J. Durand and D. Massey (eds), *Crossing the Border*, New York: Russell Sage Foundation: 63–320.
Rajan, R. and A. Subramanian (2005) 'What Undermines Aid's Impact on Growth?', NBER Working Paper No. 11657.
Ratha. D. (2003) 'Workers' Remittances: An Important and Stable Source of External Development Finance', in *Global Development Finance*, ch. 7, World Bank.
Ratha. D. (2007) 'Leveraging Remittances for Development', Migration Policy Institute Policy Brief.
Ratha, D. and W. Shaw (2007) 'South–South Migration and Remittances', World Bank Working Paper No. 112, Development Prospects Group, World Bank, Washington, DC.
Sander, C. (2003) 'Migrant Remittances to Developing Countries: A Scoping Study', Prepared for the UK Department of International Development; Available at: http://www.bannock.co.uk/PDF/Remittances.pdf.
Sen, A. (1992) *Inequality Reexamined*, Cambridge, Mass.: Harvard University Press.
Singh, A. (1999a) 'Should Africa Promote Stock Market Capitalism?', *Journal of International Development*, 11: 343–65.
Singh, A. (1999b) 'Asian Capitalism and Financial Crisis,' in J. Grieve Smith and J. Michie (eds), *Global Instability and World Economic Governance*, London: Routledge.
Singh, A. (2002) 'Competition and Competition Policy in Emerging Markets: International and Developmental Dimensions', G24 Discussion Paper No 18.
Singh, A. (2006) 'Stock Market and Economic Development', *The Elgar Companion to Development Studies*, Cheltenham, UK, and Northampton, Mass.: Edward Elgar: 584–90.
Singh, A. and B. Weisse (1998) 'Emerging Stock Markets, Portfolio Capital Flows and Long Term Economic Growth: Micro and Macroeconomic Perspectives', *World Development* 26 (4): 607–22.
Singh, A. and A. Zammit (2006) 'Corporate Governance, Crony Capitalism and Economic Crises: Should the US Business Model Replace the Asian Way of Doing Business?', *Corporate Governance: An International Review*, 14 (4): 220–33.
Solimano, A. (2004) 'Remittances by Emigrants: Issues and Evidence', in A. B. Atkinson (ed.), *New Sources of Development Financing*, Oxford: Oxford University Press.

Stark, O. and E. Taylor (1986) 'Remittances and Inequality.' *Economic Journal*, 96 (383): 722–40.

World Bank (2006) 'Trends, Determinants, and Macroeconomic Effects of Remittances', *Global Economic Prospects*, Washington, DC: World Bank.

World Bank (2007) *Global Development Finance, 2007.*,Washington, DC: World Bank.

World Bank Development Policy Grant (DPG) (2007) Remittances Data Set. Available at: http://siteresources.worldbank.org.EXTDECPROSPECTS/Resources/476882- 1157133580628/RemittancesData_updated2007.xls.

Yang, D. (2003) 'Remittances and Human Capital Investment: Chile Schooling and Chile Labor in the Origin Households of Overseas Filipino Workers'. Available at: http://www.people.fas.harvard.edu/~dyang/papers/yang_remittances.pdf.

8

Ownership, Institutions and Technological Intensities: Automotive and Electronic Component Firms in East Asia

Rajah Rasiah[1]

Introduction

The theoretical arguments over the role of foreign multinationals in spillovers have remained inconclusive. Whereas the discourse on the significance of foreign direct investment (FDI) has moved from being ideological to empirical, the neoclassical assumptions and instruments used to examine it remain problematical. Critics argue that asymmetric relations between globalized giant firms and weak governments reproduce harmful effects from defensive conduct (see Lall and Streeten, 1977), which include oligopolistic control of markets (see Hymer, 1960) and the acquisition and crowding-out of efficient local firms. In addition to static capital and employment benefits, supporters point to the potential these firms bring to developing economies – for example, technology, scale and competitive discipline (see Dunning, 1958; Hirschman, 1958). Helleiner (1973) had shown evidence of MNCs decomposing production and relocating the assembly and processing of the labour-intensive segments of their latest products to dismiss Vernon's (1966) product-cycle model, arguing that only mature production will be relocated at developing sites. Lall (1979), Rasiah (1992, 1996), Cantwell (1995) and Ernst (2006) provided evidence of foreign MNCs offshoring R&D activities in developing economies.

Multinational companies (MNCs), through licensing, human capital transfers, subcontracting links, alliances and direct investment, offer the potential for the transmission of know-how to local firms. Apart from economies facing poor labour, resource, infrastructure and domestic market endowments, most other developing economies that are secure and stable enjoy at least some degree of bargaining opportunity to be able to frame strategies to appropriate knowledge spillover from foreign MNCs. Institution building – the *sine qua non* for sustained growth and structural change – can only be achieved when governments create and co-ordinate the conditions through appropriate interventions. Host governments have a big responsibility to drive institutional change to facilitate learning and innovation domestically (Nelson and Winter, 1982; Rasiah, 1992). Kaldor (1967) and Singh (1989) argued for developing economies to shift the focus of growth to industrialization to drive increasing returns.

This chapter assumes that the learning potential of local firms from FDI depends on the composition of technology, and the strength of the embedding institutional and systemic support (IS) at host sites. It takes the evolutionary assumption that taxonomies and trajectories matter in technological catch-ups, and it varies with the types of industries, technologies and the strength of the support institutions at host sites.

The rest of the chapter is organized as follows. The second section reviews some of the leading arguments on the developmental impact of FDI on developing economies. The third section introduces the methodology to examine gaps in technologies by industry between foreign and local firms, and the relationship between IS and technological intensities. The fourth section presents the findings and analysis, while the fifth section rounds off the chapter with the conclusions. Automotive and electronic component firms were chosen because of the medium high-tech and high-tech nature of operations respectively in China, Indonesia, Malaysia, the Philippines and Taiwan.

Multinationals and technological spillovers

This section explores two major branches of economic theory that examine spillovers: one, neoclassical, and the other, evolutionary.

Neoclassical theory

Early neoclassical work on FDI relaxed the immobile factor conditions imposed in the Heckscher–Ohlin model (see Leamer, 1995) to allow for international capital movements (Bhagwati, 1979). However, this framework simply assumed that the outflow of capital from a capital-surplus and labour-scarce economy (the United States) to a capital-scarce and labour-surplus economy (Mexico) will eventually lead to the equalization of interests and wages, and with that there will be a convergence of development between these economies. Markets are deemed to automatically drive equalization of factor prices across borders.

Driven by the notion that relative prices will attract FDI, the implicit assumptions of neoclassical production function models assume that the changing structure of prices as capital flows from rich to poor countries will offer optimal conditions for spillover to take place at host sites. Caves (1974) adapted Solow's (1956) production function model to first estimate spillovers from a foreign presence.

However, the neoclassical evidence on spillovers is mixed. On the one hand, Caves (1974), Blomstrom and Persson (1983) and Blomstrom and Sjoholm (1999) produced evidence of positive spillovers from the presence of foreign firms in Australia, Mexico and Indonesia, respectively. On the other hand, Haddad and Harrison (1993), Kokko *et al.* (1996) and Aitkin and Harrison (1999) show a lack of spillovers to domestic firms from a foreign presence in Morocco, Uruguay and Venezuela, respectively. These contradictory findings not only show problems with neoclassical estimation methods but also a disjuncture between theory and reality.

The underlying neoclassical assumptions that markets are efficient and economic agents enjoy equal access, as well as processing and decision-making abilities, are wrong. Instead of assuming that proactive and stable governments attempt to create or use market instruments to drive allocation and co-ordination, it assumes that the unleashing of market forces will resolve government failures. By arguing that all governments had to do was to leave markets to co-ordinate resource and factor allocation, neoclassical theory continues to discourage the institutional upgrading essential to speed up technical change.

The contradictory findings on spillovers are also a result of methodological weaknesses. The use of the production function is undermined by at least three problems. First, the residue in the production function used to measure total factor productivity, as Romer (1994), Nelson (1994) and Vaitsos (2003) have argued, does not capture technology or technical change. Second, spillover is a dynamic concept that refers to systemic effects captured by economic agents (including workers) external to the firms studied, and hence often do not appear in pecuniary measures (see Rasiah, 1992). Third, spillovers enjoy differences in intensity – including positive and negative elements, thus making aggregation impossible.

In addition, production function models analysing the technological gap estimate it wrongly, using the value of machinery and equipment of firms, capital expenditure or productivity differences between foreign and local firms. Differences in the stock of knowledge – embodied in human capital, machinery and equipment, and relationships – cannot be estimated in this way. In addition, efforts to draw policy conclusions from mere differences in productivity and technological levels do not take into consideration the structural interdependence between industries and complementarities (see Kaldor, 1979).

Heterodox approaches

Industrial policy (for example Hamilton, 1791; List, 1885; Gerschenkron, 1962; Reinert, 2007), evolutionary (for example, Nelson and Winter, 1982; Freeman, 1989; Lundvall, 1988, 1992; Lall, 1992), and development economists (for example Myrdal, 1957; Hirschman, 1958) introduced trajectories, sequencing, institutions and linkages in engendering the conditions systematically to drive catch-up. Central to this literature is a national or regional strategy on accumulation that focuses on building domestic capability. While it is the domestic economic agents that are targeted for catch-up, efforts to develop them combines access to foreign knowledge with the development of local knowledge. Because knowledge has cumulative and path-dependent features, accessing it from mature sources initially will be economic and faster than developing it. What is critical from foreign sources is access to knowledge that can be drawn through FDI, imitation or licensing, acquisition of foreign firms and the hiring of human capital carrying tacit knowledge. Latecomers such as Japan, Taiwan and Korea relied extensively on the latter two modes to absorb foreign knowledge to hasten catch-up in local firms (Johnson, 1982; Edquist and Jacobssen, 1987; Amsden, 1989; Wade, 1990; Chang, 1994; Rasiah and Lin, 2005). Singapore and Ireland have continued to rely on FDI extensively (Best, 2001). To this literature should be added the use of motives and benefits by business scholars to explain the conduct of MNCs at host sites (see Dunning, 1988; Narula, 1996; Cantwell and Mudambi, 2001).

Consistent with Marshall (1890), evolutionary economists offered a systemic understanding of knowledge flows (Nelson and Winter, 1982, p. 63). Scitovsky (1964) and Rosenstein-Rodan (1984) distinguished technical from pecuniary external economies. Nelson (2007) discussed the imperfect, and co-ordinated and uncoordinated nature of knowledge flows. Knowledge flows from interaction between workers, and the movement of human capital to drive systemic synergies. Mature firms in open integrated clusters gain new ideas to support continuous organizational change as older employees are retired to make way for fresh ones, while new firms benefit from the released entrepreneurial and technical human capital to start new firms (Rasiah, 1992; Best, 2001). Rasiah (1992, 1994) and Saxenian (1994) documented the development and movement of human capital, which supported new firm creation in Penang and the Silicon Valley, respectively.

Using the experience of Japan, Freeman (1989) demonstrated that international flows of stocks of knowledge from developed to developing economies take a sequential movement from import to adaptation, assimilation and innovation. The development of a typology of technological capabilities by Lall (1992), Bell and Pavitt (1995), Figueiredo (2003) and Rasiah (2004) on the basis of taxonomies and trajectories (see Dosi, 1982; Pavitt, 1984) has facilitated the identification of technological gaps to formulate learning and innovation strategies for driving catch-ups. Lall (1992), Rasiah (1992, 1994, 2004) and Figueiredo (2003) showed how firms move up the technology trajectory by acquiring initially simple and later complex technological capabilities before eventually participating in R&D activities.

Successful spillover outcomes from foreign to local firms show that latecomer firms benefit from the foreign presence. What is clear is that foreign firms need to show higher levels of technological capability for such a spillover to become useful for local firms. The capacity of the local firm to absorb such knowledge is then critical for it to occur. Using evidence from Korea, Kim (1997) had argued that the appropriation is maximized when local firms can switch from duplicative to creative imitation capabilities. Indeed, the first steps for rooting MNC-based learning and innovation will be to identify the firms with the relevant technologies, appropriable benefits and requisite institutions for absorption.

Hirschman (1958; 1970) had canvassed strongly for export orientation to attract the discipline and scale effects of larger markets to promote competition and backward linkages. Critical in Hirschman's (1970) accounts of FDI is the emphasis on backward linkages, arguing that rising exports will expand the scale of production and competitiveness to raise backward-linkage opportunities. Hirschman argued that the initial entry of FDI to underdeveloped locations often created serious demand–supply imbalances because of the lack of capable suppliers, and hence policies are essential to develop domestic supply capabilities. Although the capacity to absorb new knowledge is easier when the gap between the leader and learner is narrow, Hirschman (1958; 1970) argued that the greater the gap, the larger will be the potential for catch-up. What is obvious in Hirschman's (1970) work is that it is the potential benefits that are critical when developing economies seek FDI.

Industrial policy, evolutionary and development economists paved the way for understanding catch-up, but it was business scholars who offered some understanding of when FDI would provide tangible technological benefits at developing host sites. Dunning's (1988) eclectic approach of ownership, location and internalization (OLI) to explain the internationalization of production addresses potential spillover at host sites. However, such a framework should include Vernon's (1966) argument on national factors, and OECD (1998) and Amsden *et al.* (2001: 5) showed evidence of low incidence and intensity of R&D investment outside national borders.

This chapter uses the evolutionary approach, but with contributions from Hirschman's (1970) logic of learning, Dunning's (1988) ownership influences and Vernon's (1966) emphasis on national factors, to examine the following hypotheses:

1. Because of ownership benefits, human resource (HR) and process technology (PT) intensities of foreign firms will be higher than local firms at host sites, and that the relationship between these variables and IS will only be significant in the local sample.
2. Because of the influence of national institutions, RD intensities of local firms are expected to be higher at host sites than of foreign firms, though a positive relationship is expected in both.

Methodology and data

This section discusses the methodology that will be used to examine the hypotheses identified in the previous section. The focus is on examining differences in technological intensity between foreign and local firms, and its relationship with the embedding institutional and systemic strength.

Basic and high-tech infrastructure

The IS of Taiwan is superior to those of China, Malaysia, the Philippines or Indonesia (see Table 8.1). Given the difficulty firms have in evaluating IS against what are available abroad, firm-level assessments are confined only to national assessments. These figures are then adjusted with the national index scores on basic infrastructure (BI) and R&D infrastructure (RDI) derived from normalizations using related proxies where sufficient data are available.

BI is estimated using the proxies of healthcare support (hospitals and clinics), primary and secondary schools and transport and telecommunications. RDI is measured using the proxies of R&D scientists and engineers per million people and R&D expenditure in gross national investment.

Table 8.1 Basic and high-tech infrastructure (BI and HTI), 2001

	BI	HTI
China	0.337	0.102
Indonesia	0.111	0.020
Taiwan	0.625	0.500
Malaysia	0.437	0.042
Philippines	0.121	0.034

Note: BI calculated using the proxies of adult literacy rate (education), doctors per thousand people (health) and main telephone lines per thousand people (communication) using the normalization formula $(X_i - X_{min})/(X_{max} - X_{min})$ (where X_i, X_{min} and X_{max} refer to the *i*th, minimum and maximum value of the variable), and the 96 countries where data were available from World Bank (2003). The same approach was used to calculate HTI using the proxies of R&D scientists and engineers per million people, and R&D investment in gross domestic investment and 55 countries where the data was available from World Bank (2003) and national ministries. Both BI and HTI were adjusted by dividing the scores with the highest observation so that the figures fall within $0 \leq X \leq 1$.
Source: Computed from World Bank (2003); Taiwan (2004); Malaysia (2004).

Table 8.2 List of variables and their relationship with the dependent variables, 2001

		Dependent variables		
Independent variables	**Acronym**	**HR**	**PT**	**RD**
Export	$X/Y, X$	+ve	+ve	+ve
Institutional and systemic support	*IS*	+ve	+ve	+ve
Union	*U*	Unclear	Unclear	Unclear
Foreign ownership share	*FOS*	Unclear	Unclear	−ve
Size	*S*	Unclear	Unclear	Unclear
Age	*A*	Unclear	Unclear	Unclear

Specification of variables

The variables used in the chapter are specified in this subsection, and their expected relationships with technological intensities are shown in Table 8.2.

Technological intensities

Three types of technologies are examined in this chapter, namely, HR, PT and RD. It is methodologically better to integrate related proxies into a composite set of indexes, which will not only help to minimize double counting, but also reduce collinearity problems in statistical analysis. In addition, adjusting a firm's responses with related proxies will offer a better approximation of its intensity than any single proxy – for example, R&D expense in sales or R&D staff in the workforce. Because there are no prior reasons to attach greater significance to any of the proxies, the normalization procedure used is not weighted. The following technological intensities are specified:

Human resources

Consistent with the first hypothesis, where HR differences are significant, foreign firms are expected to show higher intensities than local firms in underdeveloped sites.

HR practices were measured as:

$$HR_i = 1/3[TM_i,\ TE_i,\ CHR_i]$$

TM, *TE* and *CHR* refer to training mode, training expense in payroll and cutting edge HR practices, respectively, of firm *i*. *TM* was measured as a multinomial logistic variable of 1 when staff are exposed to external training; 2 when external staff are used to train employees; 3 when staff with training responsibilities are on the payroll; 4 when a separate training department is used; 5 when a separate training centre is used; and 0 when no formal training is undertaken. *CHR* was measured by a score of one for each of these practices: (i) team-working; (ii) small group activities to stimulate innovation; (iii) multi-skilling; (iv) interaction with marketing, customer service and R&D department; (v) life-long learning; and (vi) upward mobility. Because all the proxies were evenly weighted, HR was divided by 3. Skills intensity was excluded from this index, as the formal qualifications of employees are often determined before they are employed by the firms.

The proxies were normalized using the following formula:

$$\text{Normalization Score} = (X_i - X_{min})/(X_{max} - X_{min})$$

X_i, X_{min} and X_{max} refer to the *i*th, minimum and maximum values, respectively, of the proxy, *X*. The normalization procedure raises the highest observation among the five countries to one and the lowest to zero. Caution must be placed in the interpretation of the normalized data as they represent relative values against the highest and lowest observations.

Process technology

Consistent with the first hypothesis, foreign firms are expected to show higher PT intensities than local firms in underdeveloped sites.

Data on three proxies facilitated the computation of PT:

$$PT_i = 1/2[EM_i, IQC_i]$$

where *EM* and *IQC* refer, respectively, to equipment and machinery, and inventory control and quality control methods of firm *i*. *EM* was computed as a multinomial logistic variable with an average age of over 5 years = 0; 5 years = 1; 4 years = 2; 3 years = 3; 2 years = 4; and 1 year or less = 5. Each cutting-edge inventory and quality control method reported by firm *i* was counted for *IQC*: (i) just-in-time or minimum stock turnaround; (ii) statistical process control; (iii) total preventive maintenance; (iv) materials or integrated materials resource planning; (v) quality-control circles; (v) small-group activity; and (vi) zero or low defects in parts per million. Because the proxies were evenly weighted, *PT* was divided by 2.

R&D

Firm-level R&D is focused largely on process technology and product development. Given the weak IS, mean RD are expected to be low in China, Malaysia, the Philippines and Indonesia. Because foreign firms enjoy access to R&D facilities at parent sites, their RD intensity is expected to be lower than in local firms, particularly in Taiwan, where IS is strong. RD is also expected to be positively correlated with X/Y because of competition in export markets.

The data collected allowed the computation of two R&D proxies. It was not possible from the ADB sample data to disentangle investment advanced between process and product R&D, and hence this proxy was measured to relate to both product and process R&D, and was measured as:

$$RD_i = 1/2[RD_{expi}, R_{Dempi}]$$

where RD_{exp} and RD_{emp} refer to R&D expense in sales and R&D personnel in the workforce, respectively, of firm i. Because the proxies were evenly weighted, *RD* was divided by 2.

Institutional and systemic support

Given differences in IS across the economies examined, firms are likely to show higher RD means in Taiwan than in China, Malaysia, the Philippines and Indonesia. Although firms have access to stocks of knowledge from foreign national innovation systems – for example, publications, education, licensing arrangements and foreign affiliates – because of proprietary obligations and greater support given to national firms, they rely more on their own national institutions to participate in R&D activities (see Vernon, 1971; Rasiah, 2004).

The technology components of HR, PT and RD are expected to be positively correlated with IS in all three samples. However, the relationship of IS, and HR and PT is expected to be positive and significant only in the local sample, because of the access foreign firms enjoy to their parent plants. Foreign firms tend to retain new product development at parent sites – preferring to participate largely in adaptations at host sites. Offshoring of R&D take place when endowments exists or the operation is resource-driven. Hence, RD is expected to show higher impact on IS in the local than in the foreign sample.

IS_{BI} is measured as follows:

$$IS_{BIi} = 1/3BI_k([H_i,\ PS_i,\ TT_i])$$

where IS_{BI}, BI_k, H, PS and TT refer to institutional and systemic support from basic infrastructure institutions, national *BI* factor of country *k*, and firms' assessment of basic infrastructure support for health care, primary and secondary schools, and transport and telecommunication institutions, respectively. Likert scale scores of 1–5 were used to measure the strength. IS_{BI} is divided by 3 because of to the number of proxies used.

IS_{RDI} is measured as follows:

$$IS_{RDIi} = 1/3RDI_k[RD_{Ui},\ RD_{Li},\ RD_{IGi}]$$

where IS_{RDI}, RDI_k, RD_U, RD_L and RD_{IG} refer to institutional and systemic support involving R&D infrastructure, national *RDI* factor of country k, R&D support from universities, labs, and government incentives and programmes. Likert scale scores of 1–5 were used to measure the strength. IS_{RDI} is divided by the number of proxies used (that is, 3).

IS is measured as follows:

$$IS_i = IS_{BIi} + IS_{RDIi}$$

IS_{BI} and IS_{RDI} can have both positive and negative implications. While it helps to draw firms' assessments of the quality of connections and co-ordination with the relevant institutions involved, including explaining the geographical dispersion in institutional support across individual economies, it also can introduce perceptive biases. The national consultants who faced the officials of all the responding firms were asked to rate their assessment strictly on the basis of what they think should be the worst (1) and the best (5).

Exports

Competition, scale and scope make export markets a driver of technical change (Hirschman, 1977; Rasiah, 2004). Exports are measured using intensities for automotive parts firms, and incidence for electronic components:

$$\text{Export intensity } = X_i/Y_i.$$

$$\text{Export incidence, } X_i = 1 \text{ if firms exported; } X_i = 0 \text{ otherwise.}$$

The latter was unavoidable because of the poor response rate for gross output and export values. Where X and Y refer to exports and gross output respectively of firm i.

Union

Owing to collinearity problems between wages (W) and IS, union (U) was used to represent labour market conditions (see Appendix Table 8.A1). Institutional representation, which is strong in automotive firms and weak in electronics firms, is expected to produce a positive link and no link, respectively, between U and technological intensities. Union was measured as:

$$U_i = 1 \text{ when firm reports yes to unionized workers; } U_i = 0 \text{ otherwise,}$$

where U refers to the union incidence of firm i.

Size

Industrial organization exponents posit that firms achieve competitiveness with a certain minimum efficiency scale (MES), which varies with industries (see Scherer, 1980, 1992; Pratten, 1971). The automotive and electronic components industries are diverse: some subsectors are scale-intensive (for example, absorbers, stereo sets, wafer fabrication, memory and microprocessor assembly, and tyres) while some are scope-intensive (for example, command navigation systems, smart-light systems, contract R&D and robotics). Where scale is unimportant – for example. small-batch components – scope rather than scale is important (Piore and Sabel, 1984; Rasiah, 1994). Audretsch (2002) offered persuasive analysis of US data to dispel arguments related to the significance of large size in efficiency and innovative activities.

Table 8.3 Breakdown of automotive and electronic component firms, 2001

	Automotive			Electronic		
	Foreign	**Local**	**Total**	**Foreign**	**Local**	**Total**
China	22	63	85	12	36	48
Indonesia	6	82	88	14	24	38
Malaysia	22	66	88	64	23	87
Philippines	10	26	36	18	9	27
Taiwan	20	56	76	5	46	51
Total	**70**	**293**	**363**	**113**	**138**	**251**

Source: ADB (2003) 'Competitiveness of Firms Survey, 2000–3', Asian Development Bank (ADB), Manila.

Two categories of size are chosen, namely, small and medium; and large, and is measured as a dummy variable:

$S_i = 1$ when employment size is 500 or fewer; $S_i = 0$ if otherwise

where S refers to size of firm i.

Ownership

Following the first hypothesis of this chapter, foreign firms are expected to enjoy higher intensities than local firms when HR and PT differences are significant in the developing sites, and the second hypothesis where local firms are expected to enjoy higher intensities than foreign firms when RD differences are significant. Two different ownership proxies are used in the paper. The first – that is, FOS – uses the foreign equity share, while the second – that is, FO – uses a 30 per cent foreign equity share to separate samples into foreign and local. FOS and FO were measured as:

FOS_i = foreign equity/total equity.

$FO_i = 1$ if foreign equity ownership of firm i is 30% or more;

$FO_i = 0$ otherwise.

The breakdown of the firms on the basis of ownership is shown in Table 8.3.

Age

Given that firms with longer experience enjoy greater experiential knowledge, age is considered to provide a positive relationship with export intensity and technological capabilities. However, the statistical relationship may not be positive if foreign firms, using superior technology from abroad and enjoying strong access to global markets, only started relocating their operations recently or when local firms migrate from other industries, a neutral relationship is assumed. The absolute age of the firm is used and was measured as:

$$A_i = \text{years in operation of firm } i$$

where A refers to the age of operation of firm i.

Overall, 363 automotive and 251 electronic component firms supplied usable data (ADB, 2002; UNU-MERIT, 2002) (see Table 8.3). The national experts who collected the data were requested to follow strictly the sampling frame of the respective national statistics departments.

Statistical exercises

Two statistical exercises were carried out: the first, two-tailed t-tests of means to examine differences in technological intensities between foreign and local firms; and the second, Tobit regressions to examine the relationship between technological intensities and IS by ownership, controlling for $X/Y(X)$, S, A and U. Tobit regressions were preferred, since the dependent variables were censored on the right and left sides of the data sets as *HR*, *PT* and *RD* take a minimum value of zero and a maximum value of one. *IS* is assumed to pick up country effects, and hence country dummies were dropped.

$$Tobit: HR = \alpha + \beta_1 X/Y + \beta_2 IS + \beta_3 S + \beta_4 FOS + \beta_5 A + \beta_6 U + \mu \quad (8.1)$$

$$Tobit: PT = \alpha + \beta_1 X/Y + \beta_2 IS + \beta_3 S + \beta_4 FOS + \beta_5 A + \beta_6 U + \mu \quad (8.2)$$

$$Tobit: RD = \alpha + \beta_1 X/Y + \beta_2 IS + \beta_3 S + \beta_4 FOS + \beta_5 A + \beta_6 U + \mu \quad (8.3)$$

The regression equations above were repeated using foreign and local samples separately. Following the arguments of Smith (1776), Marshall (1920) and Young (1928), the paper assumes circular causation between *HR*, *PT*, *RD* and X/Y (X), and *IS*.

Results and discussion

This section uses the statistical instruments and the variables specified in the previous section to examine differences in technological intensity between foreign and local firms, and the relationships in which they are involved.

Table 8.4 Two-tailed *t*-tests of means, automotive and electronic component firms, 2001

	Automotives			Electronics		
	Foreign	Local	*t*	Foreign	Local	*t*
HR						
China	0.354	0.298	1.15	0.603	0.466	2.52**
Malaysia	0.346	0.290	1.84	0.475	0.454	0.33
Taiwan	0.273	0.432	−3.79*	0.319	0.421	−1.48
Indonesia	0.396	0.307	2.77*	0.429	0.305	2.81*
Philippines	0.561	0.411	2.42**	0.445	0.458	−0.53
PT						
China	0.375	0.353	3.71*	0.219	0.236	−1.17
Malaysia	0.457	0.437	0.45	0.479	0.333	2.29**
Taiwan	0.475	0.509	−1.26	0.452	0.505	−0.96
Indonesia	0.375	0.275	1.06	0.310	0.235	2.06**
Philippines	0.400	0.331	1.24	0.457	0.326	2.57**
RD						
China	0.230	0.190	1.20	0.272	0.358	−0.94
Malaysia	0.200	0.240	−1.06	0.103	0.033	1.41
Taiwan	0.470	0.690	−3.61*	0.423	0.610	−2.38**
Indonesia	0.110	0.100	0.18	0.052	0.060	−0.31
Philippines	0.020	0.110	−3.41*	0.036	0.087	−2.01**

Note: * and ** refer to 1% and 5% levels of significance, respectively.
Source: Computed from ADB, UNU-MERIT Survey (2003) using SPSS package.

Statistical differences

Results of the two-tailed *t*-tests of means are shown in Table 8.4.

Automotive components

Differences in HR are statistically significant in Indonesia, the Philippines and Taiwan. Foreign firms enjoyed higher HR than local firms in the Philippines and Indonesia. in particular, Japanese suppliers have introduced cutting-edge HR practices in these countries to reduce defects and downtime. It is the opposite in Taiwan, as the HR of local firms is higher than that of foreign firms. Interviews show that local firms face higher competition in replacement markets than foreign firms who had tie-ups with host-site assemblers.

Process technology differences are significant only in China, where foreign firms enjoyed higher PT means than local firms. Interviews show that foreign firms have been forced to upgrade their machinery and equipment because of policy pressures to access the domestic market.

Local firms enjoyed higher RD means in Taiwan and the Philippines. Interviews show that local firms in Taiwan managed to marry the world class industries of machinery and electronics to produce frontier automotive components with significant numbers of patents taken in the US. RD means in the Philippines were extremely low. Interviews show that these firms are engaged in the adaptation of equipment and products (for example, wire harness).

Electronic components

The two-tailed *t*-test of differences in means between foreign and local firms shows foreign firms enjoying higher means over local firms among the statistically significant production technology results. Foreign firms enjoyed higher HR means than local firms in China and Indonesia, and PT means in Malaysia, Indonesia and the Philippines. Interviews confirm the transfer of best practices by foreign firms from abroad.

Local firms show higher RD means than foreign firms in Taiwan and the Philippines. Whereas foreign firms offshore R&D activities to take advantage of endowments already there, local firms utilize host-site endowments much more. Grants supporting R&D activities in Taiwan have gone only to local firms or joint ventures having local equity participation. Local firms are engaged in the adaptation of equipment and components in the Philippines much more than are foreign firms.

Taken together, the results show that foreign firms in underdeveloped sites enjoy higher HR and PT intensities than local firms because of access to superior plants abroad. Best practices and participation in higher-precision activities give foreign firms an edge over local firms in underdeveloped sites. However, where the host site is developed, as in Taiwan, there are typically no obvious statistical difference between foreign and local firms in production technologies. Local firms enjoyed higher HR means than foreign automotive firms in Taiwan as a result of differences in market orientation. The picture is completely different in the case of RD. Local firms show higher means than foreign firms in Taiwan and the Philippines in both industries.

Statistical relationships

This section examines the statistical relationships involving technological intensity variables. All the regressions reported in Table 8.5 passed

Table 8.5 Technological intensity regressions, automotive and electronic component firms, 2001

	Automotive									Electronic											
	HR			*PT*			*RD*			*HR*			*PT*			*RD*			*All*		
	All	FO	Local	All	FO	Local	All	FO	Local	All	FO	Local	All	FO	Local	All	FO	Local	HR	PT	RD
X/Y,	0.025	−0.087	0.060	0.079	0.027	0.103	0.266	0.269	0.255	0.012	−0.057	−0.017	0.053	0.065	0.035	0.144	0.257	0.203	0.042	0.089	0.328
X	(0.8)	(−1.4)	(1.7)	(2.9)*	(0.6)	(3.3)*	(5.7)*	(2.6)*	(4.8)*	(0.4)	(−0.8)	(−0.4)	(1.4)	(0.9)	(0.8)	(2.9)*	(2.3)**	(3.1)*	(1.2)	(2.5)*	(6.5)*
IS	0.019	−0.039	0.041	0.050	0.033	0.058	0.195	0.172	0.192	0.058	0.065	0.081	0.053	0.028	0.065	0.195	0.223	0.242			
	(1.4)	(−1.4)	(2.7)*	(4.2)*	(1.6)	(4.2)*	(9.6)*	(3.7)*	(8.2)*	(3.1)*	(1.6)	(4.0)*	(2.8)*	(0.7)	(2.8)*	(8.0)*	(4.3)*	(4.4)*			
FOS	0.037			0.041			−0.151												−0.002	−0.040	−0.306
	(1.2)			(1.5)			(−3.2)*												(−0.1)	(−1.4)	(−7.8)*
U	0.037	−0.008	0.067	0.059	0.041	0.072	0.078	0.139	0.056	−0.000	−0.002	−0.000	0.000	0.002	0.000	0.000	0.001	0.002	0.000	0.000	0.000
	(2.0)**	(−0.3)	(3.1)*	(3.6)*	(1.7)	(3.6)*	(2.8)*	(2.5)**	(1.7)	(−0.3)	(−1.1)	(−0.8)	(2.0)**	(1.3)	(1.3)	(0.4)	(0.7)	(0.6)	(−0.6)	(1.9)	(0.6)
A	−0.001	−0.001	−0.001	−0.000	−0.001	−0.000	−0.000	−0.003	0.001	−0.002	0.000	−0.004	0.002	0.000	0.001	0.001	−0.000	−0.000	−0.002	0.002	0.003
	(−0.7)	(−0.7)	(−1.2)	(−0.4)	(−0.9)	(−0.2)	(−0.3)	(−1.00)	(0.9)	(−1.6)	(0.2)	(−2.0)**	(1.2)	(1.0)	(0.5)	(0.3)	(−0.9)	(−0.4)	(−1.6)	(1.3)	(1.3)
S	0.122	0.136	0.102	0.100	0.175	0.070	0.150	0.205	0.126	0.117	0.059	0.146	0.148	0.148	0.203	−0.018	0.040	−0.033	0.109	0.147	0.003
	(6.2)*	(3.7)*	(4.4)*	(5.7)*	(6.3)*	(3.3)*	(5.0)*	(3.3)*	(3.5)*	(4.9)*	(1.6)	(5.0)*	(6.1)*	(6.1)*	(6.2)*	(−0.6)	(0.8)	(−0.7)	(4.5)*	(5.9)*	(0.1)
μ	0.285	0.419	0.262	0.276	0.336	0.264	−0.040	−0.106	−0.063	0.428	0.495	0.395	0.226	0.226	0.246	−0.163	−0.121	0.070	0.467	0.261	−0.053
	(13.4)*	(9.1)*	(11.6)*	(14.6)*	(9.6)*	(12.7)*	(−1.2)	(−1.3)	(−1.8)	(11.6)*	(10.2)*	(10.7)*	(5.9)*	(5.9)*	(5.9)*	(−3.1)*	(−1.8)	(1.2)	(13.2)	(7.2)*	(−1.0)
N	492	105	387	492	105	387	492	105	387	251	113	138	251	113	138	251	113	138	251	251	251
LR $\chi 2$	136.7*	43.6*	102.8*	186.3*	73.1*	127.2*	−142.7*	−25.1*	−117.9*	71.8*	26.3*	53.1*	59.3*	28.5*	32.6*	−38.2*	−24.9*	-26.7*	67.1*	56.5*	−38.3*

Note: * and ** refer to 1% and 5% levels of significance.
Source: UNU-MERIT (2003) survey.

the White test for heteroskedasticity and the chi-square statistics for model fit.

Automotive components

IS in the HR regression is statistically highly significant and its coefficient is positive in the local sample (see Table 8.5) but not in the foreign sample – though the partial scatter plot shows no obvious relationship (see Appendix Figures 8.A1 and 8.A2). The lack of statistical significance of *FOS* in the overall sample shows that no obvious ownership differences exist once controlled for other variables. Whereas HR in local firms depends strongly on host-site IS, foreign firms transfer best practices from abroad. HR enjoyed no statistically significant relationship with *X*/*Y* in all three samples. The coefficient of size is positive and highly significant in all the samples, demonstrating that scale is important in the use of cutting-edge HR practices and training. Union has the right positive sign.

Similarly, the relationship between IS and PT is statistically significant only in the local sample, though the partial scatter plot shows no obvious link (see Appendix Figures 8.A3 and 8.A4). Whereas PT in local firms is influenced by host-site IS, foreign firms transfer best practices from abroad. The lack of a significant relationship between *FOS* and PT shows that no obvious ownership-based differences existed once other variables are controlled for. The relationship between *X*/*Y* and PT is also significant in the local sample. Union incidence has the right positive sign. Size is positively correlated in all three samples, demonstrating that scale is important in PT intensities.

The relationship between IS and RD is positive and highly significant in all three samples, showing that the strength of the embedding environment mattered in firms' participation in R&D, irrespective of ownership. Indeed, the partial scatter plot shows a strong relationship between IS and RD, with the link looking much stronger in the local than in the foreign sample (see Appendix Figures 8.A5 and 8.A6). The higher coefficient of IS in the local sample shows that local firms depend more on host-site IS than do foreign firms. The relationship between RD and *X*/*Y* is statistically highly significant and positive in all three samples. The strong and negative coefficient of *FOS* in the RD regression points to higher RD intensities in local than in foreign firms. Union has the right positive sign. The relationship between RD and size is positive and statistically highly significant, demonstrating that large firms are more R&D-intensive than small and medium-sized firms among the automotive component firms in East Asia.

Electronic components

Because *FOS* is correlated with IS, separate regressions were run to examine relationships in the electronic components sample (see Table 8.5 and Appendix Table 8.A1).

IS showed a strong and positive relationship with HR in the local sample in electronic component firms (see Table 8.5), though the partial scatter plot only shows some link (see Appendix Figures 8.A7 and 8.A8). The lack of a statistical relationship in the foreign sample and the *FOS* in the overall sample shows that foreign firms transfer best practices irrespective of IS. *X* has a positive relationship with HR. Union has no relationship with HR. The strong and positive *S* shows that scale is important in HR intensity.

IS showed a strong and positive relationship with PT in the local sample in electronic component firms, though this is not obvious from the partial scatter plot (see Appendix Figures 8.A9 and 8.A10). The lack of statistical significance in the foreign sample and the *FOS* in the overall sample shows that foreign firms transfer best practices irrespective of IS. *X* has a positive relationship with PT. Union has no relationship with PT. The strong and positive *S* shows that scale is important in PT intensities.

The relationship between IS and RD is positive, strong and statistically significant in all three samples, but the coefficient of IS in the local sample exceeded that in the foreign sample – which is confirmed by the partial scatter plot (see Appendix Figures 8.A11 and 8.A12). These results show that participation in R&D activities at host sites rise as IS becomes stronger, irrespective of ownership, but local firms continue to utilize it far more than foreign firms. *FOS* shows a strong and inverse relationship with RD, demonstrating that local firms show more R&D effort than foreign firms at host sites. *X*/*Y* has a positive relationship with RD. Union has no relationship with HR. The lack of a statistical relationship between *S* and RD shows that scale is unimportant in R&D of electronic component firms.

Overall, the relationship between IS, and HR, PT and RD is positive and strong in the local samples. Only RD is correlated strongly with IS in the foreign sample. *FOS* is correlated inversely with RD in both overall samples. Hence, while foreign firms do offshore R&D, the development of R&D at host sites depend much more on the efforts of local firms. *X*/*Y* (*X*) is also important in driving RD in the foreign samples, but not statistically significant in the HR and PT regressions. Whereas IS shows a positive and statistically significant relationship with RD in both samples, it is higher in the local sample. The results underline the importance of IS at host sites in driving RD intensities.

Summary and conclusions

This chapter has examined differences in technological intensities between foreign and local automotive and electronic component firms in East Asia, and the statistical relationships involving them.

Only in the automotive sample and in the most advanced IS environment of Taiwan, local firms enjoyed higher HR intensities than foreign firms and even that owing to differences in market orientation. Foreign firms show higher HR intensity in the Philippines and Indonesia in automotive components, in China and Indonesia in electronics components, and PT intensities in China in automotive component firms, and Malaysia, Indonesia and the Philippines in electronics component firms. HR and PT intensities of local firms depend much more on host-site IS than foreign firms as the regression results show a positive and strong relationship only in the former. Nevertheless, the higher HR and PT intensities of foreign firms over local firms in the less-developed sites suggest that foreign firms can provide significant demonstration effects and technology diffusion of production technologies to local firms.

The picture is significantly different with RD. The only statistically significant result shows higher RD intensities in local firms than in foreign firms in Taiwan and the Philippines. The regression results also confirm the influence of IS on RD in both foreign and local samples. IS had a greater impact on RD in the local than in the foreign samples. Although foreign firms do offshore R&D because of policy preferences for national firms and the presence of sophisticated IS at parent sites, the evidence shows that they are less likely to invest extensively in such activities at host sites compared to local firms. The statistically significant but low RD mean in the Philippines arises from incremental engineering activities. Hence, whereas human capital exposed to management and production technology in foreign MNCs is important for local firms (through interactions and hiring), participation in R&D requires strong institutional focus targeted at local firms. The Taiwanese experience shows that local institutional support, acquisition of foreign firms, licensing and hiring of local personnel working in foreign firms rather than direct foreign investment could be the route that developing economies should take to stimulate local firms' participation in R&D activities.

The highly significant and positive coefficient of exports in the local sample shows that technological intensities and exports drive each other. Hence, local firms seem to be utilizing host-site IS and export markets far more than foreign firms to learn and innovate. Consistent with the catch-up school, these results show that governments should emphasize the development of local-firm-driven R&D eventually to stimulate their movement towards the technology frontier. The asset-specific advantages of foreign firms as advanced by Dunning (1988) and national factors advanced by Vernon (1966) seem to explain these differences. However, contrary to Vernon's (1966) model, the results show that RD in foreign firms rise when host-site IS becomes stronger.

These results should provide the motivation necessary to carry out a more representative innovation survey to test the evolutionary argument about the relationship between IS, and embodied technology in firms. Policy focus should target strengthening the IS facing firms, as it will enhance learning and innovation in firms. The strategies for individual economies and industries would obviously differ with their specific endowments and their technological taxonomies and trajectories.

Appendix

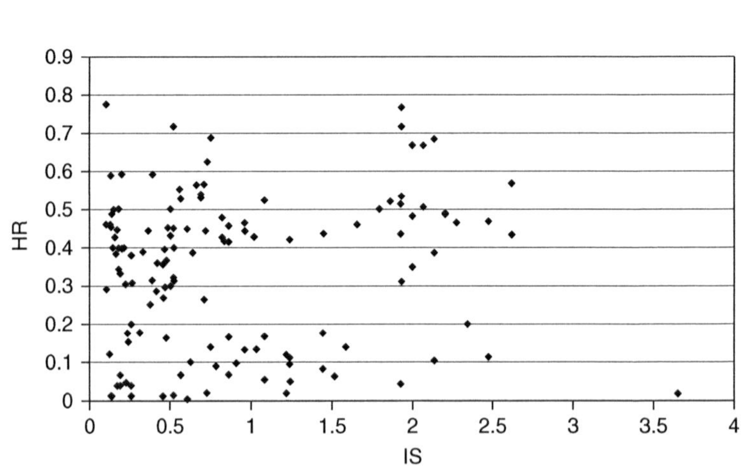

Figure 8.A1 Relationship between HR and IS, local auto component firms, 2001

Table 8.A1 Correlation coefficients of independent variables, 2001.

	Automotive components							**Electronic components**						
	X/Y	***IS***	***A***	***U***	***FOS***	***S***	***W***	***X***	***IS***	***A***	***U***	***FOS***	***S***	***W***
X/Y, X		0.157	−0.003	0.044	0.166	0.035	0.134		0.296	0.273	−0.217	0.192	0.249	0.099
IS	0.157		0.134	−0.041	0.063	−0.055	0.568*	0.296		−0.005	−0.200	−0.485*	−0.079	0.319*
A	−0.003	0.134		0.281	−0.188	0.295	0.088	0.273	−0.005		0.024	0.192	0.137	−0.022
U	0.044	−0.041	0.281		0.025	0.283	−0.105	−0.217	−0.200	0.024		0.095	0.064	0.220
FOS	0.166	0.063	−0.188	0.025		−0.002	0.004	0.192	−0.485*	0.192	0.095		0.229	−0.196
S	0.035	−0.055	0.295	0.283	−0.002		−0.178	0.249	−0.079	0.137	0.064	0.229		−0.157
W	0.134	0.568*	0.088	−0.105	0.004	−0.178		0.099	0.319*	−0.022	0.220	−0.196	−0.157	

Note: * = too high correlation.
Source: UNU-MERIT (2003) survey.

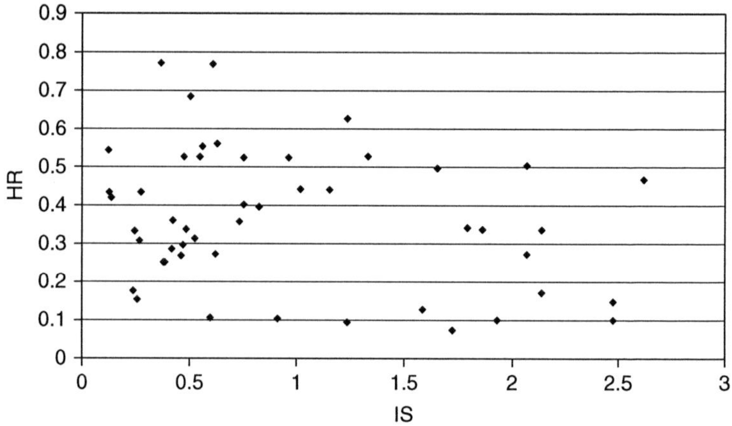

Figure 8.A2 Relationship between HR and IS, foreign auto component firms, 2001

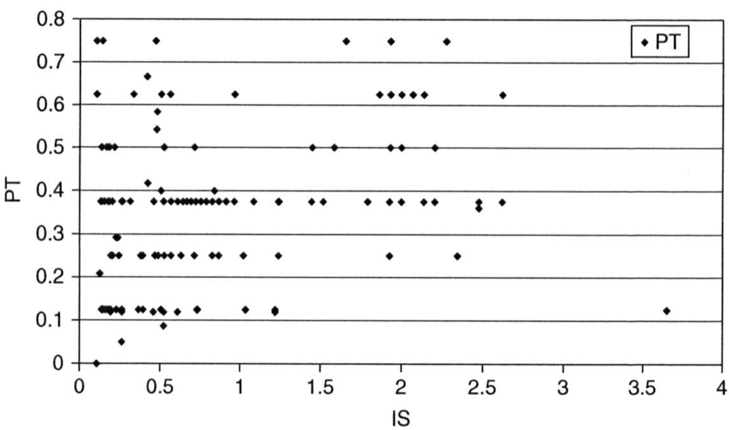

Figure 8.A3 Relationship between PT and IS, local auto components, 2001

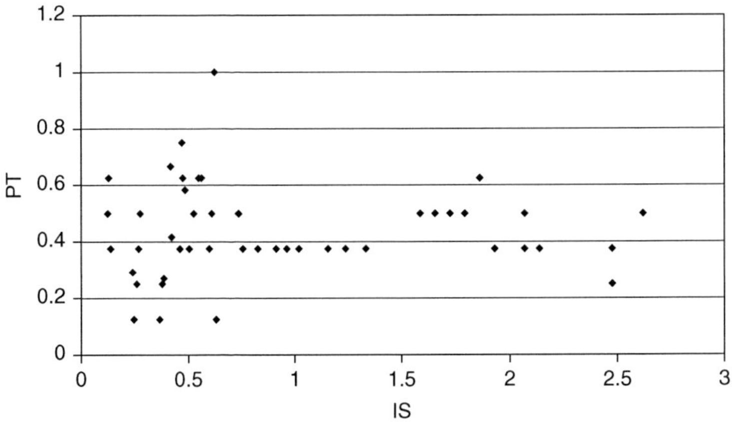

Figure 8.A4 Relationship between PT and IS, foreign auto component firms, 2001

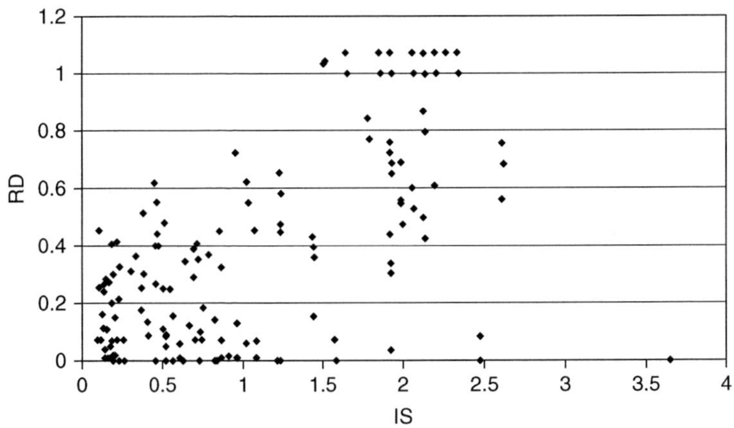

Figure 8.A5 Relationship between RD and IS, local auto component firms, 2001

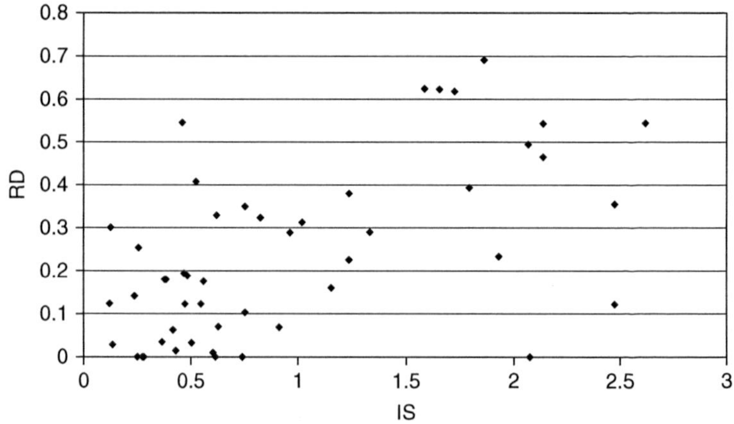

Figure 8.A6 Relationship between RD and IS, foreign auto component firms, 2001

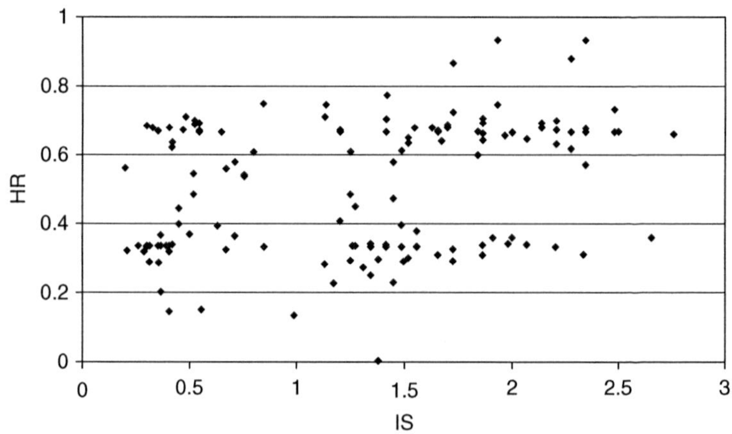

Figure 8.A7 Relationship between HR and IS, local electronic component firms, 2001

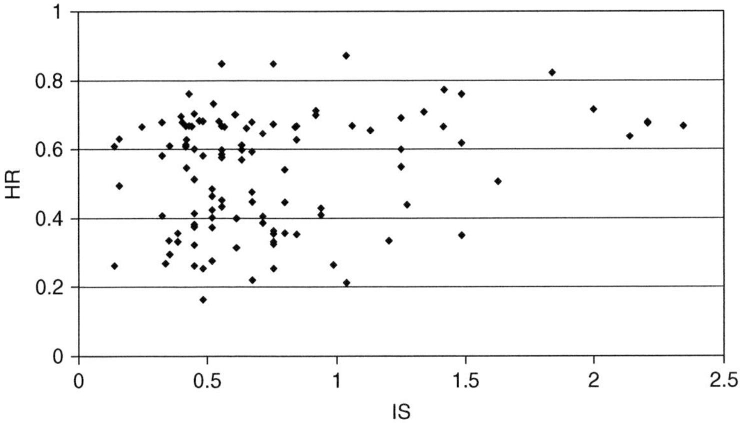

Figure 8.A8 Relationship between HR and IS, foreign electronic component firms, 2001

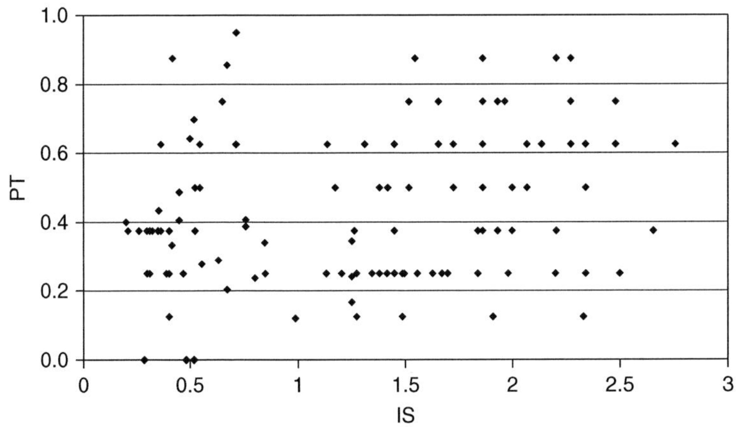

Figure 8.A9 Relationship between PT and IS, local electronic component firms, 2001

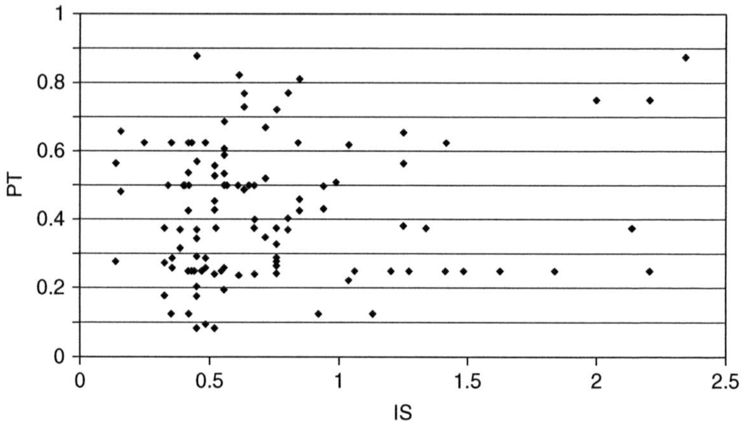

Figure 8.A10 Relationship between PT and IS, foreign electronic component firms, 2001

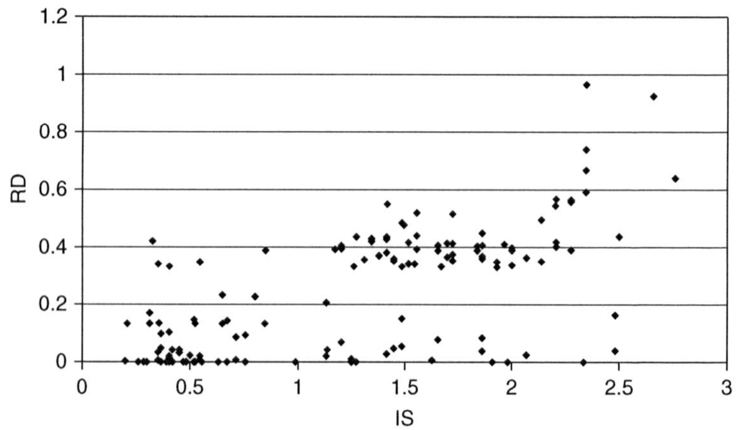

Figure 8.A11 Relationship between RD and IS, local electronic component firms, 2001

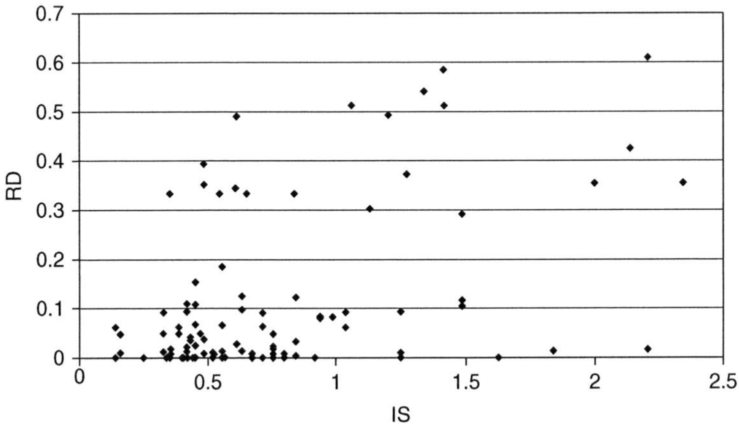

Figure 8.A12 Relationship between RD and IS, foreign electronic component firms, 2001

Note

1. I am grateful to Sanjaya Lall and Ajit Singh for encouraging me in this exercise as well as Richard Nelson and Adrian Wood for their comments.

References

Aitkin, B. and A. Harrison, (1999) 'Do Domestic Firms Benefit from Direct Foreign Investment? Evidence from Venezuela', *American Economic Review*, 89 (3): 605–18.

Amsden, A. (1989) *Asia's Next Giant: South Korea and Late Industrialization*, New York: Oxford University Press.

Amsden, A., T. Tschang and A. Goto (2001) 'Do Foreign Companies Conduct R&D in Developing Countries?', ADBI Working Paper No. 14, Tokyo.

Audretsch, D. (2002) 'The Dynamic Role of Small Firms: Evidence from U.S.', *Small Business Economics*, 18 (1–3): 13-40.

ADB (2002) 'Unpublished Export-competitiveness Survey', Manila: Asian Development Bank.

Bell, M. and Pavitt, K. (1995) 'The Development of Technological Capabilities', in I. U. Haque (ed.), *Trade, Technology and International Competitiveness*, (Washington, DC, World Bank).

Best, M. (2001) *The New Competitive Advantage*, Oxford: Oxford University Press).

Bhagwati, J. (1979) 'International Factor Movements and National Advantage', *Indian Economic Review*, 14 (2): 73–100.

Blomstrom, M. and H. Persson (1983) 'Foreign Investment and Spillover Efficiency in an Undeveloped Economy: Evidence from Mexican Manufacturing Industry', *World Development*, 11 (6): 493–501.

Blomstrom, M. and F. Sjoholm (1999) 'Technology Transfer and Spillovers: Does Local Participation with Multinationals Matter?', *European Economic Review*, 43: 915–23.

Cantwell, J. (1995) 'The Globalization of Technology: What Remains of the Product Cycle Model', *Cambridge Journal of Economics*, 19 (1): 155–74.

Cantwell, J. and R. Mudambi (2001) 'MNE Competence-creating Subsidiary Mandates: An Empirical Investigation', International Investment and Management Discussion Paper, No. 285, Reading University.

Caves, R. (1974) 'Multinational Firms, Competition and Productivity in Host Country Markets', *Economica*, 41 (162): 176–93.

Chang, H. J. (1994) *The Political Economy of Industrial Policy*, London: Macmillan.

Dosi, G. (1982) 'Technological Paradigms and Technological Trajectories', *Research Policy*, 11 (3): 147–62.

Dunning, J. (1958) *American Investment in British Manufacturing Industry*, London: Allen & Unwin.

Dunning, J. (1988) *Explaining International Production*, London: Unwin Hyman.

Edquist, C. and S. Jacobssen (1987) 'The Integrated Circuit Industries in India and South Korea in an International Techno-economic Context', *Industry and Development*, 21: 1–62.

Ernst, D. (2006) 'Innovation Offshoring: Asia's Emerging Role in Global Innovation Networks', East–West Center Special Report 10, East–West Center, Hawaii.

Figueiredo, P. N. (2003) 'Learning, Capability Accumulation and Firms Differences: Evidence from Latecomer Steel', *Industrial and Corporate Change*, 12 (3): 607–43.

Fransman, M. (1985) 'International Competitiveness, Technical Change and the State: The Machine Tool Industries in Taiwan and Japan', *World Development*, 14 (12): 1375–96.

Freeman, C. (1989) 'New Technology and Catching-Up', *European Journal of Development Research*, 1 (1): 85–99.

Gerschenkron, A. (1962) *Economic Backwardness in Historical Perspective: A Book of Essays*, Cambridge, Mass.: Belknap Press of Harvard University Press.

Haddad, M. and A. Harrison (1993) 'Are There Positive Spillovers from Foreign Direct Investment? Evidence from Panel Data from Morocco', *Journal of Development Economics*, 42: 51–74.

Hamilton, A. (1791) 'Report on Manufactures', 5 December; available at: http://www.oberlin.edu/~gkornbl/Hist258/ReportMfres.html – downloaded 13 December 2005.

Helleiner G. (1973) 'Manufactured Exports from Less-developed Countries and Multinational Firms', *Economic Journal*, 83(329): 21–47.

Hirschman, A. (1958) *The Strategy of Economic Development*, New Haven, Conn.: Yale University Press.

Hirschman, A. (1970) *Exit, Voice and Loyalty: Responses to Decline in Firms, Organizations, and State*, Cambridge, Mass.: Harvard University Press.

Hymer, S. (1960) The International Operations of National Firms: A Study of Direct Foreign Investment', PhD Dissertation submitted to MIT (published by MIT Press, Cambridge, Mass., 1976).

Johnson, C. (1982)*MITI and the Japanese Miracle*, Stanford, Calif.: Stanford University Press.

Kaldor, N. (1967) *Strategic Factors in Economic Development*, Ithaca, NY: Cornell University Press.

Kaldor, N. (1979) 'Equilibrium Theory and Growth Theory', in M. Boskin (ed.), *Economics and Human Welfare: Essays in Honor of Tibor Scitovsky*, New York: Academic Press.

Kim, L. (1997) *From Imitation to Innovation*; Cambridge, Mass., Harvard Business School Press.

Kokko, A., R. Tansini and M. Zejan (1996) 'Local Technological Capability and Productivity Spillovers from FDI in the Uruguayan Manufacturing Sector', *Journal of Development Studies*, 32 (4): 602–11.

Lall, S. (1979) 'The International Allocation of Research Activity by US Multinationals', *Oxford Bulletin of Economics and Statistics*, 41 (4): 313–31.
Lall, S. (1992) 'Technological Capabilities and Industrialisation', *World Development*, 20 (2): 165–86.
Lall, S. and P. Streeten (1977) *Foreign Investment, Transnational Corporations and Developing Countries*, Boulder, Col.: Westview Press.
Leamer, E. (1995) *The Heckscher–Ohlin Model in Theory and Practice*, Princeton, NJ: Princeton University Press.
List, F. (1885) *The National System of Political Economy*, London: Longmans, Green & Co.
Lundvall, B. A. (1988) 'Innovation as an Interactive Process: From User–Producer interaction to the National System of Innovation', in G. Dosi, C. Freeman, G. Silverberg and L. Soete (eds), *Technical Change and Economic Geography*, London: Frances Pinter.
Lundvall, B. A. (1992) *National Systems of Innovation: Towards a Theory of Innovation and Interactive Learning*, London: Frances Pinter.
Marshall, A. (1890) *Principles of Economics*, London: Macmillan.
Marshall A. (1920) *Principles of Economics*, London: Macmillan.
Malaysia (2004) *Economic Report 2004–2005*, Kuala Lumpur: Government Printers.
Myrdal, G. (1957) *Economic Theory and Under-Developed Regions*, New York: Methuen.
Narula, R. (1996) *Multinational Investment and Economic Structure*, London: Routledge.
Nelson, R. (ed.) (1993) *National Innovation Systems*, New York: Oxford University Press.
Nelson, R. (1994) 'What has been the Matter with Neoclassical Growth Theory?', in Silverberg, G. and Soete, L. (eds), *The Economics of Growth and Technical Change*, Aldershot: Edward Elgar.
Nelson, R. (2007) 'Economic Development from the Perspective of Evolutionary Theory', Paper presented at the Sanjaya Lall Memorial Conference, UNCTAD, 8–9 March, Geneva.
Nelson, R. R. and S. G. Winter (1982) *An Evolutionary Theory of Economic Change*, Cambridge, Mass., Harvard University Press.
OECD (1998) *The Internationalization of Industrial R&D: Patterns and Trends*, Paris: Organisation for Economic Co-operation and Development (OECD).
Pavitt, K. (1984) 'Sectoral Patterns of Technical Change: Towards a Taxonomy and a Theory', *Research Policy*, 13 (6): 343–73.
Piore, M. and C. Sabel (1984) *The Second Industrial Divide: Possibilities for Prosperity*, New York, Basic Books.
Pratten, C. (1971) *Economies of Scale in Manufacturing Industry*, Cambridge: Cambridge University Press.
Rasiah, R. (1992) 'Foreign Capital and Industrialization in Malaysia', Doctoral thesis approved by Cambridge University. Published 1995, London: Macmillan.
Rasiah, R. (1994) 'Flexible Production Systems and Local Machine Tool Subcontracting: Electronics Transnationals in Malaysia', *Cambridge Journal of Economics*, 18 (3): 279–98.
Rasiah, R. (2002) 'Systemic Coordination and the Knowledge Economy: Human Capital Development in MNC-driven Electronics Clusters in Malaysia', *Transnational Corporations*, 11 (3): 89–130.
Rasiah, R. (2004) 'Technological Capabilities in East and Southeast Asian Electronics Firms: Does Network Strength Matter?', *Oxford Development Studies*, 32 (3): 433–54.

Rasiah, R. (1996) 'Institutions and Innovations: Moving Towards the Technology Frontier in the Electronics Industry in Malaysia', *Industry and Innovation*, 3(2): 79–102.

Rasiah, R. and Y. Lin (2005) 'Learning and Innovation: The Role of Market, Government and Trust in the Information Hardware Industry in Taiwan', *International Journal of Technology and Globalization*, 1 (3/4): 400–32.

Reinert, E. S. (1994) 'Catching-up from Way Behind: A Third World Perspective on First World History', in J. Fagerberg, B. Verspagen and N. V. Tunzelmann (eds), *The Dynamics of Technology, Trade and Growth*, Aldershot: Edward Elgar.

Reinert, E. (2007) *How Rich Countries Got Rich ... and Why Poor Countries Stay Poor*, New York: Carroll and Graf Publishers.

Romer, P. (1994) 'The Origins of Endogenous Growth', *Journal of Economic Perspectives*, 8: 3–22.

Rosenstein-Rodan, P. N. (1984) 'Natura Facit Saltum: Analysis of the Disequilibrium Growth Process', in G. M. Meier and D. Seers (eds), *Pioneers in Development*, New York: Oxford University Press.

Saxenian, A. L. (1994) *The Regional Advantage: Culture and Competition in Silicon Valley and Route 128*, Cambridge, Mass.: Harvard University Press.

Scherer, F. M. (1980) *Industrial Market Structure and Economic Performance*, Chicago: Rand McNally.

Scherer, F. (1992) *International High Technology Competition*, Cambridge, Mass.: Harvard University Press.

Scitovsky, T. (1964) *Papers on Welfare and Growth*, London: Allen & Unwin.

Singh, A. (1989) 'Third World Competition and De-industrialisation in Advanced Countries', *Cambridge Journal of Economics*, 13 (1): 103–20.

Smith, A. (1776) *The Wealth of the Nations*, London: Strahan and Cadell.

Solow, R. (1956) 'A Contribution to the Theory of Economic Growth', *Quarterly Journal of Economics*, 70(1): 65–94.

Taiwan (2004) Investment Statistics, unpublished (Taipei, Central Bank of Taiwan).

UNU-MERIT (2002) *'Unpublished Malaysian Industrial Firm Surveys'*, Maastricht: UNU-MERIT.

UNU-MERIT (2003) 'Technological Capability Building and Economic Performance Survey of Firms', funded by the Maastricht Educational Institute of Social and Economic Research and Training Centre on Innovation and Technology (MERIT), United Nations University (UNU), Maastricht.

Vaitsos, C. (2003) 'Growth Theories Revisted: Enduring Questions with Changing Answers', INTECH Discussion Paper No. 9, United Nations University, Maastricht.

Vernon, R. (1966) 'International Investment and International Trade in the Product Cycle', *Quarterly Journal of Economics*, 80: 190–207.

Vernon, R. (1971) *Sovereignty at Bay: The Multinational Spread of U.S. Enterprises*, New York, Basic Books.

Wade, R. (1990) *Governing the Market*, Princeton, NJ: Princeton University Press.

World Bank (1993) *The East Asian Miracle*, New York: Oxford University Press/World Bank.

World Bank (2003) 'World Development Report Statistics', Washington DC: World Bank Institute.

Young, A. (1928) 'Increasing Returns and Economic Progress', *Economic Journal*, 38 (152): 527–42.

9
Competition and Industrial Rates of Return

Anwar Shaikh

Introduction

I first met Ajit in 1978 when I spent a year at Cambridge as a visitor to the Faculty of Economics. It was a heady time in the economics profession, and it was personally gratifying for me to meet Joan Robinson, Nicholas Kaldor, Richard Kahn, Richard Goodwin, Geoffrey Harcourt and Luigi Pasinetti, among others, not to mention the young turks such as Ajit, Francis Cripps and John Eatwell. Karl Marx had once again been 'rediscovered' as an economist, as happens periodically, and Piero Sraffa's famous little book (Sraffa, 1963) had helped to spark a revival of interest in the classical analysis of competition.

The analysis of competition has always played an important role in Ajit's work. A quick look at his homepage showed that fully one-third of his listed articles refer to that subject, dated from 1968 to as recently as 2005. And within this subject, the analysis of profit rates has always been one of his central concerns. This is also the topic of my own contribution to this volume, which I hope will help to further Ajit's ongoing project.

Profit rate equalization in the classical-Marxian theory of competition

The classical theory of competition conceives of profit rate equalization as a dynamic and turbulent process. Investment flows into an industry are motivated by the expected rates of return on those potential new investments that embody the best-practice conditions of production (Cohen *et al.*, 1987, p. 387). I shall call these the expected rates of return of *regulating capitals*, where the term 'regulating' refers to the lowest-cost methods operating under generally reproducible conditions.

Higher-cost methods, which are represented most often by older technologies, are excluded even though they are reproducible, because they are not competitive. On the other hand, conditions of production that rely on special locations and the like are also excluded because they are non-reproducible.

Evaluations of potential profitability are made by a heterogeneous set of investors. There is no single expected rate of return in any given industry, but rather a diverse set of expected returns that are revised continually in the light of actual outcomes.[1] Hence classical economics typically focuses on actual outcomes rather than on the various expectations that might have motivated them. In a growing economy, new capital flows are generally positive. But if the regulating profit rates in a given industry are higher than the economy-wide average, production in this industry will accelerate until the supply in the industry grows more rapidly than its demand. The rising excess supply will in turn drive down the industry's relative price, thereby reducing its regulating rate of profit. The latter may well fall below the general rate, which would then cause supply to grow less rapidly than demand, and so on. It should be noted that the changes in rate of growth of production that drive this process are brought about initially by changes the utilization of existing capacity and only later, if necessary, by changes in the rate of growth of capacity itself.[2] The end result is the turbulent equalization of actual rates of profit on new investments, over some period of 'fat and lean years' whose precise length depends on the industry in question (Botwinick, 1993, ch. 5; Mueller, 1990, pp. 1–3; 1986, p. 8; Shaikh, 1998). As Marx emphasizes, there is never a moment in which all profit rates converge to some 'uniform' rate of profit. On the contrary, in fact:

> all this involves a very complex movement in which, on the one hand, the market prices in each particular sphere, the relative [prices of production] of the different commodities, the position with regard to demand and supply within each individual sphere, and, on the other hand, competition among the capitalists in the different spheres, play a part, and, in addition, the speed of the equalisation process, whether it is quicker or slower, depends on the particular organic composition of the different capitals (more fixed or circulating capital, for example) and on the particular nature of their commodities, that is, whether their nature as use-values facilitates rapid withdrawal from the market and the diminution or increase of supply, in accordance with the level of the market prices ... These are some of the reasons why the *general rate of profit* appears as a hazy mirage. (Marx, 1971, pp. 464–5)

Non-regulating capitals do not participate directly in this equalization process: methods of production with higher unit costs will not be attractive to new capitals, while the non-reproducible conditions on privileged capitals make them unavailable to new capitals. Competition constantly weeds out the higher cost capitals, while technical change, which is one of the principal weapons of competition, constantly throws new ones into the fray (Shaikh, 1978, pp. 240–1). Hence there is *never a moment in which all capitals within an industry operate under the same conditions of production.*

Competition within an industry tends to enforce a common selling price. Given the existence of an array of production conditions, this implies that profit rates will generally differ within any given industry. At the same time, competition between industries leads to a process of entry and exit of capital in search of higher profit rates. This is the foundation for the equalization of profit rates across industries. But since competition 'dis-equalizes' profit rates within an industry, how can it also equalize them *between* industries? This apparent contradiction is resolved through the concept of regulating capital: it is the rate of return on the regulating capital that is of interest to new investment, and it is this regulating rate of return that is equalized by competition between industries.[3]

Two important corollaries can be derived from this approach. First, since the industry selling price will be regulated by the price of production (long-run competitive price) of the regulating firms, these firms will appear as the dominant, price-setting firms in each industry. Second, since competition dis-equalizes profit rates within an industry, and equalizes regulating rates of profit turbulently across industries, profit rates at any given moment will always appear to be different. It is only by tracking the movements of the regulating capitals over sufficiently long periods of time that we can assess whether or not these (risk-adjusted) rates are equalized in practice.

Neoclassical, Austrian, Schumpeterian and oligopolistic theories of competition

Neoclassical theory operates within a static and perfectionist framework (Mueller, 1990, p. 4). Free entry and exit is assumed, to ensure that all firms within any given industry operate with the same (most efficient) method of production, and all produce the same (homogeneous) product. Within any industry, over the 'short run', competition leads to a single common price, and since these firms are identical, to a single common profit rate for each firm. On the other hand, over the 'long run' (which, like the 'short run' is peculiarly timeless), competition between industries leads to a single common rate of profit in each industry. Since all firms within an industry have the same profit rate, and all industries have the same profit rate, so all firms everywhere must have the same profit rate. This is the fundamental neoclassical hypothesis about competition.

Sraffian theory is disappointing similar in this respect, because it typically makes three crucial assumptions. First, that all profit rates are exactly equal, which eliminates any profit rate differentials between industries. Second, only one condition of production exists in any given industry, so that the regulating conditions are also the average ones.[4] This eliminates any profit rate differentials within an industry. The one exception occurs in the theory of rent, where only the zero-rent conditions of production are the regulating ones – that is the ones that participate in profit rate equalization (Ricardo, 1951, ch. 2; Sraffa, 1963, ch. 11). The existence of more diverse types of privileged capital may therefore be viewed as a generalization of the theory of rent. And third, the capital values assigned to older vintages are assumed to be such that their profit rates are exactly the same as that on the newest vintage. In most national income accounts this is viewed as the ideal measure of the net capital stock (Gordon, 1993, p. 103). Then, under such conditions, all capital has the same profit rate, so that the average profit rate on all capital in an industry is the same as the profit rate on its new capital. As in the case of neoclassical theory, we do not have to distinguish between firms and industries in assessing differences in rates of profit.

Austrian theory takes a great step forward by emphasizing that competition is a process rather than some timeless state. A competitive process is viewed as one 'in which the forces of entry are strongly and rapidly attracted to excess profits . . . and in which they rapidly bid these profits away' (Mueller, 1986, p. 4). Implicit is the notion that the process is stable. Hence, while the test of the neoclassical model is whether profit rates are more or less equal at any given moment, the test of the Austrian theory of competition is 'whether markets are stable and quick' (Geroski, 1990, p. 28). Schumpeterian economics emphasizes the constant creation, adoption and displacement of technologies, much as Marx did earlier. But unlike Marxian theory, the Schumpeterian approach tends to have little to say about intertemporal profit rate differentials. Evolutionary economics, with its similar emphasis on innovation and adaptation, also tends to suffer from the same lack of specificity. Mueller (1990, pp. 3–4) subsumes both of them under a general Austrian approach in which empirical analysis involves estimating the long-run centres of gravity of actual profit rates, testing for their risk-adjusted equality, and estimating their speed of adjustment.

The generalized Austrian model of competition shares many features with the classical-Marxian one, except that it makes no distinction between regulating and non-regulating capital. Thus, in the Austrian case, the null hypothesis is 'that all individual company profit rates converge to a single, competitive level' (Mueller, 1986, p. 13). As a result, empirically observed persistent differences in firm-level profit rates are viewed as prima facie evidence of non-competitive conditions (Mueller, 1986 pp. 9–12, 31–3, 130). This is quite different from the classical-Marxian argument, in which profit rates are always expected to differ at any given moment, with only regulating rates turbulently expected to be equalized over sufficient lengths of time.

In practice, profit rates differ between industries, multiple methods of production coexist within any given industry, and vintages are seldom valued at the 'ideal' level. Indeed, direct measures of capital stocks are not usually available, so they are constructed from observed gross investment flows on the basis of highly simplified assumptions about service lives and retirement patterns.[5] This introduces an unknown and possibly large error in the estimation of long-run levels of the rate of profit. Hence, if we are to consider the issue of profit-rate equalization from a classical viewpoint, we must find a way to measure the rate of return on regulating capitals.

Defining measures of average and regulating rates of profit

Even within a single firm, one must distinguish between the rate of profit on total capital and that on more recent investment. The cost differences between older and newer capital imply that they will have different profit margins, and if we evaluate their profit rates in terms of the initial capitals advanced for each type[6] (appropriately adjusted for inflation), which is known in national accounts as the gross capital stock concept (OECD, 2001, p. 31), their profit rates will also generally differ. This means that one cannot treat the average rate of profit in a firm as a proxy for its regulating rate. A similar problem exists at the level of an industry.[7] In both cases, it is the rate of profit on recent investment that is relevant to competition between industries.

The rate of profit on total capital is the ratio of total profits to the current-cost value of the capital stock. Using the current-cost value of capital makes this a real; that is, an inflation-adjusted measure, since both the numerator and denominator are in current dollars. This is evident if we divide both numerator and denominator by a common price index:

$$r_{K_t} = \frac{P_t}{K_t} \quad \text{[average rate of profit]} \tag{9.1}$$

But the rate of profit on total capital is itself the average of the current rates of profit on different types of capital in the overall stock, including the profit rate on the newest types; that is, on regulating capital. From our point of view, it is the latter that matters, because it represents the current rate of return on recent investment (r_{It}). At any given moment, the current profit P_t earned by a firm is the sum of the current profit on the most recent investment (P_{It}) and the current profit on all earlier vintages (P'_t), the latter being the profit that would have accrued in the absence of recent investment I_{t-1}:

$$P_t = P_{I_t} + P'_t \tag{9.2}$$

Subtracting lagged profits from both sides and rearranging this allows us to express the profits of new capital as the sum of the increment in total profits and an 'adjustment' term incorporating the effects of changes in prices, wages, efficiency, scale and capacity utilization on the surviving elements of the previous year's capital (that is, current 'older' capital):

$$P_{I_t} = (P_t - P_{t-1}) + \left(P_{t-1} - P'_t\right) = \Delta P_t + P_{t-1}\left(1 - \frac{P'_t}{P_{t-1}}\right) \tag{9.3}$$

The problem of estimating the profit on new capital therefore boils down to estimating the current profit of the older stock of capital relative to what it had been in the previous period. Let p_t, w_t, wr_t and t_t represent the output price, nominal wage, real wage and indirect business tax rate, and Yr_t, L_t and yr_t real output, employment and productivity of older capital, respectively. As before, variables pertaining to older capital are denoted by wr'_t, Yr'_t etc. Let economic capacity and corresponding employment and productivity be denoted by Ycr_t, Lc_t, ycr_t, etc., where capacity refers to the economically desirable point of production in a competitive long run. (Kurz, 1986). Finally, let $u_t = Yr_t/Ycr_t$ = the capacity utilization rate. If employment and output move together when utilization changes, $L_t/Lc_t = u_t$ too. Since profit is the difference between the money value of output net of indirect business taxes and the money wage bill, we can write the relative profit of older capital as the product of four distinct terms, the general contribution of each being expressed by the sign above it, as discussed below:

$$\frac{P'_t}{P_{t-1}} = \frac{p_t Yr'_t (1 - t_t) - w'_t L'_t}{p_{t-1} Yr_{t-1} (1 - t_{t-1}) - w_{t-1} L_{t-1}}$$

$$= \left(\frac{\overset{+}{p_t}}{p_{t-1}}\right)\left(\frac{Y^{-} cr'_t}{Ycr_{t-1}}\right)\left(\frac{u'^{\pm}_t}{u_{t-1}}\right)\left(\frac{m'^{\pm}_t}{m_{t-1}}\right)$$

$$m'_t = \left(1 - t_t - \frac{wr'_t}{yr'_t}\right) = \text{the current profit margin on older capital, and} \tag{9.4}$$

$$m_{t-1} = \left(1 - t_{t-1} - \frac{wr_{t-1}}{yr_{t-1}}\right) = \text{the previous year's profit margin on all capital}$$

The first term on the right-hand side of Equation (9.4) is the gross rate of change of prices, which in a generally inflationary environment is likely to have a positive impact on the profit ratio; that is, it will tend to raise it above one. The second term is the ratio of the current capacity of older capital to the capacity of the previous year's total capital, which will tend to be below one because of the retirement of some capital. The third term is the ratio of the capacity utilization rates of older and previous-year capitals, and if older and newer capitals in a given year have roughly similar rates, this ratio is the same as the gross rate of change of capacity utilization (u_t/u_{t-1}), which is likely to have a neutral impact in any interval long enough for capacity utilization to gravitate around its normal level. Finally, if the real product-wages ($wr = w/p$) of workers in particular plants are linked to the profitability and hence the labour productivity of these plants,[8] then, since tax rates tend to be stable over this interval, the last term is likely to be close to one and may safely be ignored.

Thus the first term will tend to raise the profit ratio above one, the second will tend to lower it below one, and the remaining two terms will tend to make the profit ratio fluctuate around one. For example, for the private sector as a whole between 1987 and 2005, the estimated average profit ratio (P'_t/P_{t1}) = 1.003, and lies almost entirely within +/− 5 per cent of this value. *Hence it is an excellent first approximation to assume that this ratio is roughly equal to one*, as I do here. In this case, we can estimate directly the current gross profits of newer capital from Equation (9.3) as the change in overall gross profit, and the rate of profit on newer capital as the ratio of this profit to the previous period's gross investment; that is, as *the incremental rate of profit* (Elton and Gruber, 1991, p. 454):[9]

$$P_{I_t} \approx \Delta P_t \tag{9.5}$$

$$r_{I_t} \approx \frac{\Delta P_t}{IG_{t-1}} \quad \text{[Incremental Rate of Profit]} \tag{9.6}$$

In my earliest work on this subject, I used this approximation to estimate the rate of return on new, non-financial corporate capital, and showed that this measure closely tracked the stock market rate of return and even had essentially the same mean and standard deviation (Shaikh, 1998, p. 397). The use of the incremental return as a proxy for the regulating rate return was subsequently applied by Christodoulopoulos (1995) to OECD countries (which we consider below), by Schroeder (2004) to the Asian Crisis of the 1990s, and by Tsoulfidis and Tsaliki (2005) to manufacturing in Greece.

The incremental rate of profit has two major virtues. First, it is estimated easily because its two components, gross profit and gross investment, are widely available across countries and over time: gross profit is defined as gross operating surplus (see below), while gross investment is observed directly, unlike the laboriously constructed measures of the capital stock required to calculate the average rate of profit. Second, the incremental rate of profit has a direct interpretation as the 'marginal' return on capital (Damodaran, 2001, p. 695; Elton and Gruber, 1991, p. 454), provided one understands that, like all real 'marginals', it is turbulent, spiky and discontinuous.

Empirical evidence for OECD countries

The 1994 *International Sectoral Database* (ISDB) (OECD, 1994) contained annual data, now discontinued, from which it was possible to derive measures of gross profit (gross operating surplus – that is, GDP *minus* indirect business taxes (net of subsidies) *minus* employee compensation), gross capital stock, and gross investment for various OECD countries. This was used by Christodoulopoulos (1995) to derive measures of average and incremental rates of profit by world industry. I thank him for providing the data and for detailing the steps involved, as listed in Appendix 1. In order to achieve comparability and consistency across countries and industries, the analysis was limited to the period 1970–90 and focused on the profitability of eight manufacturing industries (Food, Textiles, Paper, Chemicals, Minerals, Metals, Metal Products, Machinery

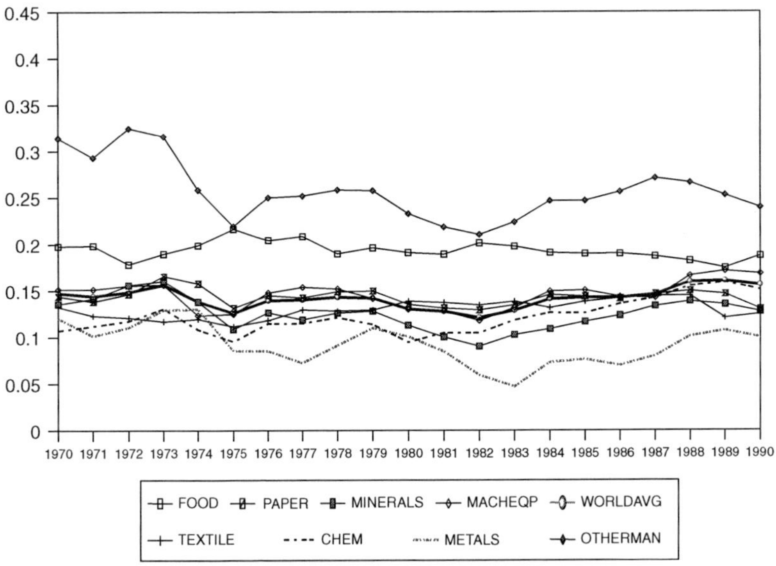

Figure 9.1 Average rates of profit of world manufacturing industries, 1970–1990 (OECD Data, ISDB 1994: 3-yr. centred average)

and Equipment, and Other Manufacturing products) across eight countries (USA, Japan, Canada, Germany, France, Italy, Belgium, Norway). World totals for gross profits, gross capital stock and gross investment were calculated for each industry, using PPP exchange rates to make the translation into US dollars. This data was then used to calculate average and incremental profit rates for each industry at the (developed) world level.

Figure 9.1 displays average rates of profit on total capital for world manufacturing industries for 1970–90, expressed as 3-year, centred moving averages to smooth the data. As is often the case with average rates, most of them cluster around a common level, but there are some that remain persistently above or below. Given the many problems associated with measurement of capital stock, it is not easy to distinguish between actual differences and statistical artefacts. Figure 9.2 displays the 3-year moving averages of the corresponding incremental rates of profit. We now see a very different pattern, with the rates crossing back and forth in exactly the manner anticipated by the classical theory of profit rate equalization.

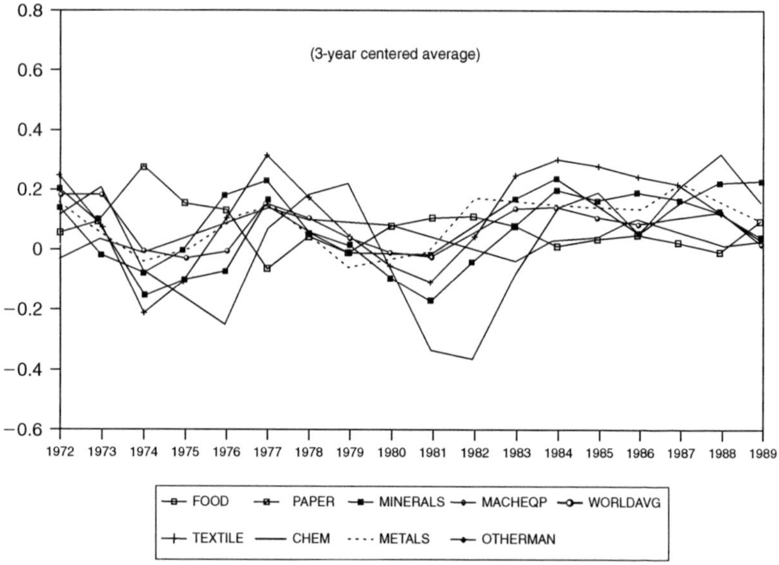

Figure 9.2 Incremental rates of profit of world manufacturing industries, 1970–1990 (OECD Data, ISDB 1994: 3-yr. centered average)

Figures 9.3 and 9.4 depict the annual total and incremental profit rates for US manufacturing alone for 1960–90, but not smoothed this time. As in the previous case, the rates of profit on total capital exhibit some persistent differences in levels, whereas the incremental rates of profit exhibit considerable cross-over.

Recent data for US industries

Data for more recent periods is derived from the US National Income and Product Accounts (NIPA) for 1987–2005. Five important innovations are introduced in this chapter. First, because gross operating surplus counts *all* the income of proprietors and partners as profit, a better measure of gross profit is derived by subtracting the estimated wage-equivalent (WEQ) of proprietors and partners.[10] This adjustment reduces the measured long-term profit rate in all sectors, the greatest effect being in industries with large numbers of self-employed people. For example, in Construction it reduces the measured profit rate from 90.5 per cent to 20.7 per cent. Second, I remove the fictitious measures of gross profits,

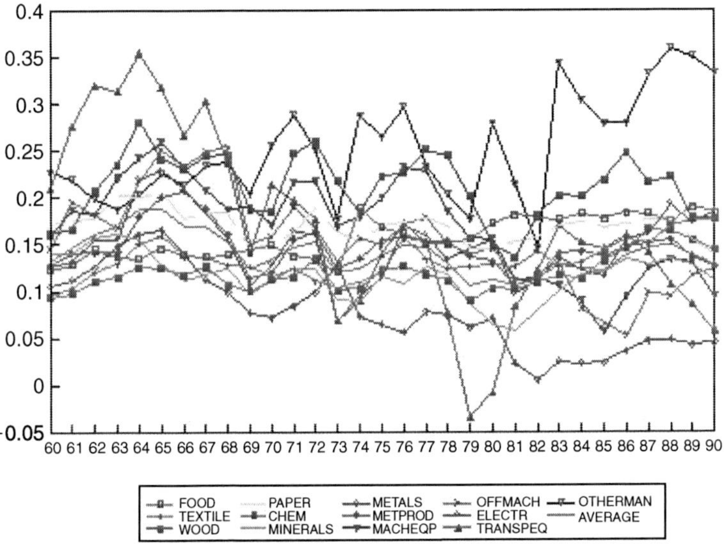

Figure 9.3 Average rates of profit of US manufacturing industries, 1960–1990 (OECD Data, ISDB 1994: annual rates)

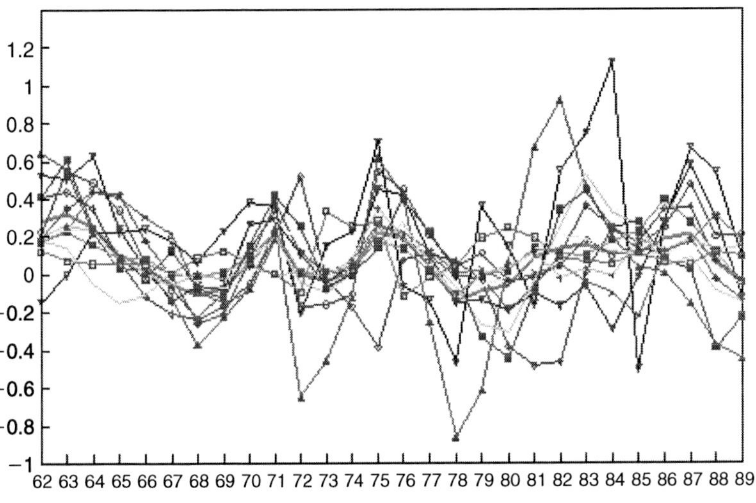

Figure 9.4 Incremental rates of profit of US manufacturing industries, 1960–1990 (OECD Data, ISDB 1994: annual rates)

investment and capital stock inserted by NIPA as a result of its treatment of homeowners as businesses renting their homes to themselves (Mayerhauser and Reinsdorf, 2007; Shaikh and Tonak, 1994, pp. 253–4, 267). In the case of the real estate industry between 1988 and 2005, this imputed gross operating surplus amounts to 55.5 per cent, and imputed capital stock amounts to fully 76 per cent, of the corresponding industry totals. Third, where possible, estimated normal inventories were added to measures of fixed capital stock, and estimated normal inventory investment added to fixed investment flows. These were based on NIPA data for manufacturing and wholesale/retail trade; on partial census data for the construction industry; and on Flow of Funds data for the Insurance and Banking industries, in order to account for normal reserves (Panico, 1983, p. 182). Fourthly, the inclusion of reserves raises the banking and finance industry capital stock by almost 50 per cent, which, in combination with the effect of the wage-equivalent adjustment reduces the measured industry profit rate from 41.8 per cent to 17.7 per cent. Finally, a particular effort was made to focus on industries that were composed mainly of profit-driven enterprises and were deemed to be competitive internationally. This led to the exclusion of thirty-one of the original sixty-one private industries on one of three grounds: because they were dominated by non-profit activities enterprises, as in arts, museums, educational services and social services; because we lacked sufficient data for an adequate measure of the wages of proprietors and partners, as in legal, medical and computer services; or because the industries in question were non-competitive internationally, so that their rate of return on investments would not qualify as potential regulating rates, as was the case with textiles, mining and domestic oil production. All further details can be found in Appendix 2.

Figure 9.5 presents the evidence on average profit rates between 198 and 2005 for thirty US industries. It is apparent that the previously noted patterns are repeated: rates of profit on total capital cluster around some central tendency, but a substantial number remain persistently above or below the average (defined by the overall profit rate of all private industries included).

This pattern is clearer in Figure 9.6, which displays the deviations of individual sectoral profit rates from the average rate of profit. Industries whose profit rates *cross* the average rate have deviations which change sign, which can be seen by the fact that these deviations cross the zero line shown on the corresponding charts. Of the 30 industries in this sample, 18 display this tendency, while 12 do not (7 remain persistently above and 5 persistently below). It is instructive to note in industries

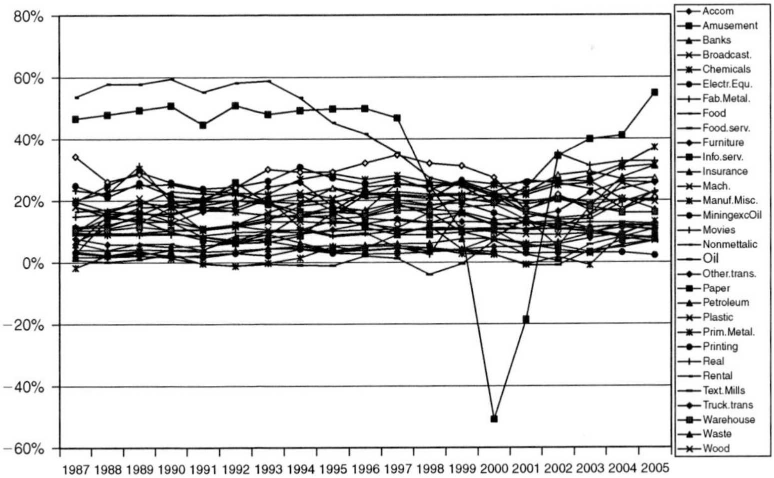

Figure 9.5 Rates of profit, US industries 1987–2005 (see Appendix 2 for sources)

whose deviations are highly trended, such as Nonmetallic Minerals, Machinery, Printing and Rentals, their period-average deviations can be bad proxies for their econometrically estimated long term values even though their deviations do cross over at least once,.

Figures 9.7 and 9.8 examine the incremental rate of profit in the same manner. Figure 9.7 shows that, unlike average profit rates, incremental rates of profit do 'cross over' a great deal. This is clearest in Figure 9.8, which displays the deviations of individual industry incremental profit rates from the overall average. *In every case, individual incremental rates of profit cross back and forth relative to the average incremental rate*: the smallest number of such crossing is four (Fabricated Metals), while the largest is twelve (Broadcast). This is a radically different picture from that presented by average rates of profit in the same sample.

There remains the interesting question of how rates of return might be linked to risk, and how growth rates of capital might in turn be linked to rates of return. We have already seen from the charts in Figure 9.8 that the period-average of an industry's rate of return may not be a good proxy for its long-term equilibrium level. None the less, since econometric investigation is beyond the scope of this chapter, it is interesting to see in Figure 9.9 that period-averages of industry incremental rates of return are positively correlated with the standard deviations of these incremental rates. Finally, I noted in the first section of the chapter that the first response to persistently increasing rates of return on new investment

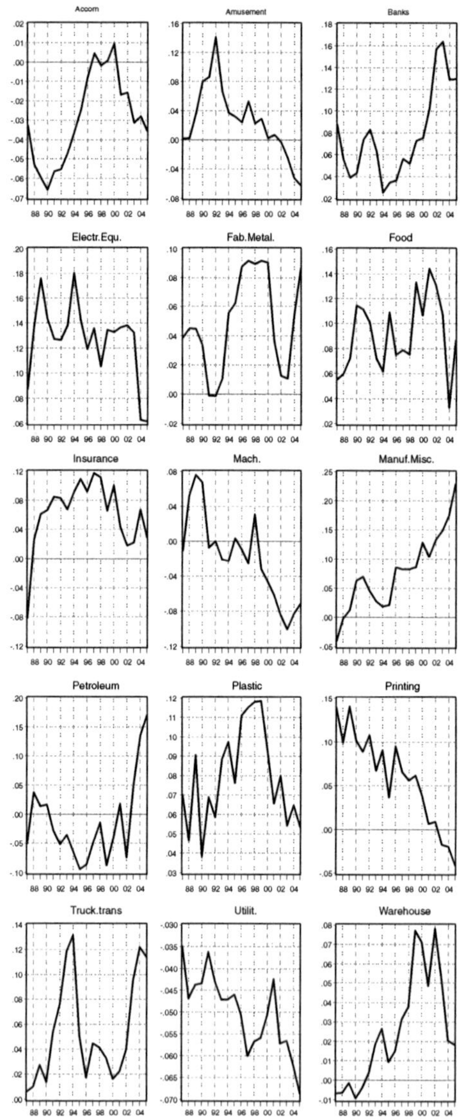

Figure 9.6 Deviations of average rates of profit from the average, US 1987–2005 (see Appendix 2 for sources)

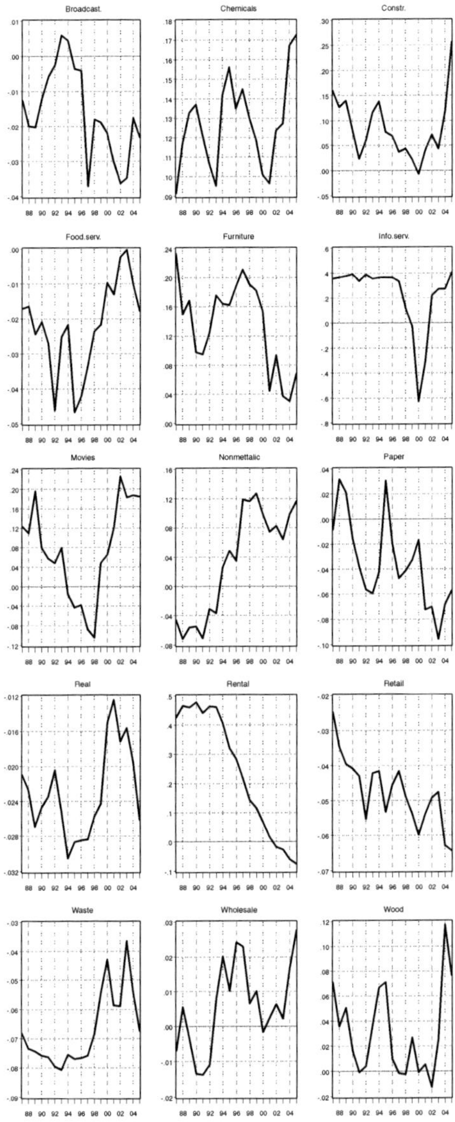

Figure 9.6 Continued

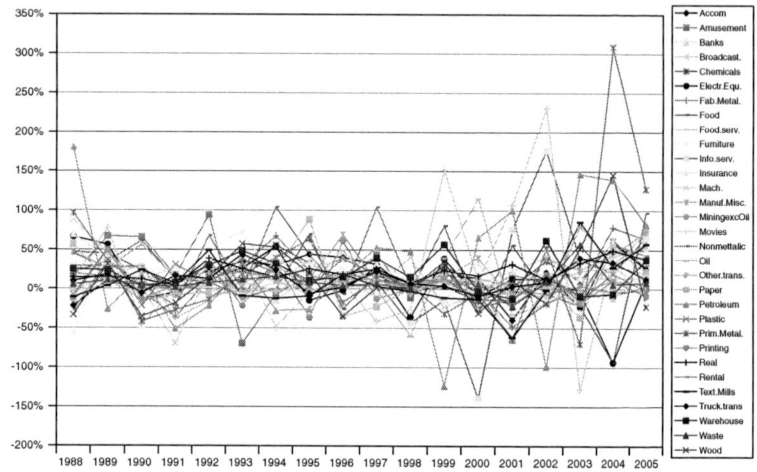

Figure 9.7 Incremental rates of profit, US industries 1988–2005 (see Appendix 2 for sources)

will be an acceleration in output as a result of the increased utilization of existing capacity, followed subsequently, if at all, by changes in the rate of growth of capacity itself. But if new investment in a particular industry is more profitable than the average new investment for any extended period of time, this would gradually raise the average rate of profit in the industry. At the same time, any resulting acceleration in real investment would gradually raise the industry's rate of growth of real capital. Thus we would expect to see a positive correlation between period averages of industry average rates of profit and the corresponding growth rates of real capital. Figure 9.10 shows that such a correlation does indeed exist.

Summary and conclusions

Profit rate equalization is a central concept in all theories of competition. This chapter has outlined a classical view of industrial competition, in which profit rate equalization is conceived as a dynamic and turbulent process involving ceaseless fluctuations around a moving centre of gravity. New capitals are constantly entering the battle of competition as older ones fall away. This perpetual fray gives rise to profit rates that generally differ across capitals. But what is relevant for competition is the profit rate on new investment, which is different from that on older capitals.

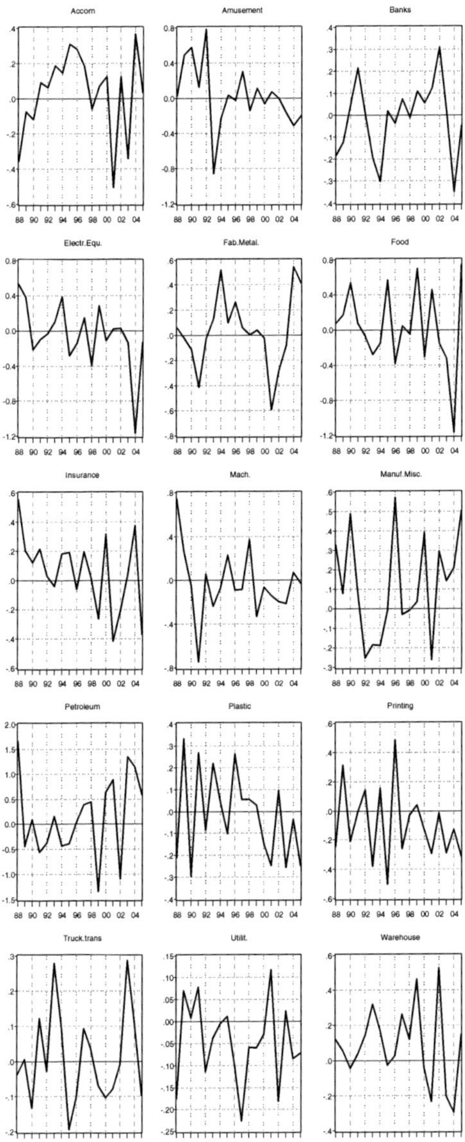

Figure 9.8 Deviations of incremental rates of profit from the average incremental rate, US 1988–2005 (see Appendix 2 for sources)

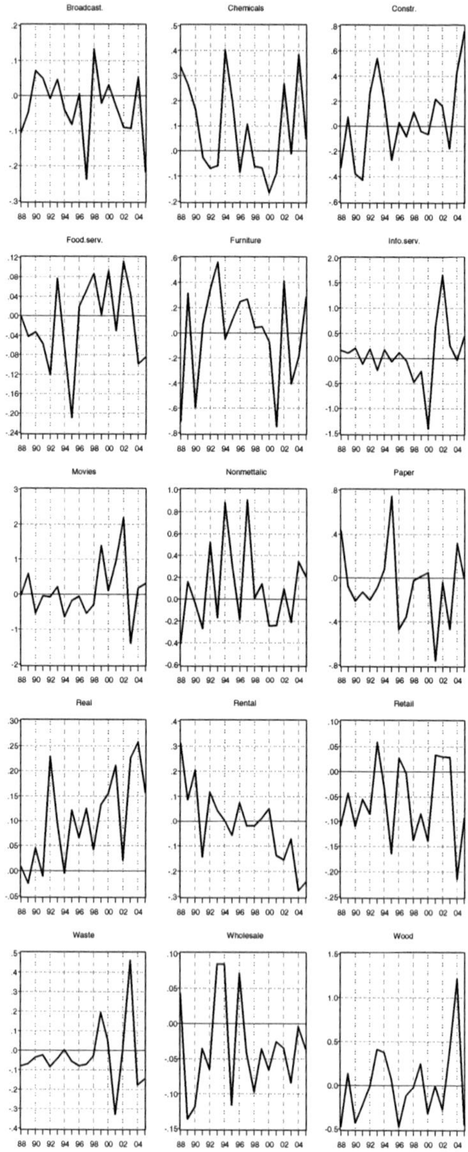

Figure 9.8 *Continued*

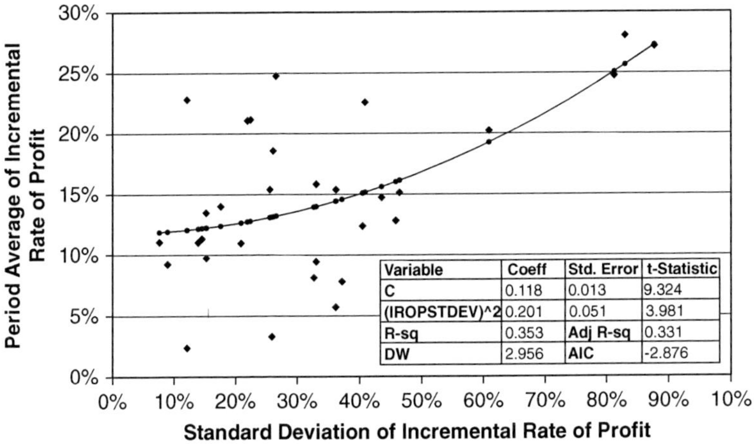

Figure 9.9 Risk and return: incremental rate of profit vs. standard deviation US industries, period-averages 1988–2005 (see Appendix 2 for sources)

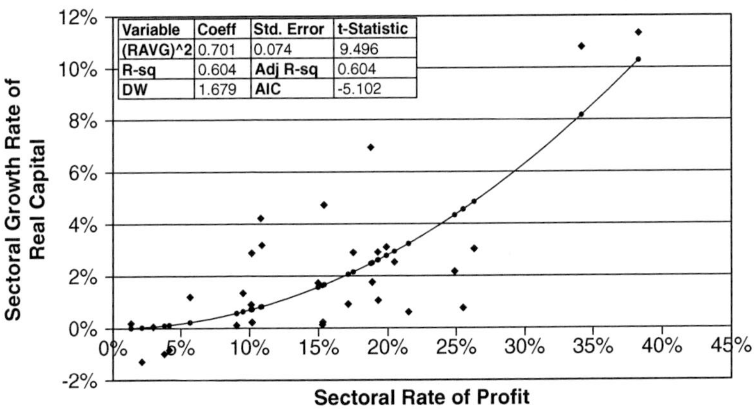

Figure 9.10 Growth and return: growth rate of real net capital vs rate of profit US industries, period-averages 1988–2005 (see Appendix 2 for sources)

The profit rate on total capital is simply the ratio of profits to capital stock. I develop a measure for the profit rate on recent investment, and argue on theoretical and empirical grounds that this can be well approximated by the incremental rate of profit, defined here as the ratio of the change in gross profits to the previous period's gross investment flows. At an empirical level, average and incremental measures both require measures of gross profits, data for which is nowadays available across industries and countries. But the rate of profit on total capital also requires the prior estimation of capital stocks, and this is considerably more problematical, because such measures are notoriously dependent on a widely criticized set of simplifying assumptions whose use imparts an unknown degree of error to estimates of the average rate of profit. By contrast, the incremental profit rate is fairly easy to measure, since the only additional data it requires is that on gross investment, which is directly observed and is widely available.

The empirical section of this chapter first examined the evidence on average and incremental rates of profit for eight developed-world manufacturing industries (Food, Textiles, Paper, Chemicals, Minerals, Metals, Metal Products, Machinery and Equipment, and Other Manufacturing products) aggregated across eight OECD countries (USA, Japan, Canada, Germany, France, Italy, Belgium and Norway). Similar data is presented for US manufacturing alone, from 1979–90, and subsequently for thirty US industries from 1987–2005. While most rates of profit on total capital cluster around a common mean, several remain persistently above or below that level. On the other hand, incremental rates of profit consistently cross back and forth, as would be expected from the classical theory of turbulent profit rate equalization. While period-average incremental rates of return in each industry are generally poor proxies for the theoretical long-term rates, it is encouraging that they seem to be positively correlated with risk (as measured by the standard deviation of incremental rates of return). An analytical examination of the process of profit rate equalization also leads us to expect a positive correlation between period-averages of industry profit rates and the corresponding growth rates in real capital, and this too is borne out by the data. Subsequent work will focus on econometric specifications of the adjustment process, and tests of the properties of estimated long-run profit rates on both average capital and new investment. So far, at least, the results are supportive of the classical theory of competition.

Appendix 1: OECD data, 1970–90, for Figures 9.1–9.4

Data for Figures 9.1–9.4 comes from the OECD *International Sectoral Data Base* (ISDB) of 1994. This contains annual data for several categories of fourteen OECD countries. For the detailed analysis of the production and use of goods and services, the economy is divided into approximately thirty branches according to *International Standard Industrial Classification* (ISIC) used in the National Accounts publication by OECD.[11] In order to achieve comparability and consistency across countries and industries we had to limit our sample to eight manufacturing industries (Food, Textiles, Paper, Chemicals, Minerals, Metals, Metal Products, Machinery and Equipment, and Other Manufacturing products) across eight countries (USA, Japan, Canada, Germany, France, Italy, Belgium and Norway).[12]

For each country, nominal gross operating surplus (GOS) in each industry was calculated as nominal GDP *minus* employee compensation *minus* indirect business taxes, while nominal gross capital stock was calculated by reflating the real gross capital stock through the investment deflator (which was itself calculated as the ratio of nominal to real gross investment). For world industries, gross operating surplus in local currency in any given industry was converted into US dollars, using annual GDP PPP-ratios, while corresponding nominal capital stock and gross investment were converted using annual gross investment PPP-ratios. The world average rate of profit in each industry was calculated as the ratio of its total world gross operating surplus to its total world gross capital stock, while the incremental rate of profit was calculated as the ratio of the change in nominal world gross operating surplus to the previous period's gross investment. For US measures, the nominal US variables were used directly. Further details are in Christodoulopoulos (1995, app. A).

Appendix 2: US data, 1987–2005, for Figures 9.5–9.12

Since the US Bureau of Economic Analysis (BEA) now only calculates net capital stock, the rate of profit on total capital is defined here as the ratio of nominal net profits (gross profits minus depreciation) to current-cost net capital stock On the other hand, since gross investment figures are widely available and are independent of the debatable assumptions needed to estimate capital stocks, the incremental rate of profit is defined as the ratio of the change in nominal gross profits to lagged nominal gross investment. Further details of the derivation and use of these and other relevant variables are listed below.

1. The basic flow variables were taken from the US Bureau of Economic Analysis (BEA) Gross Domestic Product (GDP) by Industry tables 1947–97 GDPbyInd_VA_NAICS and 1998–2005 GDPbyInd_VA_NAICS, available at http://www.bea.gov/industry/gdpbyind_data.htm. From these were calculated current gross value added (GVA), employee compensation (EC), gross operating surplus (GOS),[13] the price index for GVA (VAPI) which was used to create real

GVA (GVAR), and employment data on full and part-time employees (FTPE), self-employed persons (SEP), and full-time equivalent employees (FEE). All of these were available for 1987–2005 except SEP and FEE, which were only available for 1998–2005.

2. For each sector, a wage equivalent (WEQ) was calculated by applying the average full-time wage per worker (w ≡ EC/FEE) to SEP, and the resulting value was subtracted from GOS to create gross profits (PG). This was done because the NIPA calculation of GOS implicitly treats all of the income of proprietors and partners (that is, of self-employed persons) as profit-type income. Since SEP and FEE were only available for 1998–2005, the 1987 ratios of FEE/FTPE and PEP/FTPE were used along with 1987–97 values of FTPE to fill in these earlier years.
3. Current cost capital stock (K), gross investment (GI), and current cost depreciation (DEP) for each sector, and the quantity index for net capital stock (KQI) were taken from the following BEA Wealth tables: Table 3.1ES. Current-Cost Net Stock of Private Fixed Assets by Industry; Table 3.4ES. Current-Cost Depreciation of Private Fixed Assets by Industry; Table 3.7ES. Historical-Cost Investment in Private Fixed Assets by Industry; and Table 3.8ES. Chain-Type Quantity Indexes for Investment in Private Fixed Assets by Industry, all downloaded on 11 August 2007, last revised on 8 August 2007. The industries in the Wealth tables were matched to those in the NIPA accounts, which required aggregating sectors 50–51 and 69–70 in the former tables. Real capital stocks (KR) were created by scaling up the quantity index using the base-year (2000) values of current cost stocks.
4. Imputed values for owner-occupied-housing (OOH) were removed from the real estate industry values of GVA (space rent line 134 *minus* intermediate input line 135), GOS (GVA *minus* taxes net of subsidies (line 135 *minus* line 136), and DEP (line 140), there being no imputation made for EC, using NIPA Table 7.12. Imputations in the National Income and Product Accounts, Bureau of Economic Analysis (downloaded on 11 April 2007, last revised 1 August 2007). But whereas the BEA NIPA accounts now allocate all imputed values for OOH to the real estate sector, it still splits the Wealth stock components of OOH imputations between Farms and Real Estate, which had to be removed using Table 5.1. Current-Cost Net Stock of Residential Fixed Assets by Type of Owner, Legal Form of Organization, Industry, and Tenure Group, lines 15–16, respectively. A similar adjustment was made for GI, using Table 5.7. Historical-Cost Investment in Residential Fixed Assets by Type of Owner, Legal Form of Organization, Industry, and Tenure Group, lines 15–16.

5. Inventories were added to the capital stocks of manufacturing and wholesale/retail trade industries, using NIPA Table 1BU. Real Manufacturing and Trade Inventories, (http://www.bea.gov/national/nipaweb/nipa_underlying/SelectTable.asp) and Table 2AUI, Implicit Price Deflators for Manufacturing and Trade Sales, both downloaded on 11 August 2007, last revised 3 February 2004. The 1987–2005 average ratio of real inventories to real capital stock in each sector was taken to be its normal ratio, and this was used in conjunction with annual real capital stocks to create annual normal inventories for each sector. These were then converted to current-cost inventories using the implicit price deflators for manufacturing and trade sales.

   For the Construction industry, data on inventories of materials and supplies was available from the 1992, 1997, 2002 Economic Census of Construction, Table 3. The value of construction work was available for establishments reporting inventories; reporting no inventories; and non-reporting. The ratio of the Construction sales of the first two sets was used to split the last set into subcomponents, with and without inventories, the inventory sales ratio of the first set was applied to the first subcomponent of the last set to estimate its inventory levels, and this was added to reported inventories to achieve an overall total. The average inventory/GVA ratio for 1992, 1997, 2002 (which was stable at around 4 per cent) was then used to define a normal ratio, and this was used to estimate annual normal inventory stocks in the construction sector. The same ratio was also applied to the sector's fixed investment in order to estimate normal inventory investment. Total capital and investment were defined as the sums of their fixed and inventory components.

   In the Insurance and Related Activities industry, total reserves were calculated as the sum of checkable deposits and currency, money-market funds and security RPs in US Flow of Funds Tables L.116, Property-Casualty Insurance Companies (lines 2–3) and L.117, Life Insurance Companies (lines 2–3), downloaded 1/08/08. Since the ratio of reserves to net current-cost capital declined over time and fluctuated from one year to the next, its normal level was defined by its exponential trend. This trend value was then applied to annual capital stocks to obtain the normal reserve stocks, and to annual investment flows to obtain the normal investment in reserves, the resulting figures being added to fixed capital stocks and investment to get the total capital stock and investment. A similar procedure was followed for the Banking and Finance industry, which encompasses

Table 9.A1 Full list of excluded industries

Industry No.	Industry level	Industry title
1	Agriculture	Farms
2	Agriculture	Forestry, fishing, and related activities
3	Mining	Oil and gas extraction
4	Mining	Mining, except oil and gas
5	Mining	Support activities for mining
10	Manufacturing D	Primary metals
13	Manufacturing D	Computers and electronic products
15	Manufacturing D	Motor vehicles, bodies and trailers, and parts
16	Manufacturing D	Other transportation equipment
20	Manufacturing ND	Textile mills and textile product mills
21	Manufacturing ND	Apparel and leather and allied products
29	Transportation	Air transportation
30	Transportation	Rail transportation
31	Transportation	Water transportation
33	Transportation	Transit and ground passenger transportation
34	Transportation	Pipeline transportation
35	Transportation	Other transportation and support activities
37	Info	Publishing industries (includes software)
42	Finance	Securities, commodity contracts, and investments
44	Finance	Funds, trusts, and other financial vehicles
47	Profess.	Legal services
48	Profess.	Computer systems design and related services
49	Profess.	Miscellaneous professional, scientific, and technical services
50	Management	Management of companies and enterprises
51	Admn&Waste	Administrative and support services
53	Educ.	Educational services
54	Health&Soc.	Ambulatory health care services
55	Health&Soc.	Hospitals and nursing and residential care facilities
56	Health&Soc.	Social assistance
57	Arts	Performing arts, spectator sports, museums, and related activities
61	Other Services	Other services, except government

commercial banks, savings banks and credit unions, with reserves defined as the sum of vault cash and currency, reserves at the Federal Reserve, banks' own checkable and time deposits and currency (but not that of their customers), and Fed Funds and RPs, as taken from US Flow of Funds Table L.109 (lines 2–4), L.114 (lines 2–5), and L.115 (lines 2–4), downloaded 1/08/08.

6. The NAICS dataset has sixty-one individual private industries, plus an overall aggregate (All Private Industries) and several subaggregates such as Total, Durable, and Nondurable Manufacturing. Detailed descriptions of each industry are available online (StatCanada, 1997). Particular care was taken to focus on industries that were dominated by profit-driven enterprises and were also competitive on a world scale. This led to the exclusion of thirty-one the original sixty-one private industries, with a concomitant redefinition of the overall rate of profit and incremental rate of profit. The first set of industries were excluded if they were dominated by non-profit activities enterprises (for example, arts, museums, educational services, social services) or if the available data on the wages of employees significantly understated the wage-equivalent of the proprietors and partners (as, say, in the case of law firms or medical offices).[14] Such considerations applied to Administrative and Support Services, Ambulatory Health Care Services, Educational Services; Funds and Other Financial Vehicles, Hospitals and Nursing and Residential Care Facilities; Other Service Except Government (which include Religion, Grant Making, Civic, Professional and Similar Organizations); Performing Arts, Spectator Sports, Museums, and Related Activities; Legal Services, Computer Systems Design and Related Services, and Miscellaneous Professional, Scientific, and Technical Services; Publishing Industries; and Social Assistance. These sectors typically had either extremely low or negative 'profit rates' (for example, Educational Services), or very high ones (for example, Administrative and Support Services, and the various subsectors of Professional, Scientific, and Technical Services). Finally, another eighteen industries were excluded because either their average or incremental rates of profit had period-averages below 5 per cent (several even had negative or near-zero averages).[15] These were deemed to be uncompetitive internationally on a world scale. See Table 9.A1 for the full list of excluded industries.

Notes

1. In traditional finance theory, the focus is on 'the' prospective rate of return, defined as the *constant-over-time* internal rate of return (IRR) implicit in any expected future cash flows. But heterogeneous investors will have different evaluations of any given project. Hence there is no such thing as 'the' expected rate of return (Lutz, 1968, p. 218). In the end, the hypothesis of

arbitrage across investments – that is, of profit rate equalization – must refer to the *ex-post* process.

2. I thank Adrian Wood for directing my attention to the role of capacity utilization in profitability measures, and Randall Wray for suggesting an examination of the relations between profitability, risk and growth.
3. The notion of regulating capital is quite different from Steindl's idea of a marginal capital. His marginal capitals are those with the highest cost, and he assumes that they earn zero net profit; that is, that 'they just cover costs' (Steindl, 1976, p. 39). But a regulating capital always earns some profit, and in the long run it earns a normal rate of profit. Moreover, in the case of industry, it embodies the *lowest* generally reproducible costs. In the case of agriculture and mining, to the extent that better conditions of production are not reproducible, the regulating capitals may well have the highest costs, as in Ricardo's producer on marginal land (Ricardo, 1951, ch. 2). But, even here, there may be different technologies in use on the marginal land, in which case the lowest-cost producer on the marginal land is the regulating capital.
4. Alternatively, if two methods of production for a given commodity coexist at some given real wage, it is assumed that they can do so in competitive equilibrium only if they have the same rate of profit (Sraffa, 1963, pp. 38–9).
5. Although the validity of these assumptions has been questioned widely, they continue to be used in most countries because of their great computational convenience (OECD, 2001, ch. 8, pp. 75–81).
6. Vintages and types are two separate issues. Every type of capital may exist in different vintages, depending on how long it has been in operation.
7. Moreover, since an industry may itself be global, the international equalization of regulating rates is consistent with persistent national differences in average rates of profit for a given industry (see the next section).
8. An aggregate connection between real wages and productivity is a common theme in many different traditions (Shaikh, 2003). A classical take on the microeconomics of wage-setting is given by Botwinick (1993, ch. 6–7).
9. In the definition of the incremental rate of profit, the numerator ΔP_t is a proxy for the current profit (P_{new}) and past investment I_{t-1} is a proxy for the current cost of recent capital (K_{new}). Just like the current cost average rate of profit, the current cost incremental rate of profit is simultaneously a real rate.
10. We used this procedure in Shaikh and Tonak (1994, pp. 110–13). It has recently been incorporated into the Annual Macro-Economic Database (AMECO) of the European Commission's Directorate General for Economic and Financial Affairs, available at http://europa.eu.int/comm/economy_finance/indicators/annual_macro_economic_database/ameco_contents.htm.
11. Branches are defined as groups of units of homogeneous production, each engaged in a single activity. The use of the word 'branch' here is synonymous to industry.
12. Compensation of employee data is not obtainable for the years prior to 1970, while capital stock and gross fixed capital formation data is available only for some industries of some countries in the ISDB database.
13. Gross operating surplus = gross value added –employee compensation – taxes on production and imports.

14. We wish to thank George Smith and Denise McBride of the Bureau of Economic Analysis for helping us to identify potential sectors. However, the final decisions were ours.
15. Duménil and Lévy (2004, pp. 84–5) argue that, in two of these industries, Pipeline Transportation and Railroad Transportation, the extremely low measured rates of profit were primarily because the BEA methods yield excessively high values for their capital stocks as a result of the very long service lives the BEA assigns to pipelines and rail tracks.

References

Botwinick, H. (1993) *Persistent Inequalities: Wage Disparities under Capitalist Competition*, Princeton, N.J.: Princeton University Press.

Christodoulopoulos, George (1995) 'International Competition and Industrial Rates of Return', Department of Economics, New School for Social Research, New York.

Cohen, Jerome B.; Edward D. Zinbarg and Arthur Zeikel (1987) *Investment Analysis and Portfolio Management*, Homewood, Ill.: Irwin.

Damodaran, Aswath (2001) *Corporate Finance: Theory and Practice*, New York: John Wiley.

Duménil, Gérard and Dominique Lévy (2004) 'The Real and Financial Components of Profitability (United States, 1952–2000)', *Review of Radical Political Economics*, 36 (1): 82–110.

Elton, Edwin J. and Martin J. Gruber (1991) *Modern Portfolio Theory and Investment Analysis*, New York: John Wiley.

Geroski, Paul A. (1990) 'Modeling Persistent Profitability', in Dennis C. Mueller, *The Dynamics of Company Profits: An International Comparison*, Cambridge: Cambridge University Press: 15–34.

Gordon, Robert J. (1993) 'Reply: The Concept of Capital', *Review of Income and Wealth*, Series 39 (1): 103–10.

Kurz, Heinz (1986) 'Normal Positions and Capital Utilization', *Political Economy: Studies in the Surplus Approach*, 2 (1): 37–54.

Lutz, Friedich A. (1968) *The Theory of Interest*, Chicago: Aldine.

Marx, Karl (1971) *Theories of Surplus Value, Part 3*, Moscow: Progress.

Mayerhauser, Nicole and Marshall Reinsdorf(2007) 'Housing Services in the National Income Accounts', Bureau of Economic Analysis, U.S. Department of Commerce : 1–4.

Mueller, Dennis C. (ed.) (1990) *The Dynamics of Company Profits: An International Comparison*, Cambridge: Cambridge University Press.

Mueller, Dennis C. (1986) *Profits in the Long Run*, Cambridge: Cambridge University Press.

OECD(1994) *The International Sectoral Database*, Paris: OECD.

OECD (2001) *OECD Manual: Measurement of Capital Stock, Consumption of Fixed Capital and Capital Services* Paris, OECD.

Panico, Carlo (1983) 'Marx's Analysis of the Relationship between the Rate of Interest and the Rate of Profits', New York: Duckworth: 167–86.

Ricardo, David (1951) *Principles of Political Economy and Taxation*, ed. Piero Sraffa, Cambridge: Cambridge University Press.

Schroeder, Susan K. (2004) 'Political Economic Forecasting of Financial Crises', Department of Economics, New York: New School for Social Research.

Shaikh, Anwar (2003) 'Labor Market Dynamics within Rival Macroeconomic Frameworks', in George Argyrous, Gary Mongiovi and Mathew Forstater, *Growth, Distribution and Effective Demand: Alternatives to Economic Orthodoxy*, Armonk, NY: M. E. Sharpe: 127–43.

Shaikh, Anwar (1978) 'Political Economy and Capitalism: Notes on Dobb's Theory of Crisis', *Cambridge Journal of Economics*, 2: 233–51.

Shaikh, Anwar (1998) 'The Stock Market and the Corporate Sector: A Profit-Based Approach', in Malcolm Sawyer, Philip Arestis and Gabriel Palma, *Festschrift for Geoffrey Harcourt*, London: Routledge & Kegan Paul.

Shaikh, Anwar and E. Ahmet Tonak (1994) *Measuring the Wealth of Nations: The Political Economy of National Accounts*, Cambridge: Cambridge University Press.

Sraffa, Piero (1963) *Production of Commodities by Means of Commodities*, Cambridge: Cambridge University Press.

StatCanada (1997) 'North American Industry Classification (NAICS) 1997'.

Steindl, Josef (1976) *Maturity and Stagnation in American Capitalism*, New York: Monthly Review Press.

Tsoulfidis, Lefteris and Persefoni Tsaliki (2005) 'Marxian Theory of Competition and the Concept of Regulating Capital: Evidence from Greek Manufacturing', *Review of Radical Political Economics*, 37 (1): 5–22.

10
Accounting for Business Combinations

Geoff Meeks and Geoff Whittington

Introduction

Ajit Singh's monograph '*Takeovers: Their Relevance to the Stock Market and the Theory of the Firm*' (1971) was a pioneering study of the link between takeovers and the performance of the participants before and after the deal. A large literature has since developed on the characteristics of taken-over firms, and of post-merger performance. One line of development has focused on the choice of statistical technique. Ajit Singh pioneered the use of discriminant analysis for the identification of the characteristics of taken-over firms and, since then, alternatives have included logit and probit analysis, factor analysis, and neural networks. A second line of development has been on the research question. Some later studies have tended to regard the prediction of the takeover event as an end in itself, rather than regarding takeover studies as tests of theories of the firm, the central concern of the Singh study. This narrower remit can be understood in the light of the substantial gains to be made from accurate prediction: takeover targets typically experience share price rises of around 25 per cent in the days preceding the bid, so predicting that event offers the prospect of major financial gains (see Hughes, 1993). The third line of development has been to shift the focus of performance measurement, from accounting data to share price movements on the stock market (see, for example, Agrawal *et al.* (1992), Andrade *et al.* (2001), Gregory (1997)). Ajit Singh measured market valuations as well as accounting profitability, but many subsequent studies have reported only share price data – because such data are more easily accessible or because of concerns about the reliability of accounting data. Some studies have persisted with accounting data, however – for example, Chatterjee and Meeks (1996); Cosh *et al.* (1989); Dickerson *et al.* (1997); Kumar

(1984); Meeks (1977); Mueller (1980); Ravenscraft and Scherer (1987), partly because such data do not conflate track record and expectations, in the way that share price movements do, and partly because of doubts about the informational efficiency of the stock markets that generate those share price data.[1]

This chapter considers the measurement of the performance of bidders and targets ahead of a combination, and of the combined company afterwards. It addresses some of the challenges presented for accounts-based work because of the evolution of accounting measurement since Ajit Singh completed his classic work. This evolution has resulted partly from the interplay, on the one hand, of 'creative accountants' seeking to flatter their companies' performance by accounting manipulation, sometimes to influence the terms of a takeover, and sometimes to flatter post-merger performance; and, on the other hand, of regulators seeking to outlaw misleading accounting practice and harmonize accounting methods. As a result, some accounting variables used in Ajit Singh's work have now changed their meaning; some have disappeared; new ones have emerged; and the quality of some of the variables has changed over time. These developments affect the inferences that could be drawn in subsequent work from using the tests he carried out.[2]

To explore these developments, the chapter gives a brief history of the evolution of accounting standards relating to business combinations from 1970 onwards, showing in particular how changes to standards have been designed to counter abuse by parties to takeovers. This discussion concentrates on the UK, the source of Ajit Singh's data and that of many subsequent studies, but experience in the US and in international accounting standards has been broadly similar[3] It then considers the problems of accounting measurement in the context of one of the principal explanatory variables used in the Singh (1971) study – the accounting rate of return – which can be affected by the earnings management practices that have been associated with takeovers.

Accounting, and creative accounting, for business combinations in the UK before 1990

The takeover boom of the late 1960s could be said to have been responsible for the introduction of a formal accounting standard-setting system in the UK. Before 1970, UK financial accounting was governed by 'generally accepted accounting practice', which was, at the time, a rather permissive and ill-defined set of practices based on the Companies Act's minimal requirements, a few rather loose Recommendations by the

Institute of Chartered Accountants in England and Wales, and a broad consensus established by practitioners. It allowed for a great deal of discretion and choice, and the opportunities that it offered for flattering performance were exploited ruthlessly in the increasingly competitive capital markets of the late 1960s (Kynaston, 2001), particularly in relation to the market for corporate control. This led to various accounting scandals, which finally provoked the accounting profession to establish an accounting standard-setting body – the Accounting Standards Steering Committee (ASSC) – in 1970. Two of the most prominent of these scandals involved takeovers: the acquisition of Pergamon by Leasco, and the acquisition of AEI by GEC. In these cases, the acquired company had boosted its reported or forecast pre-merger profits by overestimating the most recent value of its stock and work-in-progress, thus allegedly inducing the acquiring company to overbid. AEI's forecast profits of £10 million for 1967 turned out in fact to be a loss of £4.5 million. Of the difference, £9.5 million was a result of adjustments attributable to differences in the principles used in accounting for contracts (Stamp (1969, fn 10).

The ASSC and its successor body, the ASC, worked through the 1970s and 1980s to produce thirty-four accounting standards and revisions of standards, but there was still concern about creative accounting, much of it associated with the growth of financial engineering. This, in turn, was often associated with takeover bids and defences, and with reporting post-combination performance. Terry Smith's controversial book, *Accounting for Growth* (1992), which describes and illustrates many of the creative accounting techniques used in the 1980s, devotes an entire section (Part II, chs 3–5) to accounting techniques used on the acquisition and disposal of subsidiaries. Again, the 1990 paper by Tweedie and Whittington identified accounting for business combinations as one of four core problems of financial reporting at that time. The techniques of creative accounting for business combinations that gave rise to concern were focused first on the choice of model (acquisition accounting or merger accounting), and second on accounting choices available within the acquisition accounting model. These choices could have a significant impact on the profit numerators and asset denominators of performance ratios such as those used by Ajit Singh.

The choice of model was determined partly by the nature of the acquisition. Merger accounting (alternatively known as pooling of interests accounting) could be applied only when the consideration for the transaction was shares of the acquiring company. This model treats the combination of the two businesses as a merger, which is analogous to the formation of a partnership. The accounting book values of both parties are preserved (unless there is a voluntary revaluation, which could take place even in the absence of a merger), and the equity issued as consideration is valued at book value rather than market value.[4] This preserves the comparability of the pre- and post-merger valuation practices of both businesses and might seem to provide a useful basis for comparing pre- and post-merger performance: if they are consistent over time, the flaws in the pre-merger and post-merger valuations may to some extent net out when the change alone is analysed (see Penman (2001)). But what this approach ignores are the terms of the merger transaction itself, except in the rare cases where the consideration paid is exactly equal to book value. In most cases, the value of this consideration will exceed book value, the excess representing a combination of undervaluation of the assets at book value and the non-recognition of goodwill in the acquired entity. Thus merger accounting does not fully reflect management's accountability for the business combination transaction: the opportunity cost of the funds used by the acquirer is not fully represented. From management's perspective, this offers the prospect of reporting higher post-merger profits, because it avoids the revaluation of stocks, fixed assets and goodwill, which would typically raise the costs charged in the income statement after the merger. Merger accounting also affords greater flexibility over dividend payments, as well as boosting profits for the year of acquisition, relative to the alternative method – acquisition accounting – which incorporates profits of the new subsidiary only from the date of acquisition rather than the beginning of the accounting year in which the acquisition took place.[5]

Acquisition accounting (alternatively known as purchase accounting) treats the business combination as an acquisition of the target company by the bidding company, rather than as a merger or pooling of interests, and it therefore recognizes the consideration at its current value. When the consideration is cash, acquisition accounting is the only option, because the disbursement of cash to the acquired entity's proprietors has to be accounted for. The assets and liabilities of the acquired entity are revalued at current value (often described as 'fair value') and the resulting amount is compared with the consideration paid. Any surplus of consideration over revalued net assets acquired is treated as goodwill.[6] Clearly, the acquisition model can lead to lower post-merger profits and rates of return because of its higher valuations at the point of takeover, which create higher future costs or depreciation charges when the assets are consumed or sold. The same increased valuations additionally depress the post-combination rate of return by increasing its denominator.

Often, the impact of this accounting choice on the performance measure will be material. For the US, Ayers *et al.* (2000) report that, in combinations reported as mergers in 1992–7, 'unrecognized' goodwill averaged over 30 per cent of the bidder's book value.[7] Taking a particular UK example, Li (2005) estimates that, had BP treated its combination with Amoco using acquisition rather than merger accounting, and recognized the goodwill implicit in the terms of the deal, that goodwill would have amounted to almost 50 per cent of BP and Amoco's revalued net assets, and the subsequent accounting rate of return on investment would have been depressed by as much as half. In these circumstances, it is not surprising that the newly-combined group adopted merger accounting, despite the combination appearing to many independent observers to have the characteristics of an acquisition of Amoco by BP.[8] Some accounting studies in the Singh tradition allow for these choices. Meeks (1977) adjusts the accounts for the different accounting treatments, while Ravenscraft and Scherer segment the two approaches and report separate results according to accounting method. But the accounting choice does not just affect measurement; sometimes it affects behaviour and expenditure too. Directors will sometimes go to great lengths to avoid the impact of acquisition accounting on reported performance. Lys and Vincent (1995) analyse the acquisition of NCR by AT&T: AT&T offered up to US$500 million more for NCR if they could structure the deal so that it could be accounted for as a merger rather than an acquisition.[9]

However, acquisition accounting presents its own opportunities for the acquirer to flatter post-combination performance. This is because of the options within acquisition accounting referred to earlier. In the late 1980s, there were three areas that offered opportunities to the creative accountant: provisions for reorganization; the fair value of assets; and the treatment of goodwill.

Provisions for reorganization have sometimes been made at the time of the combination: they reduce the valuation of the net assets acquired and increase goodwill (the difference between net assets acquired and purchase consideration). The provision is then available to offset post-acquisition costs, on the grounds that these were necessarily incurred as a result of the reorganization of the business to accommodate the merger. This obviously has the effect of enhancing post-merger profits. To take an extreme example, Smith (1992, p. 209) analyses the contribution of such provisions to the post-merger profits of Coloroll in 1988–9, after a string of acquisitions. Reported profit was £56 million; but, of this, no less than £52 million could be attributed to the use of these provisions. More recently, in the US, Feder and Schiesel (2002) suggest that WorldCom – subsequently to become the biggest bankruptcy in world history – had been setting up excessive reserves at the time of takeover, against which routine operating expenses were charged in subsequent years in order to relieve the income statement of those expenses. This was part of a package of devices totalling as much as US$5 billion.

Attributing a fair value to the assets acquired involves a great deal of judgement, and this allows discretion to the preparer of the financial statements (management). In some cases, management may wish to show generous fair values – for example, to lower the apparent gearing ratio when it has borrowed heavily to fund the acquisition.[10] More often, management will be more concerned to report strong post-merger profits, in which case it will be tempted to understate fair value in order to reduce the costs charged against subsequent profits.

The treatment of goodwill is the aspect of accounting for business combinations that has caused the greatest difficulties for accounting standard-setters over the years. Goodwill arises on acquisition because it represents a valuation, at the time of the business combination, of the target firm in aggregate, rather than of its separate recognized assets. It is thus an amalgam of measurement error, intangible assets that are not recognized in the accounts and, what might be described as 'pure goodwill' – the difference between the going-concern value of the business and the sum of the separate assets.[11] Whatever its composition, it is something that is not recognized in accounts other than as a result of the acquisition of a business; that is, only when it is 'purchased' and not when it is 'internally generated' (for example, through advertising to develop a brand); and it is one of the possible advantages of merger accounting that it sidesteps the problem: it avoids the need to recognize goodwill, even in a business combination. Thus there has been considerable doubt and controversy among accountants about how purchased goodwill should be treated. Some do not regard it as an asset at all, or at least not one reliable enough to be reported in the accounts, and would prefer to write it off against reserves immediately it is acquired, so that it is treated consistently with internally generated goodwill. Others say that this treatment would fail to hold management accountable for their expenditure on goodwill. They would prefer to treat purchased goodwill initially as an asset but amortize it over its useful life (the period over which the acquired entity is expected to generate returns from it) as a charge against profits. A third school of thought would recognize goodwill in the balance sheet, on acquisition, but would not require subsequent amortization, on the grounds that it is not usually possible to identify the useful life and appropriate amortization pattern of purchased goodwill. Moreover, purchased goodwill is often replaced by internally generated goodwill as the entity sustains the business, and the cost of doing this will be charged against profits. Therefore this third school of thought would argue that goodwill should only be written down in value when an impairment test shows that its carrying value is no longer justified.

By 1990, the ASC had closed only one of these options. Its standard 'Accounting for Goodwill' (SSAP 22) was developed after much controversy and closed only the third approach: capitalization and non-amortization[12] With acquisition accounting, a choice between the first two models was allowed, immediate write-off against reserves or capitalization and subsequent amortization. The latter would lead to lower post-merger profits, but a higher initial balance sheet value which would show a more favourable gearing ratio.[13]

This accounting choice left huge scope for choice by preparers, and those choices could have a significant impact on the performance and financing measures used both by analysts in the market and by academic studies such as Ajit Singh's. It was one of several issues on which the ASC's performance in combating creative accounting was held to be inadequate. In 1990, following the Dearing Report (1988), the ASC was replaced by the ASB, which had greater powers and more independence from the accounting profession.

Attempts to improve accounting for business combinations since 1990

The new ASB, led by David Tweedie, set out to deal with the perceived abuses of creative accounting, and abuses associated with business combinations were a high priority.[14] As soon as the lengthy due process could be completed it issued two new standards: FRS 6, Acquisitions and Mergers; and FRS7, Fair Values in Acquisition Accounting (September 1994), which attempted to address many of the problems described earlier. The difficult and controversial topic of goodwill took longer to resolve through two further standards: FRS10, Goodwill and Intangible Assets (December 1997); and FRS11, Impairment of Fixed Assets and Goodwill (July 1998).

The ASB's approach to the choice of model was not to ban either merger accounting or acquisition accounting, but to limit the use of merger accounting. FRS6 put five broad constraints on the circumstances in which merger accounting would apply, and asserted that these circumstances were likely to be rare. Essentially, these defined a merger of equals, in which the parties were of similar size, shareholders of both merging entities retained their interests, and the managements participated more or less equally in the post-merger entity. As intended, the number of business combinations qualifying for merger accounting fell drastically (Wilson *et al.* (2001), pp. 323–4), although some of the mergers involved were very large, as would be expected of mergers of equals. Moreover, although it restricted the scope for arbitrage between the two methods of accounting, FRS6 still preserved two different methods, whereas greater interfirm comparability might be achieved by having a single model for all types of combination.

With regard to the practice of acquisition accounting, FRS7 was designed to close a number of loopholes that had been potential sources of creative accounting – particularly on measuring fair values and on transaction costs that could be included in the consideration. Valuation of the acquired entity's assets and liabilities was to be based on the perspective of that entity at the time of acquisition. It should not take into account the acquirer's expectations or intentions for future action. Thus, provisions for future reorganization by the acquirer (as in the Coloroll example, above) were ruled out, as were impairments or lower valuations of assets that reflected the acquirer's future intentions rather than their value to the acquired business at the date when control was transferred.

In addition to these requirements for recognition and measurement in the accounts, FRS6 and FRS7 also required supplementary disclosure in notes of various details of merger and acquisition (M&A) transactions, to help the diligent user of accounts to understand what lay behind the headline figures in the accounts. These also led to greater transparency from the perspective of the marketplace, though they add to the bulk of the accounts and inevitably attract criticism from preparers of accounts that they are expensive and potentially confusing. However, while market participants can take full account of supplementary disclosures, either by reading them directly or by relying on reports by analysts who have read them, such data can be harder to incorporate into standardized variables for large sample studies, and empirical researchers may be tempted to use the headline numbers, ignoring the nuances in the notes.

FRS10, Goodwill and Intangible Assets, restricted the treatment of goodwill to capitalization followed by writing-off as a cost against profit over its life. The preferred procedure was amortization over useful life, where that could be determined at the time of the acquisition, but it was recognized that this might not be practical in many cases. The standard contained a rebuttable presumption that useful life does not exceed twenty years, but, in cases where this assumption could be rebutted, systematic amortization over the longer period had to be supplemented by an annual impairment test.[15] The impairment test makes a specific calculation of the erosion of goodwill in place of the mechanistic approach of amortization.[16] An impairment test entails calculating the current value of the asset as the higher of its recoverable amount (the discounted present value of expected future cash flows arising from it) and net realizable value. In the case of goodwill, net realizable value is unlikely to be reliably measurable because it cannot be realized separately from the business as a whole, so the typical current value will be a recoverable amount, based on estimated cash flows. The current value is then compared with the carrying amount in the accounts: impairment occurs to the extent that current value falls short of the carrying amount . In the case of goodwill, if the test led to an impairment in excess of amortization, that had to be charged against profit. If the useful life was indeterminate, so that an amortization rate could not be established, a full annual impairment test was required and that became the only means by which the goodwill or intangible asset was written down.

Li (2005) analyses the case of Marconi, which, impaired £3,677 m of goodwill in 2002. This was the equivalent of 85 per cent of that year's total sales; and it eliminated 48 per cent of its net assets as at the end of 2001. The effect on accounting rates of return is therefore dramatic, whether comparison is being made with prior years for Marconi (as in Singh's comparisons of profitability before and after the merger) or with other companies in a cross-sectional test (as with his comparisons of merging and non-merging companies).

Clearly, the impairment approach is an incomplete method of capturing amortization, because the impairment test compares the current value of the goodwill in the business with its current carrying amount. The cash flows used to estimate current value will inevitably include the effects of goodwill generated by the entity following the acquisition, and, because this additional goodwill is internally generated rather than purchased, it will not be included in the carrying amount in the accounts. Therefore, to the extent that the current value estimate includes the effects of this 'replacement goodwill', it understates the amortization of the goodwill acquired in the business combination. However, if the impracticality of measuring amortization reliably is acknowledged, the impairment test provides a practical – if incomplete – alternative.

The ASB introduced a raft of other measures to support their new regulation of M&A accounting. FRS10 pre-empted accounting arbitrage between goodwill and other intangible assets acquired in a combination. FRS11 provided a consistent framework for impairment testing; and supplementary disclosures were required to inform the (potentially subjective) estimates of market values and future cash flows used in that testing. FRS12 restricted drastically the use of provisions for future costs or losses – previously a notorious area of earnings management. And FRS3 made much more transparent those movements in reserves that had no counterpart in the profit and loss account – for example, asset revaluations. As a result, the diligent investment analyst was much better informed of the substance of M&A transactions. But not all the new information would be captured in the summary accounting measures traditionally used by statistical researchers.

The advent of international standards and the current state of accounting for business combinations

The ASB had reformed accounting for business combinations to limit the range of possible accounting practices and mitigate the opportunities for earnings management by preparers of accounts. However, it rejected one possibly revolutionary change: the treatment of all business combinations as acquisitions, ruling out merger accounting entirely. This solution had been favoured in particular by some commentators in the US, where there was concern about the abuse of the merger accounting ('pooling of interests') option, and it was proposed in a discussion paper published by the 'G4+1'[17] group of standard-setters in 1998.

In 2000, a momentous decision by the governments of the European Union (EU) countries meant that the consolidated accounts of all listed companies in the EU would be prepared according to international accounting standards (IAS), which were set, at that time, by the International Accounting Standards Committee (IASC). These standards were, in most respects and certainly with respect to business combinations, similar to those of the ASB, so this decision was not necessarily revolutionary from the perspective of the UK. However, a new body, the International Accounting Standards Board (IASB) was set up to replace the IASC in 2001 and established a close working relationship with the US standard-setter, the FASB, with a view to achieving convergence between the standards of the two bodies. It was also keen to establish convergence internationally and therefore wished to provide a sound foundation for resolving the existing international diversity in accounting for business combinations: the internationalization of national capital (and hence takeover) markets was proceeding rapidly,[18] and stark differences were to be found in accounting arrangements in different jurisdictions. Nobes (1997) gives the example of Daimler-Benz ahead of its New York listing: net income using German conventions for 1993 was DM615 million, but under US conventions it was minus DM1,893 million.

The IASB shadowed the FASB's development of a new business combinations standard and issued its own standard, IFRS3, which had substantially similar requirements, in March 2004. The two central features of this standard were, first, that all business combinations were to be accounted for in the same manner, as acquisitions rather than mergers; and, second, that goodwill could no longer be amortized but was instead to be subject only to an annual impairment test. This is now standard accounting practice for the consolidated accounts of listed companies in the EU (including the UK) and for the many other companies throughout the world that are required, or volunteer, to follow IASB standards.

The elimination of merger (pooling of interests) accounting does achieve comparability of accounting method across all business combinations. This is bought at the price of having to make a rather arbitrary judgement (supported by guidelines in the standard) as to which entity is the acquirer when there really is a merger of equals. In these circumstances, 'fresh-start' accounting has some attractions. This would regard the combination as the acquisition of both combining entities by a new entity and thus would involve fair valuing ALL of the assets and liabilities acquired. This approach has theoretical appeal but would be a radical change of practice, and preparers of accounts would probably be strongly opposed to it on grounds of cost and practicality.[19] Standard-setters have therefore been reluctant previously to support fresh-start accounting, but it may be considered in the future. For statistical studies of the sort in Ajit Singh's monograph, the procedure would have mixed benefits: after the fresh start, data would be more reliable; but comparisons with the same firms before the fresh start, or with other firms that had not experienced a fresh start, would be more difficult.

The difficulties of acquisition accounting remain. They hinge on the difficulties of identifying and valuing the assets and liabilities acquired and, in some cases, even the purchase consideration.[20] The most difficult area is perhaps goodwill, because this is affected by any residual errors in the measurement of the other components.

In summary, over recent years there have been many changes in the accounting associated with business combinations. These have affected in particular the valuation of assets and the measurement of profit, causing difficulty in comparing pre- and post-merger performance, and comparing targets or acquisitive companies with others. Accounting standards have turned increasingly to additional disclosures to elaborate on the uncertainties and composition of accounting numbers, and a proper interpretation of those numbers takes into account this information. The current prevailing practice in the UK and internationally is to use acquisition accounting for all combinations, but this has been the case only since 2004. Acquisition accounting causes significant changes in accounting values in the acquired entity. It also leads to the recognition of purchased goodwill, which changes the net assets and leads to possible future reductions in reported profits, as well as adding to the measurement uncertainty of the accounts. Many of the changes in accounting standards have been in response to the actual or potential manipulation of accounts to show a favourable picture of performance – in particular, to show high post-merger profits or rates of return. This type of activity is directed towards influencing the stock market, but it is equally a trap for the economic researcher who uses the data without due care. To illustrate this, we shall examine briefly a common metric used in takeover studies: the rate of return.

Consequences for the rate of return

The rate of return is a much-used measure in empirical studies of the performance of business firms, including both those of takeovers and the assessment of post-merger performance (early examples are Singh, 1971; and Meeks, 1977). There is an extensive literature on the relationship between the economist's ideal rate of return and the accounting rate of return, which will not be reviewed here (see Whittington, 1997). Instead, we shall assume that there is such a relationship, and that, over limited periods, this is best captured by measurement at current value (such as replacement cost) in the accounts (a case argued by Edwards *et al.*, 1987). We shall consider how the accounting rate of return might be biased from this ideal by the use of different accounting practices.

The accounting rate of return has profit as its numerator. We concluded that the application of acquisition accounting would be expected to increase depreciation and amortization charges, reducing profits, post-combination, in so far as the fair valuation and recognition of goodwill increase valuations. However, this result was not certain, and there have been many creative accounting devices that have enabled managements to increase post-combination profits, some of which remain. Merger accounting creates less disturbance in profit measurement but is still susceptible to the routine techniques of earnings management. With regard to pre-acquisition profits, these also are subject to earnings management and may be particularly subject to this during a bidder's takeover preparation and the target's takeover defence. Irrespective of earnings management, the mixture of historical cost and current values in accounts will lead to a degree of random variation of profit from our ideal as well as some systematic errors. If we assume that historical costs typically understate current costs, then costs, particularly long-term costs such as depreciation charges, will be too low, and operating profits will be overstated. 'Clean surplus' total profit, which includes revaluations, will tend to be understated because not all assets and liabilities are revalued, and the prudent tendencies of accountants encourage them to report losses less reluctantly than gains. Hence we conclude that conventional accounts will typically tend to overstate operating profit and understate 'clean surplus' profit, but this depends very much on circumstances (for example, 'clean surplus' profit can be very high in a year in which revaluation takes place, because gains from previous years may be included), and, despite the efforts of standard setters, the creative accountant still has scope for managing earnings in a way that contradicts these generalizations. In large-sample statistical studies, the main challenge is to allow in longitudinal work for systematic changes in the degree of misvaluation at the point of takeover, and in cross-sectional work for different degrees of misvaluation between merging companies and benchmark or control groups.

A similar challenge arises with the denominator of the rate of return, net assets. The net asset measure in accounts is affected by non-recognition and mismeasurement of assets and liabilities. Thus, typically, net assets might be expected to be understated, but this is not necessarily the case, especially when the possible overstatement of liabilities under historical cost is considered. With regard to the accounting consequences of takeovers, acquisition accounting is likely to lead to a discontinuity between pre- and post-acquisition net assets, with post-acquisition net assets being more likely to be increased by revaluation, and the recognition of goodwill and other previously unrecognized intangible assets. However, it is possible for the acquired business to be bought for less than the book value of net assets, and it is also possible to write down goodwill on grounds of overpayment, so the consequences of acquisition accounting are not predictable with any certainty. The merger accounting approach, which is no longer permitted by IASB standards, introduces no discontinuity between pre- and post-merger net assets, but this method preserves all the imperfections of historical cost measurement. For those wishing to compare pre- and post-merger economic performance, the ideal solution might be that the pre-acquisition accounting is restated on a current value basis; but the more expedient method might be to adjust post-acquisition accounts for revaluations, so that both pre- and post-merger performance are on a like-for-like basis (see Meeks, 1977).

In summary, it is difficult to generalize about the direction or extent of distortions in the rate of return that result from accounting practices. A comfortable conclusion for the empirical researcher might be that these errors can therefore be treated as random noise in the estimation process. Unfortunately, this is not a reliable escape, because the errors will be systematic in some circumstances. A more appropriate response is to take these errors into account in selecting accounting variables (for example, in the choice of clean surplus income or operating income), in devising tests (for example, differences may be relatively reliable even where levels are misleading), and in the specification of models (for example, selecting a longer time period for measurement will alleviate some of the problems, because accounting errors tend to shift items between years rather than eliminate them for ever). Careful selection of matching samples can also be helpful, having regard to whether possible sources of accounting error might affect the sample and the control group in a similar way. The much richer information now available in the notes to the accounts is helpful in this regard (for example, the notes reveal valuation policies, so that it should be possible to match firms having similar policies); and, with some effort, the information in the notes can be used to augment the basic accounts (for example, using alternative valuations of assets provided in supplementary disclosures).

Some implications for accounting studies in the Singh tradition

We have in this chapter catalogued a daunting set of problems intrinsic to measuring assets and profits around mergers and takeovers. We have outlined the evolution of accounting treatments, highlighting differences in measurement over time and inconsistencies of treatment across companies at the same time. And we have illustrated ways in which companies have systematically sought to misrepresent their performance in their accounts around takeover. Are these problems so great that such accounting studies should be abandoned? And have the problems become greater or smaller since Ajit Singh's monograph?

Part of the case for not abandoning such work is that accounts provide the most systematic data available on company financial performance, and constitute possibly the most expensive and highly regulated economic information set in existence. They are rooted in company law; they have to be published and subjected to the scrutiny of shareholders, of the press, and of a huge and skilled industry of equity researchers; they are audited by a regulated profession; and their method of construction is governed by a sophisticated system of standard-setting. Moreover, there is a huge body of empirical evidence showing that accounting numbers drive share prices.

Furthermore, some of the accounting problems we have outlined here may not be material if such studies are carefully constructed. For example, a measurement problem that persists through time (for example, an asset's value is under-recorded) may be sidestepped if a statistical test focuses on differences rather than levels.

How else could we measure performance? One approach in the literature has been to rely on share prices, on the grounds that these will impound not just accounting information, but also other relevant data. Total shareholder return – share price appreciation plus dividends – might therefore be used as a performance measure in place of an accounting rate of return. However, such a measure is fundamentally unsuited to some of the research questions asked by Ajit Singh. For example, if used as a measure of the target's performance immediately before takeover it would conflate the track record of the target management (a central issue in Singh's work) with the stock market's perception of the likelihood of the target being taken over at a premium (share prices of firms with a poor track record tend to rise ahead of takeover, in anticipation of a bid premium). Again, some of our criticisms of accounting data have been that they are amenable to manipulation by unscrupulous insiders managing earnings or mis-stating assets for their own ends. But if stock markets are at best semi-strongly efficient (the consensus in the academic literature), and if the creative accounting is opaque – skilled analysts do not have enough information to 'reverse out' the manipulation, or to 'see through' it – then share prices will be contaminated, just as accounting data are.

Indeed, the recent literature has been investigating the interplay of accounting manipulation and misinformed share prices in takeover strategies. Shleifer and Vishny (2003) present a theory of takeover in which rational executives exploit imperfectly informed equity markets. They make takeover bids when their own share price is higher than their inside information would justify, using their own equity as consideration, and hence gaining control of targets on favourable terms. As an extension of this, Shleifer and Vishny suggest that there will be incentives for executives to encourage their own share price upwards by earnings management that is not transparent to the equity market, and will therefore fool the market. Botsari and Meeks (2006) find evidence for UK acquirers (and Erikson and Wang (1999) for US acquirers) of the systematic use of accruals to manipulate earnings upwards ahead of a bid. In this literature, accounting issues are not just a measurement problem, but also form part of the motivation for, and tactics in, the takeover process.

Have the accounting problems become bigger or smaller since Ajit Singh's pioneering work on M&As? On the one hand, deals have become bigger, so the incentives to manipulate data have become stronger. And financial transactions have become more sophisticated (for example, the development of very complex and opaque financial instruments), so new opportunities to manipulate may for this reason have increased. But at the same time, accounting regulation has in that (almost) half century become vastly more strict, and the scope for accounting discretion – and hence cross-company differences in reporting – has in most cases been greatly diminished by the regulators.[21] Moreover, the supply of supplementary disclosures, to augment the basic accounts has increased greatly, offering the possibility of richer accounting studies for the researcher who is willing to go beyond statistical analysis of just the basic accounting variables. And the extra effort of such work is compensated by the dramatic improvements in computing power available compared with the 1960s, when Ajit Singh began his research.

So our conclusion is that such work is still fraught with difficulty; but there is no easy alternative way of answering the questions posed by Ajit Singh. And, on balance, it is no harder now than it was for his classic work.

Notes

1. Jensen and Ruback (1983) observe positive share-price movements, on average, for firms ahead of takeover and negative ones afterwards, and comment, 'post outcome negative abnormal returns are unsettling because they are inconsistent with market efficiency and suggest that changes in stock prices during takeover over-estimate the future efficiency gains from takeover'. Caves (1989) provides a revealing comparison of the two approaches.
2. Not only have the definitions of particular accounting variables changed, but also there have emerged a large number of supplementary disclosures in notes to the accounts: companies reveal a much richer set of information than is contained in the basic accounting variables. For example, market valuations are provided for some assets that appear in the financial statements at historic cost. The impact of such supplementary disclosures on company

and shareholder decisions is not captured by traditional statistical tests based only on data appearing on the face of the accounts.

3. Li (2007) provides a detailed historical and comparative review of the development of accounting for business combinations for three jurisdictions – the UK, the US and the domain of international standards.
4. There had been some doubt as to the legality of this practice, because it understated the premium on the issue of shares, but this uncertainty was resolved by an explicit permission under Section 131 of the 1985 Companies' Act.
5. Meeks and Meeks (1981) analyse this bias in statistical studies of the year of merger.
6. An excess of net assets over consideration (much less common in practice) gives rise to negative goodwill, which can be regarded either as a gain on the acquisition or as compensation for the cost of reorganizing the business to realize the full potential of its assets, as reflected in their valuation.
7. The deals reported using merger accounting rose from 105 (worth US$16.9 billion) in 1992 to 321 (worth US$213.8 billion) in 1997.
8. BBC News, 11 August 1998, quoted Jeremy Batstone of NatWest Stockbrokers: 'It is billed as a merger because there are accounting reasons why that would be more appropriate, but broadly speaking BP is in the top seat.' It should, however, be acknowledged that the BP/Amoco combination took place after the tightening of criteria for assessing a merger under UK standards (1994) and the judgement as to whether those criteria were met was a difficult one in this marginal case.
9. Meeks and Meeks (2001) analyse the way that accounting rules governing the reporting of transaction costs of takeover might distort takeover motives.
10. Although this will not result in a gain in assets if goodwill is taken into account:
    Goodwill = Purchase Consideration – Fair Value of Net Assets Acquired.
    Hence, the higher the fair value of assets acquired, the lower is the goodwill, the constraint being purchase consideration. It may sometimes be possible to exaggerate the fair value of purchase consideration when this is not cash or a fixed cash value. The purchase consideration can also be inflated by exaggerating acquisition costs when these are allowed to be included without strong safeguards against abuse.
11. An excellent analysis of the composition of goodwill is given by Johnson and Petrone (1998).
12. Ironically, this is now the only approach permitted by the regulators (see below).
13. Though lenders often deduct goodwill from assets when computing gearing ratios for, say, loan covenants.
14. The paper by Tweedie and Whittington (1990) was written before the ASB was established, but is a clear statement of the new chairman's priorities for reform.
15. When amortization was over a period of twenty years or less, a full impairment test was required only when a specific indicator of impairment had occurred.
16. And the resulting numbers seem to be more 'value-relevant' for equity prices than amortization figures (Li and Meeks, 2006).

17. The G4+1 standard-setters were the IASC plus those of the US, the UK, Canada, Australia and (latterly) New Zealand.
18. UK outward investment in equities rose from around £10 billion in 1994 to around £160 billion in 2000 (Meeks, 2003).
19. Acquirers are typically bigger than targets, so the cost of revaluation would be more than double.
20. For example, part of the consideration is sometimes related to future earnings – an 'earn-out'.
21. In one important respect, recent regulatory changes have increased managerial discretion: the (now universal) impairment approach to goodwill requires insider executives to base their impairment figures on their own estimates of future cash flows (see Li and Meeks, 2006; and the example of Marconi, above). We expect this to be a focus of managerial manipulation in coming years.

References

Accounting Standards Board (ASB), London: Financial Reporting Standards (FRS):
FRS3 (1992): Reporting financial performance;
FRS6 (1994): Acquisitions and mergers;
FRS7 (1994): Fair values in acquisition accounting;
FRS10 (1997): Goodwill and intangible assets;
FRS11 (1998): Impairment of fixed assets and goodwill;
FRS12 (1998): Provisions, contingent liabilities and contingent assets.

Accounting Standards Committee (ASC) (1990) *SSAP 22: Statement of Standard Accounting Practice 22, Accounting for Goodwill*, London: ASC.

Agrawal, A., J. Jaffe and G. Mandelker (1992) 'The Post-merger Performance of Acquiring Firms', *Journal of Finance*, 47: 1605–21.

Andrade, G., M. Mitchell, and E. Stafford (2001) 'New Evidence and Perspectives on Mergers', *Journal of Economic Perspectives*, 15 (2): 103–20.

Ayers, B., C. Lefanowicx and J. Robinson (2000) 'The Financial Statement Effects of Eliminating the Pooling-of-Interests Method of Acquisition Accounting', *Accounting Horizons*, 14: 1–19.

Botsari, A. and G. Meeks (2006) 'Do Acquirers Overstate Earnings Prior to a Share for Share Bid?', SSRN; available at: http://ssrn.com/abstract=952215.

Caves, R. (1989) 'Mergers, Takeovers and Economic Efficiency: Foresight vs. Hindsight', *International Journal of Industrial Organisation*, 7.

Chatterjee, R. and G. Meeks (1996) 'The Financial Effects of Takeover: Accounting Rates of Return and Accounting Regulation', *Journal of Business Finance and Accounting*, 23: 851–68.

Cosh, A., A. Hughes, K. Lee and A. Singh (1989) 'Institutional Investment, Mergers, and the Market for Corporate Control', *International Journal of Industrial Organisation*, 7: 73–100.

Dearing Report (1988) *The Making of Accounting Standards, Report of the Review Committee under the Chairmanship of Sir Ron Dearing CB*, London: Institute of Chartered Accountants in England and Wales.

Dickerson, A., H. Gibson and E. Tsakalotos (1997) 'The Impact of Acquisitions on Company Performance: Evidence from a Large Panel of UK Firms', *Oxford Economic Papers*, 49: 344–61.

Edwards, J., J. Kay and C. Mayer (1987) *The Economic Analysis of Accounting Profitability*, Oxford: Clarendon Press.

Erikson, M. and S. Wang (1999) 'Earnings Management by Acquiring Firms in Stock for Stock Mergers', *Journal of Accounting and Economics*, 27: 149–76.

Feder, B. J. and S. Schiesel (2002) 'WorldCom Finds $3.3 billion More in Irregularities', *New York Times*, 9 August.

G4+1 (1998) 'Discussion Paper: Business Combinations', Accounting Standards Board, London.

Gregory, A. (1997) 'An Examination of the Long-run Performance of UK Acquiring Firms', *Journal of Business Finance and Accounting*, 24: 971–1002.

Hughes, A. (1993) 'Mergers and Economic Performance in the U.K.', in M. Bishop and J. Kay (eds), *European Mergers and Merger Policy*, Oxford: Oxford University Press.

International Accounting Standards Board (2004) *IFRS3: International Financial Reporting Standard 3: Business Combinations*, London: IASCF.:

Jensen, M. and R. Ruback (1983) 'The Market for Corporate Control', *Journal of Financial Economics*, 11: 1–50.

Johnson, T. and K. Petrone (1998) 'Is Goodwill an Asset?', *Accounting Horizons*, 12 (September): 293–303.

Kumar, M. (1984) *Growth, Acquisition and Investment*, Cambridge: Cambridge University Press.

Kynaston, D. (2001) *The City of London, Vol. 4: A Club No More, 1945–2000*, London: Chatto & Windus.

Li, K. (2005) 'The Stock Market Reaction to Accounting for Goodwill', Ph.D. dissertation, University of Cambridge.

Li, K. (2007) 'Trends in Accounting for Business Combinations: A Sixty-year Review of Three Jurisdictions', Working paper, Judge Business School, Cambridge, UK.

Li, K. and G. Meeks (2006) 'The Impairment of Purchased Goodwill: Effects on Market Value', SSRN; available at: http://papers.ssrn.com/abstract=930979.

Lys, T. and L. Vincent (1995) 'An Analysis of Value Destruction in AT&T's Acquisition of NCR', *Journal of Financial Economics*, 39: 353–78.

Marris, R. (1964) *The Economic Theory of Managerial Capitalism*, London: Macmillan.

Meeks, G. (1977) *Disappointing Marriage: A Study of the Gains from Merger*, Cambridge: Cambridge University Press.

Meeks, G. (2003) 'Reporting to Shareholders: The Proposals in the Company Law Review', *Journal of Corporate Law Studies*, 3: 191–200.

Meeks, G. and J. Meeks (1981) 'Profitability Measures as Indicators of Post-merger Performance', *Journal of Industrial Economics*, 29: 335–44.

Meeks, G. and J. G. Meeks (2001) 'The Loser's Curse: Accounting for the Transaction Costs of Takeover and the Distortion of Takeover Motives', *Abacus*, 37: 389–400.

Mueller, D. (1980) *The Determinants and Effects of Mergers*, Cambridge, Mass.: Oelgeschlager, Gunn and Hain.

Nobes, C. (1997) *German Accounting Explained*, London: FT Finance.
Penman, S. H. (2001) *Financial Statement Analysis and Security Valuation*, Boston, Mass.: IrwinMcGraw-Hill.
Ravenscraft, D. and M. Scherer (1987) *Mergers, Sell-offs and Economic Efficiency*, Washington, DC: Brookings Institution.
Scherer, F. M. (1988) 'Corporate Takeovers: The Efficiency Arguments', *Journal of Economic Perspectives*, 69–82.
Shleifer, A. and R. Vishny (2003) 'Stock Market Driven Acquisitions', *Journal of Financial Economics*, 70: 295–311.
Singh, A. (1971) *Takeovers: Their Relevance to the Stock Market and the Theory of the Firm*, Cambridge: Cambridge University Press.
Singh, A. (1975) 'Take-overs, Economic Natural Selection, and the Theory of the Firm', *Economic Journal*, 85: 497–515.
Singh, A. (1997) 'Financial Liberalisation, Stock Markets and Economic Development', *Economic Journal*, 107: 771–82.
Singh, A. (1997) 'Liberalisation, the Stock Market and the Market for Corporate Control: A Bridge Too Far for the Indian Economy', *Cambridge Discussion Papers in Accounting and Finance*, 35.
Smith, T. (1992) *Accounting for Growth, Stripping the Camouflage from Company Accounts*, London: Century Business, Random House.
Stamp, E. (1969) 'The Public Accountant and the Public Interest', *Journal of Business Finance*, April: 32–42.
Tobin, J. (1961) 'Money, Capital and Other Stores of Value', *American Economic Review, Papers and Proceedings*, 51 (2) (May): 26–37.
Tweedie, D. and G. Whittington (1990) 'Financial Reporting: Current Problems and their Implications for Systematic Reform', *Accounting and Business Research*, 7 (4): 87–102.
Whittington, G. (1997) 'The Economic Rate of Return and the Accountant', in P. Arestis, G. Palma, and M. Sawyer, (eds.), Markets. Unemployment and Economic Policy, Essays in honour of Geoff Harcourt, Vol. 2, London: Routledge: 97–106.
Wilson, A., M. Davis M. Curtis and G. Wilkinson-Riddle (2001) *UK & International GAAP* (7th edn), London: Ernst and Young/Tolley.

11
Takeovers after *Takeovers*

Andy Cosh and Alan Hughes

Introduction

In this chapter we reflect on the contribution Ajit Singh has made to the study of takeovers as part of the 'natural selection' process in a capitalist market economy. Our emphasis is on the seminal contributions in his 1971 book, *Takeovers: Their Relevance to the Stock Market and the Theory of the Firm* (*Takeovers* hereafter), and his subsequent article in the *Economic Journal* (Singh, 1975). We consider in particular whether the key findings and interpretations in these contributions have stood the test of time.

The study of takeovers should be rooted in a specific institutional and historical context. We therefore concentrate solely, as Ajit did, on the UK, and consider only UK institutional and regulatory changes affecting the takeover process. There is, even so, a substantial subsequent literature (to which Ajit himself contributed) spanning the three decades since the original book and article were published. In a chapter of this kind we are inevitably confined to an illustrative rather than exhaustive discussion.

Takeovers

Takeovers had its origins in 1963 and Ajit's collaboration with Robin Marris and Geoffrey Whittington. The book's publication was delayed by the preparation of another book co-authored with Geoffrey Whittington, entitled *Growth, Profitability and Valuation* (Singh and Whittington, 1968). As Ajit wrote at the time of the publication of *Takeovers*, 'A study of surviving firms took precedence over an examination of those which did not survive – it is a moot point whether this is a correct order of priorities.'

The theoretical approach to the analysis in *Takeovers* is rooted in the theories of the firm proposed by William Baumol, Robin Marris and Oliver Williamson. These were linked to the 1930s work of Adolf Berle and Gardiner Means on the development of corporations with dispersed share ownership, and professional management whose motivations did not necessarily align with those of the shareholders. A pursuit of increased size for reasons of personal aggrandizement and higher rates of remuneration would, it was argued, predispose such companies to pursue size or growth at the expense of profits. In a world in which (following Means) there was limited product market competitive pressure, the role of disciplining managers and of aligning their decision-making with the welfare of shareholders would come to rest with the stock market. It would become a market for corporate control which selected the fittest companies for survival (Manne, 1965). Marris in particular, emphasized takeovers as a disciplinary mechanism constraining managerial ambitions (Marris, 1964).

In *Takeovers* Ajit developed a set of hypotheses characterizing the market for control as a selection mechanism and used a newly constructed data set of company accounts to test them. The latter was in itself a substantial intellectual effort, carried out in collaboration with Geoffrey Whittington. It was subsequently developed and maintained through the efforts of Geoff Meeks, Joyce Wheeler and others, and has provided a rich resource for many subsequent takeover studies.

The empirical analysis in *Takeovers* seeks to compare, in turn, the performance characteristics of acquired companies relative to those companies that were not acquired; the characteristics of acquiring companies compared to the companies they acquire; and the characteristics of the acquiring companies compared to non-acquiring, non-acquired companies and companies in general. It also examines the impact of takeover on the subsequent performance of acquiring and acquired firms. In a market selection process ensuring stockholder welfare satisfaction through profit maximizing behaviour, the natural selection hypotheses are that acquiring companies will be superior profitability performers, acquired companies will be inferior performers, and takeover will improve profitability performance. Using the financial accounts for several hundred UK public quoted companies, *Takeovers* contains both univariate and multivariate analyses of the short- and long-run profit, growth and other financial characteristics of acquiring and acquired companies relative to each other, and to other companies on the stock market. The analysis is notable for its careful discussion of problems of pooling takeovers from different time periods and sectors, and for the care taken in comparing alternative methods of discriminating between groups of firms. Use is made of matched samples and of multiple discriminant analysis, with detailed checks of the robustness of the results (including, given the rather strong multivariate normality assumptions of the discriminant approach, some non-parametric checks). Analysing the impact of takeover on company performance raises the problem of the counterfactual of what the performance would have been in the absence of takeover. The counterfactual devised has been used in many subsequent studies. It involves taking the weighted combination of the companies involved in the takeover relative to their sectoral performance and comparing it with the post-takeover performance of the merged company, again normalized by sector performance.

The principal findings of the analysis in *Takeovers* were that takeovers had become the dominant form of corporate 'death'; were becoming more intense over time; were, in contrast to the US, predominantly horizontal; and varied in intensity across industries and size classes. The likelihood of acquisitions in the largest size group was substantially lower and more strongly inversely related to company size than in the smaller size groups. Size, rate of growth, rate of profitability and stock market valuation ratio were all lower for acquired firms relative to those firms that were not acquired. This is what might have been expected on the basis of natural selection arguments. However, and much more significantly, the analysis showed clearly that there was an extremely large overlap between the acquired and non-acquired firms in terms of these characteristics. As a result, the ability to discriminate successfully between acquired and other firms was very low. Acquired and non-acquired companies, matched, for example, by size and industry, revealed very little difference between the groups. Where discrimination was successful, it tended to be in terms of short-run profitability, and in particular in terms of size. The overlap in characteristics between acquired and non-acquired companies increased between the period covered by *Takeovers* (1955–60) and that covered in the 1975 article (1967–70). By the latter period, an attempt to classify companies into acquired and surviving groups based on profitability alone would have had a 46 per cent probability of misclassification. The fact that size was a better discriminator in both periods led to the somewhat perverse implication that the best way to avoid takeover for a low profitability firm was not to increase profitability, but to grow, and that making takeovers may be the fastest way to do this.

The analysis of acquiring companies suggested that they were larger, more dynamic and more profitable than the companies they acquired (but not necessarily compared to non-acquired, non-acquiring companies). Table 11.1 shows a selection of results drawn from the 1975 *Economic Journal* article, which includes key results from *Takeovers*.

Table 11.1 Differences between acquired and acquiring companies, 1955–60 and 1967–70

	1955–60		1967–70	
Variable	***d/s***	***t*-statistics**	***d/s***	***t*-statistics**
Size (logarithms)	−1.50	−10.60*	−1.35*	−6.21*
2-year average profitability	−0.41	−2.93*	−0.29	−1.33
Growth	−0.69	−4.91*	−0.35	−1.60
2-year change in profitability	n.a.	n.a.	−0.70	−3.20*

Notes: * Significance level: 1%; *d* is the difference in the means of the acquired and acquiring group, and *s* is the estimated common standard deviation. A minus sign for d/*s* indicates that acquired firms had a mean value below acquiring firms.
Source: Singh (1975).

The table shows that the most statistically significant difference is to be found when size is used as a discriminating variable. Profitability is significant only in the first of the two periods. The short-term change in profitability is, however, significant in the later period (the analysis was not carried out for the earlier years). A further detailed analysis reveals a considerable overlap between the acquired and acquiring companies, but the results provides some comfort for the proponents of a natural selection argument. However, when the impact of the takeover on performance is assessed, a disappointing result emerges. The impact on pre-tax profitability, in the period 1955–60, for example, shows that in the first year after takeover, 66 per cent of the firms have a worse post-takeover performance when compared with the combined target and acquiring firm pre-takeover relative to industry profitability. Two years afterwards, 57 per cent have a worse takeover performance, and after three years, 77 per cent have a worse takeover performance. This outcome is not consistent with the prediction of the selection models.

In addition to these central findings the analysis in *Takeovers* included an examination of a number of topics that became important issues in later research. Thus the analysis also looked at the extent to which takeovers led to executive dismissals, which might be deemed to be consistent with the selection mechanism. It revealed little difference in executive retention between successful and unsuccessful acquired firms. The analysis also contrasted hostile with friendly takeovers, again as a particular variant of the selection model, and found few differences between them.

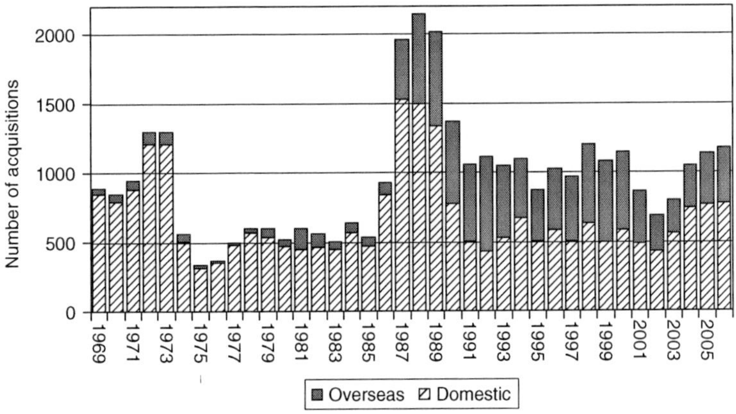

Figure 11.1 The growth and internationalization of takeovers: the number of domestic and overseas acquisitions by UK acquirers, 1969–2006
Source: Calculated from Office of National Statistics data.

As a result of these findings taken as a whole, Ajit concluded that the empirical basis for the takeover natural selection argument was very weak (Singh, 1975, p. 514).

We shall now examine how far these results and conclusions have stood the test of time.

Takeovers since *Takeovers*

The changing context of takeovers

There have been significant changes since the 1960s in both the nature of takeovers and the institutional framework in which they have occurred. Figures 11.1 and 11.2 show that takeovers have continued to occur in significant waves. The scale of these waves has, however, increased, as has the internationalization of the takeovers made by UK public companies. Figure 11.3 shows that the nature of share ownership has also changed dramatically. From the mid-1950s to the 1970s steady growth occurred in the importance of institutional investors as holders of UK equity, at the expense of individual shareholders. The decline of individuals as shareholders has continued unabated since the mid-1960s. What is most striking in Figure 11.3, however, is the major increase in overseas share ownership. The result has been that, from the early 1990s, the shares of UK institutional shareholders and pension funds have fallen. The internationalization of share ownership may potentially alter the extent to which shareholder interests are both perceived and

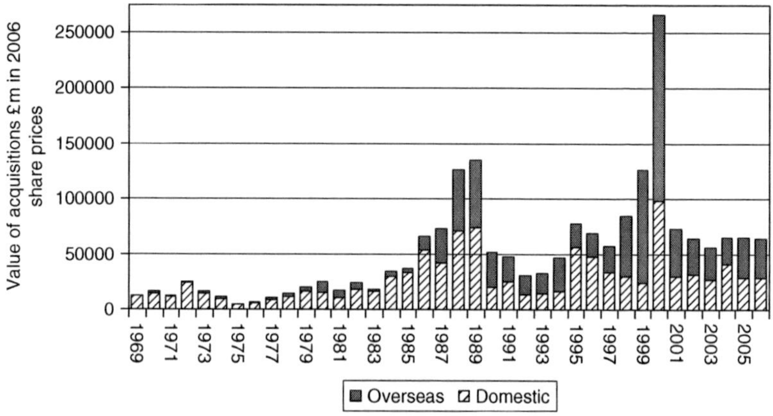

Figure 11.2 The growth and internationalization of takeovers: the value of domestic and overseas acquisitions by UK acquirers, 1969–2006 (stock market prices, 2006)
Source: Calculated from Office of National Statistics data.

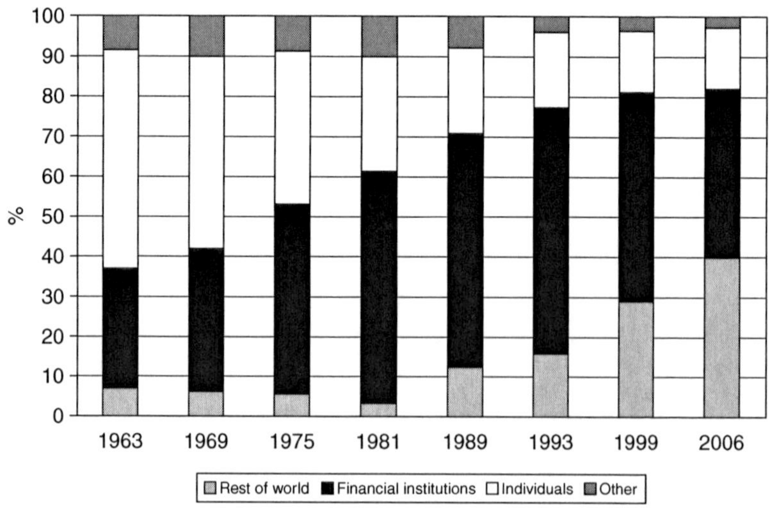

Figure 11.3 The rise and fall of institutional investors: beneficial ownership of UK shares, 1963–2006
Source: ONS (2007) *Share ownership: A Report on Ownership of Shares as at 31st December 2006, London: ONS.*

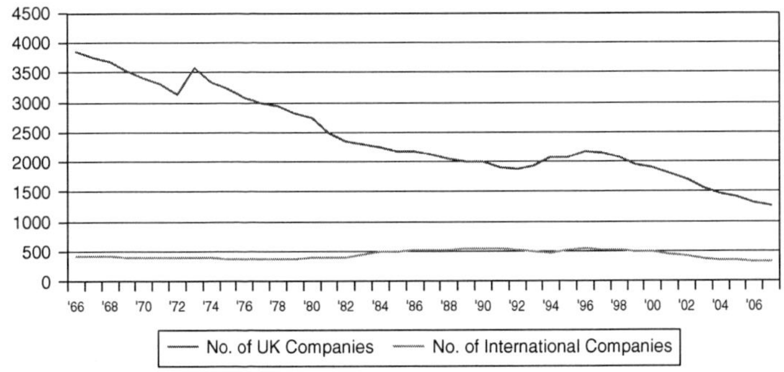

Figure 11.4 The fall and fall of UK quoted companies: numbers of quoted UK and international companies on London Stock Exchange, 1966–2007
Source: Stock Exchange historical statistics.

acted upon by investors. To the extent that overseas investors (consisting of a mix of individuals, overseas sovereign funds and overseas institutional investors) bring with them different attitudes to the nature of shareholder company relationships, then so too may the nature of the takeover process change. Equally, to the extent that collaborating action is more difficult to undertake when investors are spread internationally, the role of 'voices' may be diminished.

These developments have been accompanied by a decline in the incidence of public quoted company status. Figure 11.4 shows that the number of UK quoted companies has fallen, from almost 4,000 in the mid-1960s to fewer than 1,500 by the start of the twenty-first century. The number of international companies has remained more or less constant over this period. This trend is connected with the increasing importance of UK corporate reorganization via buy-outs, buy-ins and private equity takeovers that has led to the conversion of public companies to private status. By the start of the twenty-first century, between 20 per cent and 50 per cent of the value of total buy-out and buy-in activity was concerned with the conversion from public to private status (Wright *et al.*, 2006).

These major changes in the characteristics of the UK stock market, and the takeover process, has occurred at the same time as major changes in the regulatory framework affecting the takeover process. These changes have reflected dissatisfaction with the effectiveness of traditional forms of corporate governance in terms of board structure and function, and of the exercise of 'voice' and other direct activity by shareholders. They have also been fundamentally concerned with the operation of the takeover process itself.

These changes are reviewed in the context of governance and takeovers more generally in Cosh, Guest and Hughes (2007) 'UK Corporate Governance and Takeover Performance.'

A succession of reports in the 1990s led to the construction by 2003 of a combined code on corporate governance (Financial Reporting Council, 2003). The latest (2006) version of this combined code imposes obligations on institutional shareholders to take a responsible and active role in relation to the companies whose shares they own. In terms of board composition and board operations, the combined code emphasizes the need for a single board with collective responsibilities and a standard-setting role with a clear division of responsibilities between chairman and chief executive. In addition, at least 50 per cent of board members for larger corporates should be independent, non-executive directors. It also established procedures governing the evaluation of board effectiveness, the appointment of directors, and for setting executive remuneration and long-term incentive schemes. Remuneration is to be linked clearly to performance. An audit committee of independent directors with sufficient experience will be responsible for presenting a balanced assessment of the company's position and maintaining internal control procedures.[1] The most recent report, in 2007, which has a bearing on these issues was related in particular to private equity firms and the need for transparency in their operations (Walker, 2007).

At the same time as these persistent attempts to improve internal board government structures and the relationship between key external investors and the board, there has been the development of the City Takeover Code to regulate the actual process of takeover itself. The City Code on Takeovers and the operation of the Takeovers Panel, which enforces it in the UK, has been designed essentially to protect shareholders' interests and preserve an active market for corporate control. The focus is on shareholders alone and does not involve any discussion of wider stakeholder issues. The principal focus is on the equal treatment of stockholders. In particular, all bidders and shareholders are to be treated equally in relation to information and the timing of its release. Actions to frustrate bids that do not have shareholders' approval are particularly frowned upon.

While neither the Combined Code nor the Takeovers Panel operate with the force of law, their close links with requirements for stock market listing and accepted behaviour has meant that they have in effect come to dominate the practice of behaviour in these two areas. The rationale behind the approach adopted by the Takeover Code is implicitly, if not explicitly, that the orderly workings of the market for corporate control through takeovers are an essential part of the operation of the capital market and that they should be free to operate in as unhindered a way as possible in the interests of shareholders. One might expect that the emergence of the Code into a dominant position would have influenced the extent to which takeovers occurred in the interests of shareholders, and that this would reinforce the kinds of regulatory changes associated with the adoption of the combined governance code (Cosh *et al.*, 2007).

Pre-takeover characteristics

Hughes (1993) reviews thirteen studies that investigated the pre-takeover characteristics of acquired companies in the UK. These studies covered the period 1955 to 1986.[2] He concluded that acquired companies are always less dynamic pre-merger than control group companies, even if the difference is not always statistically significant. In relation to pre-takeover profitability, however, he concluded in particular that the differences between the acquired and control group or acquiring companies are minimized in periods of merger boom, when the groups become virtually indistinguishable. Moreover, where profitability differences do distinguish the acquired from the rest, it is in terms of short-term profitability in the years immediately preceding acquisition or declines in profit performance in those periods. In virtually all studies, size is a significant distinguishing characteristic of acquired versus acquiring companies. Acquiring companies are always larger than acquired companies. However, it is also apparent that the liability to acquisition of medium-sized to larger companies increases in merger booms.

In terms of post-takeover performance Hughes reviewed six studies of changes in accounting performance as a result of takeover, and fourteen studies reporting event study share return effects, or matched control group comparisons of measures of shareholder return based on capital gains and dividends.[3] The typical results using accounting studies and the Singh counterfactual and showing post-takeover falls are shown in Table 11.2.

Hughes concludes that there is evidence for improvements in profitability only in the case of diversifying mergers, but taken as a whole and in the case of horizontal acquisitions as a group, the impact on profitability is of a small variable, but negative movement in profitability in the post-merger compared to the pre-merger period. The studies focusing on short-term announcement effects on share returns show that any short-run gains for acquirers are outweighed by longer-term post-takeover losses. This is consistent with bids launched by acquirers

Table 11.2 Changes in normalized profitability[a] after merger in the UK, 1964–83.

	(1) Meeks 1964–71			**(2) Kumar 1967–74**			**(3) Cosh, Hughes, Lee and Singh 1981–3**	
Postmerger Year	**No. of companies (*n*)**	**Change in normalized profit**	**Percentage negative**	**No. of companies (*n*)**	**Change in normalized profit**	**Percentage negative**		
$t+3$	164	−0.06**	52.7	241	−0.08*	61†	1-year profitability	Lower n.s.
$t+5$	67	−0.11**	64.2†	186	−0.06	60†	3-year profitability	Lower n.s.
							Change in profitability	Lower sig. (10%)

Notes: †Significantly different from 50% at the 5% level. * Significantly different from the zero at the 5% level. ** Significantly different from zero at the 1% level. [a] Net income/net assets.
Source: Hughes (1993).

with 'overvalued' stock. There is some evidence that the combined short-run share price effects on acquirers and acquired company shareholders are positive or neutral because the targets receive substantial bid premiums. However, even the combined effects become negative in the longer term. He concludes that taken as a whole these studies suggest that acquirers launch their bids when their prices are relatively high (either by accident or by design). They also show that whatever positive short-term effects are associated with bids in the longer-run they are followed by cumulatively negative effects on the acquirers' shareholder performance.

There have been ten studies published since 1991, attempting to distinguish UK acquired companies from surviving companies.[4] They span the period 1948–96. Some of these studies have been carried out using similar methods to those described in *Takeovers*, but others involve using hazard function estimation procedures as well as probit and logit analysis, rather than discriminant analysis. They include the full range of financial variables considered in *Takeovers*, as well as some share return variables. The studies include several attempts to distinguish whether the profitability characteristics of firms subject to hostile bids were different from those subject to friendly bids.

In general, the results of these studies are supportive of the key findings of the results reported in *Takeovers*. In particular, attempts to discriminate in terms of rate of return between acquired companies and the rest, which use logit and probit approaches, find extremely poorly estimated models with very low rates of successful classification (Powell, 1997); Thompson, 1997; Barnes, 1999). Similarly, univariate comparisons of pre-takeover share returns or profitability show no significant differences between acquired companies and the rest (Franks and Mayer, 1996; Kennedy and Limmack, 1996; Cosh and Guest, 2001). The exception to these findings is Nuttall (1999a) who reports in an analysis of 643 UK quoted companies in the period 1989–96 that Tobin's q and the return on sales is statistically significantly negatively related to the probability of acquisition. He does not, however, report on the probabilities of misclassification arising from this analysis.

Regarding the question of hostility, Kennedy and Limmack (1996) report no difference in pre-takeover share returns between disciplinary and non-disciplinary bids, and Powell (1997) similarly finds no difference between the profitability characteristics of hostile and friendly targets. This result is echoed in Franks and Mayer (1996) and Cosh and Guest (2001). While Cosh and Guest (2001) report no pre-takeover differences in profitability between hostile and friendly targets and various control groups, they do report a significant fall in short-term profitability in hostile takeovers compared to control groups and friendly acquisitions in the year before the acquisition takes place. This analysis covering the period 1985–96 is consistent with the finding in Singh's original studies that short-term profitability falls may be related more closely to the acquisition probability than the average on medium-term rates of return before takeover. Cosh and Guest also report that the share return performance in the year before acquisition in hostile targets was significantly worse than for control groups and friendly targets, which reinforces this implication.

All the studies considered report that size is negatively related to the probability of takeover. The incidence of takeover declines with the size of the firm. In some periods, however, this may be non-linear, with the highest acquisition rates in medium-sized companies (see, for example, Dickerson *et al.*, 2002). In general, however, greater size is related to a lower likelihood of acquisition. There is some evidence that larger companies are more likely to be subject to hostile takeovers, though, as we have seen, this is not related to their profit performance (see, for example, Powell, 1997).

All the studies referred to so far have used either univariate comparisons or logit/probit models, which are closely related to the approach based on multiple discriminate analysis that Singh used in his original work on takeovers. In an interesting series of studies, however, an alternative estimation procedure has been used. These are the studies by Dickerson and colleagues, who examined the period from 1948 to 1990, making use of an updated version of the original Singh/Whittington data set.

In Dickerson *et al.* (1998) a discrete time analogue of the Cox proportional continuous time hazard function is estimated. Thus, given that a firm has survived up to any point in the data period, the method estimates the impact that a change in, say, size or profitability will have in terms of a change in its probability of takeover. They estimate this function for 2,839 UK non-financial companies in the time period 1948–70. While size is included as a variable affecting the conditional probability of acquisition along with measures of profitability, leverage, liquidity, investment, dividends and industry dummies, they do not report the change in conditional probability associated with changes in size. They do report, however, that higher dividends and higher investment both reduce significantly the conditional probability of takeover, with the impact of dividends being higher than that for investment in new assets. Since investment can increase the size of a company, they combine the total elasticity of investment and size, and show that it is only one-third as large as the effect of dividends. They conclude that the allocation of a marginal £1 of earnings by managers seeking to avoid acquisition would be to issue them in dividends rather than investing in assets. They do not regard these as being a trade-off between shareholder and manager interests, since this depends on the impact of investment of the future returns.

Dickerson *et al.* (2002) extended their analysis to the period 1970–91. This analysis covered 323 acquisitions in a sample of 892 UK-quoted companies. Using hazard function and probit analysis, they found that higher profitability, investment and dividends reduced the probability of takeover. In contrast to their findings for 1948–70, the impact of dividends is not always statistically significant. In the period after 1982 the impact of a change in profitability on the probability of being acquired was much lower. Their overall conclusion was that shareholders focus primarily on current profitability. These findings, using different estimation methods and including later time periods, confirm the important point in Singh's original work that short-run changes appear to have a much greater impact than longer-run or average effects, and confirm more generally the earlier results using univariate methods summarized in Hughes (1993).

Singh's further argument that a firm's best way to avoid acquisition is to grow through acquisition itself receives strong support in Dickerson *et al.* (2003). They showed that making a previous acquisition has a negative impact on the probability of subsequently being acquired. In the period 1948–70, the probability of subsequently being acquired fell by 27 per cent, and in the period 1975–90 it fell by 32 per cent. This effect, they argued, is mainly because of the impact of the increase in size following acquisition.

Post-takeover performance

Twenty-eight studies of the impact of acquisition on performance in the UK have been published since 1990,[5] covering takeovers occurring in the period 1948–2004. A wide range of performance variables was used in these studies. There is, however, a broad distinction between those performance analyses based on share price effects and those that focus on accounting returns.

There is a wide variation in the detail with which the share price effects are estimated. This is a result of the protracted discussions in the finance literature of the relevant benchmark to use when calculating whether the share returns experienced by a company are above what might have been expected. The other important distinction in share price studies is between those studies that focus on very short-term effects in time windows of a few days around merger events, and those that examine longer-run effects in the post-merger period (which can cover a period of up to 36 months, and occasionally longer). It is beyond the scope of this chapter to include a detailed discussion of the niceties of these alternative counterfactual estimates. There is a similar issue dealing with the appropriate accounting rate of return to use. This has also generated a distinctive methodological sub-literature, which is reviewed in recent studies of UK takeovers (see, for example, Conn *et al.*, 2005); Powell and Stark, 2005; and Cosh *et al.*, 2006).

If we focus on the returns experienced by the shareholders of acquiring companies, a fairly straightforward conclusion emerges. The announcement effects of takeover are bad for acquiring company shareholders: they most frequently lose wealth (Conn and Connell, 1990; Limmack, 1991; Sudarsanam *et al.*, 1996; Holl and Kyriazis, 1997; Sudarsanam and Maharte, 2003; Bild *et al.*, 2005; Conn *et al.*, 2005; Cosh *et al.*, 2006), or, in a few studies, are apparently made no worse off (Higson and Elliott, 1998; Cosh and Guest, 2001; Gregory and McCorriston, 2005; and Antoniou *et al.*, 2007). No studies have reported positive effects.

If we turn now to long-run post-takeover share performance, another gloomy picture emerges. There is some evidence that, in some time periods, long-run positive impacts can occur. Thus, for example, Higson and Elliott (1998) show significantly negative long-run returns to acquirers in the periods 1975–80 and 1985–90, but positive returns in the period 1981–4. Negative long-run share impacts over 12 to 36 months after the bid period are reported for acquiring companies in Limmack (1991), Kennedy and Limmack (1996), Gregory (1997), Sudarsanam and Mahate (2003), Conn *et al.* (2005) (though for private acquisitions the negative effect is statistically insignificant), Gregory and McCorriston (2005) (though the decline is insignificantly different from zero), Alexandridis *et al.* (2006), Antoniou *et al.* (2006) (although the declines are statistically insignificant), Cosh *et al.* (2006), Antoniou *et al.* (2007) and Antoniou *et al.* (2008). This is not a very happy story for the proponents of the view that the stock market selection process yields improvement in stock market performance as a result of the acquisition activity.

The studies of accounting performance as opposed to shareholder performance are more mixed. Approaches using variants of the original Singh normalization procedure typically find significantly negative impacts on most definitions of profitability. Negative impacts are found in Chatterjee and Meeks (1996) for the period 1977–84, but insignificantly positive effects for the period 1984–90 one year after the takeover is considered. They argue that the latter effects may reflect exploitation of changes in accounting standards in the mid1980s. Cosh *et al.* (1998) carried out a detailed study of profitability effects, correcting for possible selection bias in the allocation of companies into acquiring and acquired groups and allowing for regression to the norm in terms of profitability. They found that the normal tendency for profits to regress towards the mean was reinforced in the case of merging firms. Acquisition produces a deterioration in post-merger profitability compared to pre-merger profitability, which is faster than would be expected. Powell and Stark (2005), in a careful study of a variety of accounting measures and using results that allow alternatively for regression to the mean, or compare differences in normalized levels using the Singh procedures, find differences in results depending on the method and measure used. Thus, their analysis, covering the period 1985–93, shows significant improvement in operating performance in regression based models. These effects are weaker for pure cash flow measures compared to accruals-based measures. Analyses using Singh normalized rates of return show improvements that are lower than the regression model and are typically insignificantly different from zero. Bild *et al.*, studying 303 acquisitions in the UK over the period 1985–96 find that the post-takeover profitability on equity is significantly higher in the takeover year and each of the three years afterwards compared to controls. Cosh *et al.* (2006) in a detailed analysis of 363 UK public non-financial takeovers in the period 1985–96 provide an analysis of multiple accounting return measures and compare regression and normalized counterfactuals. They concluded that there is a significantly positive impact when operating profit returns are used, but an insignificantly positive impact when post-takeover cash flow returns are used.

A number of the accounting studies have touched on the issue of hostile compared to non-hostile bids. Cosh and Guest (2001), in their study of sixty-five hostile and 139 friendly takeovers in the period 1985–96 show that profitability increases significantly post-merger in hostile takeovers, but that there is no significant change in friendly takeovers. The difference in the returns between these two groups is also statistically significant. This is consistent with a more positive interpretation of the market for corporate control, and achieves some support from those long-run share price studies that have tried to distinguish between hostile and other takeovers. Thus Sudarsanam *et al.* (1996), Gregory (1997) and Higson and Elliott (1998) reported positive or less negative effects for hostile than other acquirers. Gregory and McCorriston (2005) reported no impact for hostility nor, despite their findings of significant profit differences between hostile and friendly takeovers, did Cosh and Guest (2001) find relatively improved share price performance in hostile takeovers. In fact they found insignificant negative declines in long-run returns for hostile takeovers combined with significantly negative returns for friendly takeovers. This is unrelated to the pre-acquisition performance of the target.

Taken as a whole, these results suggest that, in the short run, the shareholders of acquiring companies suffer significant wealth losses as a result of takeover. The bulk of the results also show that further long-run significant losses in shareholder wealth occur after the takeover has occurred. This does not suggest that there would be strong incentive effects for the shareholders of acquiring companies to encourage a process in which their managers are seen as the vanguard of a selection process to weed out inefficient firms. Acquisition simply makes them worse off.

If we focus instead on profit returns based on accounting data as a proxy for efficiency we find a much more mixed picture, which is clouded from the mid-1980s onwards by the possibility of accounting conventions distorting the results. For takeovers before then, Dickerson *et al.* (1997) may act as an overall summary. They analysed 1,143 acquisitions by 613 acquirers in the period 1948–77 and showed that acquisition has a significantly negative impact on profitability. The effect was a 4.07 percentage-point fall on average from the mean rate of return across all non-acquiring companies (the average being 16.45 per cent). In other words, there was a 25 per cent fall in profitability post-takeover. Dickerson *et al.* also report that these negative impacts were worsening over time and were much higher in the 1964–77 period than between 1948 and 1963.

So far, we have focused on acquisitions as single events. It is possible to argue that pooling together firms who make multiple acquisitions with firms that make a single acquisition may mask important differences between the two. Significant organizational learning effects may mean subsequent takeovers will yield better performance for the shareholders of the acquiring company than those earlier in the series. Conn *et al.* (2004) tested this hypothesis for 1,486 merger series covering 3,019 public and private acquisitions, of which only 805 involved a single acquisition. They show, by using both long-run share return and profit rate measures, that there is a steady deterioration in performance until the series ends in shareholder wealth losses.

Taking these studies as a whole we conclude that support for the idea that a selection process may be at work is strongest in the findings of profit improvements for hostile as opposed to friendly takeovers, but even these hold only for some time periods and some measures. However, acquiring company shareholders generally lose wealth no matter what the type of takeover.

Summary and conclusions

Our interpretation of the work that has been carried out on UK takeovers subsequent to Ajit Singh's seminal studies is simple. Singh's initial insight that the stock market was a very imperfect vehicle through which the natural selection process could be carried out has been supported substantially by subsequent work. This is most striking in relation to the inability to distinguish acquired companies from the rest in terms of their underlying profit or share price performance. Equally, there is very little evidence to support the view that the shareholders of acquiring companies should be motivated to support management who wish to carry out takeovers, on the grounds that they were extending their superior management skills to underperforming companies. Both the short-run and long-run share price impacts suggest that takeovers, on average, substantially worsen acquiring company shareholders' wealth. The evidence on profit impacts have become somewhat more positive over time, but depend critically on whether the period is before or after the major accounting standards changes affecting takeovers, and on whether cash flow or other methods of profit measurement are used.

The takeover process as a whole seems to be characterized more easily in terms of either the pursuit of managerial self-interest or in terms of the hubris hypothesis proposed by Roll (1986): 'If there really are no aggregate gains in takeover, the phenomenon depends on the overbearing presumption of bidders that their valuation is correct... there is little reason to expect that a particular individual bidder will refrain from bidding because he has learned from his own past errors' (p. 200).

Of course, it may be the case (as the current authors have heard argued in each successive takeover wave that has occurred) that the latest wave will be different from those preceding it. Lessons will have been learnt, and the nature of the takeover process will have changed. In terms of regulatory reform and change, it does not seem as though the nature of the process has changed dramatically despite the extent of changes we have noted in this chapter. Nevertheless, the latest version of the 'hope-springs-eternal' argument is to be found in claims at the time of writing that the role of private equity in the latest wave will show substantial gains from takeover. One of the virtues of proponents of this view while a wave is in progress is that it is difficult to evaluate the claims, because the current wave is invariably not the one that features in the current academic literature. This is partly an effect of the lags in the publication of academic results, but also of the need to allow a number of years to pass to enable the estimation of post-merger performance effects. It remains to be seen whether in five or ten years' time, when the dust has settled on the private equity boom, whether the conclusions that Ajit Singh drew in his original work will remain true. We repeat those and endorse them here: 'insofar as the neoclassical postulate of profit maximization relies on the doctrine of economic natural selection in the capital market (via the takeover mechanism) the empirical base for it is very weak' (Singh, 1975, p. 954).

Notes

1. The various reports leading up to this combined inclusion include Cadbury (1992); Greenbury (1995); Hampel (1998); Turnbull (1999); Higgs (2003).
2. These studies were Rose and Newbould (1967); Newbould (1970); Singh (1971); Buckley (1972); Kuehn (1975); Singh (1975); Davies and Kuehn (1977); Meeks (1977); Cosh *et al.* (1980); Levine and Aaronovitch (1981); Pickering (1983); Kumar (1984); Holl and Pickering (1988); Cosh *et al.* (1989).
3. The accounting studies are Singh (1971); Utton (1974); Meeks (1977); Cosh *et al.* (1980); Kumar (1984); Cosh *et al.* (1989). The share price studies also include Firth (1976, 1978, 1979, 1980); Franks *et al.* (1977); Barnes (1978); Barnes (1984); Sturgess and Wheale (1984); Dodds and Quek (1985); Franks and Harris (1986); Meadowcroft and Thompson (1986); Franks *et al.* (1988).
4. These studies are Franks and Mayer (1996); Kennedy and Limmack (1996); Powell (1997); Thompson (1997); Dickerson *et al.* (1998, 2002, 2003); Barnes (1999); Nuttall (1999); Cosh and Guest (2001).
5. These are Conn and Connell (1990); Limmack (1991); Chatterjee and Meeks (1996); Kennedy and Limmack (1996); Sudarsanam *et al.* (1996); Dickerson *et al.* (1997); Gregory (1997); Holl and Kyriazis (1997); Cosh *et al.* (1998, 2006); Higson and Elliott (1998); Manson *et al.* (2000); Cosh and Guest (2001); Tse and Soufani (2001); Raj and Forsyth (2002, 2003); Sudarsanam and Mahate (2003); Aw and Chatterjee (2004); Coakley and Thomas (2004); Abhyankaar *et al.* (2005); Bild *et al.* (2005); Conn *et al.* (2005); Gregory and McCorriston (2005); Powell and Stark (2005); Alexandridis and Antoniou (2006); Antoniou *et al.* (2006, 2007, 2008).

References

Abhyankaar, A., K.-Y. Ho, and H. Zhao (2005) 'Long-run Post-merger Stock Performance of UK Acquiring Firms: A Stochastic Dominance Perspective', *Applied Financial Economics*, 15: 679–90.

Alexandridis, G. and A. Antoniou (2006) 'Valuation Effects of Short Sale Constraints: The Case of Corporate Takeovers', *European Financial Management*, 12 (5): 747–62.

Antoniou, A., P. Arbour and H. Zhao (2006) 'The Effects of the Cross-correlation of Stock Returns on Post Merger Stock Performance', EFMA 2004 Basel Meetings Paper, Cass Business School Research Paper, September.

Antoniou, A., P. Arbour and H. Zhao (2008) 'How Much Is Too Much: Are Merger Premiums Too High?', *European Financial Management*, 14 (2): 268–87.

Antoniou, A., D. Petmezas and H. Zhao (2007) 'Bidder Gains and Losses of Firms Involved in Many Acquisitions', *Journal of Business Finance & Accounting*, 34 (7) & (8) (September/October): 1221–44.

Aw, M. S. B. and A. Chatterjee (2004) 'The Performance of UK Firms Acquiring Large Cross-border and Domestic Takeover Targets', *Applied Financial Economics*, 14: 337–49.

Barnes, P. (1999) 'Predicting UK Takeover Targets: Some Methodological Issues and an Empirical Study', *Review of Quantitative Finance and Accounting*, 12 (3): 283–301.

Barnes, P. A. (1978) 'The Effect of a Merger on the Share Price of the Attacker', *Accounting and Business Research*, 8: 162–8.

Barnes, P. A. (1984) 'The Effect of a Merger on the Share Price of the Attacker, Revisited', *Accounting and Business Research*, 15: 45–9.

Bild, N., P. Guest and M. Runsten (2005) 'The Effect of Takeover on the Fundamental Value of Acquirers', Centre for Business Research, University of Cambridge (revd version, 17 August).

Buckley, A. (1972) 'A Profile of Industrial Acquisition in 1971', *Accounting and Business Research*, 2: 243–52.

Cadbury, Sir A. (1992) *The Financial Aspects of Corporate Governance*, London: Financial Reporting Council.

Chatterjee, R. and G. Meeks (1996) 'The Financial Effects of Takeover Accounting Rates of Return and Accounting Regulation', *Journal of Business Finance & Accounting*, 23 (5) & (6): 851–68 (July).

Coakley, J. and H. M. Thomas (2004) 'Hot Markets, Momentum and Investor Sentiment in UK Acquisition', Finance Discussion Paper DP 04/09, University of Essex, January.

Conn, R. L. and F. Connell (1990) 'International Mergers: Returns to U.S. and British Firms', *Journal of Business Finance & Accounting*, 17 (5): 689–711: Winter.

Conn, R. L., A. Cosh, P. M. Guest and A. Hughes (2004) '*Why must all good things come to an end? The performance of multiple acquirers*' in Academy of Management (eds) Creating actionable knowledge: Academy of Management Best Paper Proceedings (64th), 6-11 August 2004, New Orleans, Louisiana, USA.

Conn, R. L., A. Cosh, P. M. Guest and A. Hughes (2005) 'The Impact on UK Acquirers of Domestic, Cross-border, Public and Private Acquisitions', *Journal of Business Finance & Accounting*, 32 (5) & (6): 815–70 (June/July).

Cosh, A. and P. Guest (2001) The Long-run Performance of Hostile Takeovers: UK Evidence', ESRC Centre for Business Research Working Paper No. 215, Centre for Business Research, University of Cambridge, September.

Cosh, A., P. M. Guest and A. Hughes (2006) 'Board Share-Ownership and Takeover Performance', *Journal of Business Finance & Accounting*, 33 (3) & (4) (April/May): 459–510.

Cosh, A., P. M. Guest and A. Hughes (2007) 'UK Corporate Governance and Takeover Performance', CBR Working Paper Series (December).

Cosh, A., A. Hughes and A. Singh (1980) 'The Causes and Effects of Takeovers in the United Kingdom', in D. C. Mueller, (ed.), *The Determinants and Effects of Mergers*, Cambridge, Mass.: Oelgeschlager, Gunn and Hain: 227–70.

Cosh, A., A. Hughes, K. Lee and A. Singh (1989) 'Institutional Investment, Mergers and the Market for Corporate Control', *International Journal of Industrial Organization*, March: 73–100.

Cosh, A., A. Hughes, K. Lee and A. Singh (1998) 'Takeovers, Institutional Investment and the Persistence of Profits', in I. Begg, and B. Henry (eds), *Applied Economics and Public Policy*, Department of Applied Economics Occasional Paper No. 63, Cambridge University Press.

Davies, J. R. and D. A. Kuehn (1977) 'An Investigation into the Effectiveness of a Capital Market Sanction on Poor Performance', in A. P. Jacquemin and H. W. de Jong (eds), *Welfare Aspects of Industrial Markets*, Leiden: Martinus Nijhoff.

Dickerson, A. P., H. D. Gibson and E. Tsakalotos (1997) 'The Impact of Acquisitions on Company Performance: Evidence from a Large Panel of UK Firms', *Oxford Economic Papers*, 49: 344–61.

Dickerson, A. P., H. D. Gibson and E. Tsakalotos (1998) 'Takeover Risk and Dividend Strategy: A Study of UK Firms', *The Journal of Industrial Economics*, XLVI: 281–300, September.

Dickerson, A. P., H. D. Gibson and E. Tsakalotos (2002) 'Takeover Risk and the Market of Corporate Control: The Experience of British Firms in the 1970s and 1980s', *International Journal of Industrial Organization*, 20 (8) (October): 1167–95.

Dickerson, A. P., H. D. Gibson and E. Tsakalotos (2003) 'Is Attack the Best Form of Defence? A Competing Risks Analysis of Acquisition Activity in the UK', *Cambridge Journal of Economics*, 27: 337–357.

Dodds, J. C. and J. P. Quek (1985) 'Effect of Mergers on the Share Price Movement of the Acquiring Firms: A UK Study', *Journal of Business Finance and Accounting*, 12: 285–96.

Financial Reporting Council (2003) *The Combined Code on Corporate Governance*, London: Financial Reporting Council, July.

Financial Reporting Council (2005) *Guidance on Audit Committees (The Smith Guidance)*, London: Financial Reporting Council, October.

Firth, M. (1976) *Share Prices and Mergers*, Farnborough: Saxon House/Lexington Books.

Firth, M. (1978) 'Synergism in Mergers: Some British Results', *Journal of Finance*, 33: 670–2.

Firth, M. (1979) 'The Profitability of Takeovers and Mergers', *Economic Journal*, 89: 316–28.

Firth, M. (1980) 'Takeovers, Shareholder Returns and the Theory of the Firm', *Quarterly Journal of Economics*, 94: 235–60.

Franks, J. R., J. E. Broyles and M.J. Hecht (1977) 'An Industry Study of the Profitability of Mergers in the United Kingdom', *Journal of Finance*, 32: 1513–25.

Franks, J. R. and R. S. Harris (1989) 'Shareholder Wealth Effects of Corporate Takeovers: The UK Experience 1955–85', *Journal of Financial Economics*, August: 225–49.

Franks, J. R., R. S. Harris and C. Mayer (1988) 'Means of Payment in Takeovers: Results for the United Kingdom and the Unites States', in A. J. Auerbach (ed.), *Corporate Takeovers Causes and Consequences*, Chicago: National Bureau of Economic Research/University of Chicago Press.

Franks, J. and C. Mayer (1996) 'Hostile Takeovers and the Correction of Managerial Failure', *Journal of Financial Economics*, 40: 163–81.

Franks, J., C. Mayer and L. Renneboog (2001) 'Who Disciplines Management in Poorly Performing Companies?', *Journal of Financial Intermediation*, 10 (3) & (4): 209–48.

Greenbury, Sir R. (1995) *Directors' Remuneration*, London: CBI.

Gregory, A. (1997) 'An Examination of the Long Run Performance of UK Acquiring Firms', *Journal of Business Finance & Accounting*, 24 (7) & (8): 971–1002, (September).

Gregory, A. and S. McCorriston (2005) 'Foreign Acquisitions by UK Limited Companies: Short- and Long-run Performance', *Journal of Empirical Finance*, 12: 99–125.

Hampel, R. (1998) *Committee on Corporate Governance, Final Report*, London: Gee Publishing.

Higgs, D. (2003) *Review of the Role and Effectiveness of Non-executive Directors*, London: Department of Trade and Industry.

Higson, C. and J. Elliott (1998) 'Post-takeover Returns: The UK Evidence', *Journal of Empirical Finance*, 5: 27–46.

Holl, P, and J. F. Pickering (1988) 'The Determinants and Effects of Actual Abandoned and Contested Mergers', *Managerial and Decision Economics*, 9: 1–19.

Holl, P. and D. Kyriazis (1997) 'Wealth Creation and Bid Resistance in UK Takeover Bids', *Strategic Management Journal*, 18 (6): 483–98.

Hughes, A. (1993) 'Mergers and Economic Performance in the UK: A Survey of the Empirical Evidence 1950–1990', in M. Bishop, and J. A. Kay (eds), *European Mergers and Merger Policy*, Oxford: Oxford University Press: 9–95.

Kennedy, V. A. and R. J. Limmack (1996) 'Takeover Activity, CEO Turnover, and the Market for Corporate Control', *Journal of Business Finance & Accounting*, 23 (2): 267–85, March.

Kuehn, D. A. (1975) *Takeovers and the Theory of the Firm*, London: Macmillan.

Kumar, M. S. (1984) *Growth, Acquisition and Investment*, Cambridge: Cambridge University Press.

Levine, P. and S. Aaronovitch (1981) 'The Financial Characteristics of Firms and Theories of Merger Activity', *Journal of Industrial Economics*, 30: 149–72.

Limmack, R. J. (1991) 'Corporate Mergers and Shareholder Wealth Effects: 1977–1986', *Accounting and Business Research*, 21 (83): 239–51.

Manne, H. (1965) 'Mergers and the Market for Corporate Control', *Journal of Political Economy*, 73: 110–120.

Manson, S., R. Powell, A. W. Stark and H. M. Thomas (2000) 'Identifying the Sources of Gains from Takeovers', *Accounting Forum*, 24 (4): 319–43.

Marris, R. (1964) *The Economic Theory of Managerial Capitalism*. London: Macmillan.

Meadowcroft, S. A. and D. J. Thompson (1986) 'Empirical Analysis of Returns to Pre-merger Shareholdings', Mimeo, Institute of Fiscal Studies.

Meeks, G. (1977) *Disappointing Marriage: A Study of the Gains from Merger*, Cambridge : Cambridge University Press.

Newbould, G. D. (1970) *Management and Merger Activity*, Liverpool: Guthstead.

Nuttall, R. (1999a) 'An Empirical Analysis of the Effects of the Threat of Takeover on UK Company Performance', Working Paper No. 5, Nuffield College, University of Oxford, 3 February.

Nuttall, R. (1999b) 'Takeover Likelihood Models for UK Quoted Companies', Working Paper No. 6, Nuffield College, University of Oxford, 3 January.

Pickering, J. F. (1983) 'Causes and Consequences of Abandoned Mergers', *Journal of Industrial Economics,* 31: 267–81.

Powell, R. G. (1997) 'Modelling Takeover Likelihood', *Journal of Business Finance & Accounting,* 24(7) & (8): 1009–30, (September).

Powell, R. G. and A. Stark (2005) 'Does Operating Performance Increase Post-takeover for UK Takeovers? A Comparison of Performance Measures and Benchmarks', *Journal of Corporate Finance,* 11: 293–317.

Raj, M. and M. Forsyth (2002) 'Hostile Bidders, Long-term Performance, and Restructuring Methods: Evidence from the UK', *American Business Review,* 20(1): 71–81, January.

Raj, M. and Forsyth, M. (2003) 'Hubris Amongst UK Bidders and Losses to Shareholders', *International Journal of Business,* 8 (1): 1–16.

Roll, R. (1986) The Hubris Hypothesis of Corporate Takeovers, *Journal of Business,* 59: 197–216.

Rose, H. B. and G. D. Newbould (1967) 'The 1967 Takeover Boom', *Moorgate and Wall Street,* Autumn: 5–24.

Singh, A. (1971) *Takeovers: Their Relevance to the Stock Market and the Theory of the Firm,* Cambridge: Cambridge University Press.

Singh, A. (1975) 'Take-overs, Economic Natural Selection, and the Theory of the Firm: Evidence from Postwar United Kingdom Experience', *Economic Journal,* 85 (339), September: 497–515.

Sturgess, B. and P. Wheale (1984) 'Merger Performance Evaluation: An Empirical Analysis of a Sample of UK Firms', *Journal of Economic Studies,* 11: 4.

Sudarsanam, S. and A.A. Mahate (2003) 'Glamour Acquirers, Method of Payment and Post-acquisition Performance: The UK Evidence', *Journal of Business Finance & Accounting,* 30 (1) & (2) (January/March): 299–342.

Sudarsanam, S. and A. A. Mahate (2006) 'Are Friendly Acquisitions Too Bad for Shareholders and Manager? Long-Term Value Creation and Top Management Turnover in Hostile and Friendly Acquirers', *British Journal of Management,* 17: 7–30.

Sudarsanam, S., P. Holl and A. Salami (1996) 'Shareholder Wealth Gains in Mergers: Effect of Synergy and Ownership Structure', *Journal of Business Finance & Accounting,* 23 (5) & (6): 673–98, July.

Thompson, S. (1997) 'Takeover Activity Among Financial Mutuals: An Analysis of Target Characteristics', *Journal of Banking & Finance,* 21: 37–53.

Tse, T. and K. Soufani (2001) 'Wealth Effects of Takeovers in Merger Activity Eras: Empirical Evidence from the UK', *International Journal of the Economics of Business,* 8 (3): 365–77.

Turnbull, N. (The Turnbull Report) (1999) *Internal Control: Guidance for Directors on the Combined Code,* London: Financial Reporting Council.

Utton, M. A. (1974) 'On Measuring the Effects of Industrial Mergers', *Scottish Journal of Political Economy,* 21: 13–28.

Walker, D. (2007) *Disclosure and Transparency in Private Equity,* Consultation document, July, The Walker Working Group, London.

Appendix: Ajit Singh Publications

Modern Business Enterprise, Corporate Organization, Finance and Governance in Advanced Economies and in Emerging Markets; The Theory of the Firm, Takeovers and the Stock Market; The Financial System and the Real Economy

Marris, R. L. and A. Singh (1966) 'A Measure of a Firm's Average Share Price', *Journal of the Royal Statistical Society*, Series A (General), 129, Part I.

Singh, A. and G. Whittington (1968) *Growth, Profitability and Valuation*, Cambridge: Cambridge University Press.

Singh, A. (1971) *Takeovers: Their Relevance to the Stock Market and the Theory of the Firm*, Cambridge: Cambridge University Press.

Singh, A. (1975) 'Takeovers, Economic Natural Selection and the Theory of the Firm: Evidence from the Post-War UK Experience', *Economic Journal*, 85 (339), September. (Republished in an Italian translation in *Problemi di Teoria Dell'Impressa*; and in L. Wagner (ed.), *Readings in Applied Microeconomics*, Oxford: Oxford University Press: 1981; and in G. Marchildon (ed.), *Mergers and Acquisitions*, London: Edward Elgar: 207–25, 1992.

Singh, A. and G. Whittington (1975) 'The Size and Growth of Firms', *Review of Economic Studies*, XLII (1), January. (Republished in an Italian translation in A. H. Cardani and U. Pedol (eds), *Problemi di Teoria Dell'Impressa*, Etas Libri, 1980).

Singh, A. (1976) 'Review of Douglas Kuehn, *Takeovers and the Theory of the Firm*', *Journal of Economic Literature*, 14 (2) (June).

Cosh, A., A. Hughes and A. Singh (1980) 'The Causes and Effects of Mergers in the UK: An Empirical Investigation for the late 1960s at the Microeconomic Level', in *The Determinants and Effects of Mergers: An International Comparison*, Cambridge, Mass: Oelgeschlager, Gunn & Hain.

Hughes, A., D. Mueller and A. Singh (1980) 'Hypotheses about Mergers', in *The Determinants and Effects of Mergers: An International Comparison*, Cambridge, Mass: Oelgeschlager, Gunn & Hain.

Hughes, A., D. Mueller and A. Singh (1980) 'Competition Policy in the 1980s: The Implications of the International Merger Wave', in *The Determinants and Effects of Mergers: An International Comparison*, Cambridge, Mass: Oelgeschlager, Gunn & Hain.

Hughes, A. and A. Singh (1980) 'Mergers, Concentration and Competition in Advanced Capitalist Economies: An International Perspective', in *The Determinants and Effects of Mergers: An International Comparison*, Cambridge, Mass.: Oelgeschlager, Gunn & Hain.

Cosh, A. D., A. Hughes, K. Lee and A. Singh (1989) 'Institutional Investment and the Market for Corporate Control', *International Journal of Industrial Organisation*, March.

Cosh, A. D., A. Hughes and A. Singh (1990) 'Takeovers, Short-termism and Finance-industry Relations in the UK Economy: Analytical and Policy issues', in *Takeovers and Short-termism in the UK*, London, Industrial Policy Paper No. 3, Institute of Public Policy Research.

Hughes, A. and A. Singh (1990) 'Takeovers and the Stock Market', *Contributions to Political Economy*, 6, 1987. (Republished in J. Eatwell, M. Milgate, and P. Newman (eds), *Financial Markets*, London/New York: Macmillan.)

Singh, A. (1990) 'The Institution of a Stock Market in a Socialist Economy: Notes on the Chinese Economic Reform Programme', in Dong Fureng and Peter Nolan (eds), *The Chinese Economy and its Future: Achievements and Problems of Post-Mao Reforms*, Cambridge: Polity Press.

Cosh, A. D., A. Hughes and A. Singh (1992) 'Openness, Financial Innovation and the Changing Structure of the UK and the Global Capital Markets', in Juliet Schor and Tariq Banuri (eds), *Financial Openness and National Autonomy*, Oxford: Clarendon Press.

Singh, A. (1992) 'Corporate Takeovers', in *The New Palgrave Dictionary of Money and Finance*, edited by John Eatwell, Murray Milgate and Peter Newman, London/New York: Macmillan.

Singh, A. and J. Hamid (1992) *Corporate Financial Structures in Developing Countries*, IFC Technical Paper No. 1, World Bank, Washington, DC (xii + 147 pp.). This monograph was among the first studies of its kind.

Singh, A. (1993) 'Regulation of Mergers: A New Agenda', in Roger Sugden (ed.), *Industrial Economic Regulation: A Framework and an Exploration*, London: Routledge.

Singh, A. (1993) 'The Stock Market and Economic Development: Should Developing Countries Encourage Stock Markets?', *UNCTAD Review*, 4.

Singh, A. (1993) 'Normative Relative alle Fusioni Negli USA e nel Regno Unito: Una Nuova Agenda', *Economia e Politica Industriale*, 77.

Amsden, A. and A. Singh (1994) 'The Optimal Degree of Competition and Dynamic Efficiency in Japan and Korea', *European Economic Review*, 38 (3/4): 940–51.

Amsden, A. and A. Singh, (1994) 'Concurrence Dirigée et Efficacité Dynamique en Asie; Japon; Koree du Sud; Taiwan', *Revue du Tiers-Monde*, 139, July–September: 643–57.

Singh, A. (1994) 'Takeover delle Imprese: Una Rassegna', *Economia e Politica Industriale*, 82.

Singh, A. (1994) 'How do Large Corporations in Developing Countries Finance their Growth?', in Richard O'Brien (ed.), *The AMEX Bank Prize Essays: Finance and the International Economy*, New York: Oxford University Press.

Singh, A. (1995) 'The Stock Market, Economic Efficiency and Industrial Development', in P. Arestis and V. Chick (eds), *Finance, Development and Structural Change: Post-Keynsian Perspectives*, London: Edward Elgar.

Singh, A. (1995) *Corporate Financial Patterns in Industrialising Economies: A Comparative International Study*, IFC Technical Paper No. 2, World Bank, Washington, DC (ISBN 0-8213-3231-7).

Cosh, A. D., A. Hughes, K. Lee and A. Singh (1996) 'Takeovers, Institutional Investment and the Persistence of Profits', ESRC Centre for Business Research, University of Cambridge, Working Paper No. 30, March. Subsequently published in Ian Begg and S. G. B. Henry (eds), *Applied Economics and Public Policy*, Cambridge, Cambridge University Press, 1998: 107–44.

Singh, A. (1996) 'Emerging Markets, Industrialisation and Development', in S. Sen, *Financial Fragility, Debt and Economic Reforms*, London/New York: Macmillan.

Singh, A. (1996) 'Pension Reform, the Stock Market, Capital Formation and Economic Growth: A Critical Commentary on the World Bank's Proposals', *International Social Security Review*, 49 (3): 21–44.

Singh, A. (1996) 'The Stock Market, the Financing of Corporate Growth and Indian Industrial Development', *Journal of International Finance*, 4 (2) (Fall): 1–17.

Singh, A. (1996) 'Profits, Savings, Investment and Fast Economic Growth: A Perspective on Asian Catch-up and Implications for Latin America', Department of Applied Economics, University of Cambridge, Discussion Paper in Finance and Accounting, No. AF33.

Singh, A. (1996) 'Investment, Savings and Economic Growth in East Asia', *International Capital Markets*, 16 (4) (December): 9–13.

Singh, A. (1997) 'Financial Liberalisation, the Stock Market and Economic Development', *Economic Journal*, May: 771–82. Subsequently republished in Portuguese in *Nova Economia*, (2000) 8 (1) (July) 1998; also republished in H. Dixon (ed.), *Controversies in Macro-Economics: Growth Trade and Policy*, Oxford: Blackwell: 206–18.

Singh, A. (1997) 'Portfolio Equity Flows and Stock Markets in Financial Liberalisation', *Development*, 40, (3): 22–9.

Whittington, G., V. Saporta, and A. Singh (1997) *The Effects of Hyper-Inflation on Accounting Ratios: Financing of Corporate Growth in Industrialising Economies*, IFC Technical Paper No. 3, World Bank, Washington, DC.

Singh, A. (1998) 'Savings, Investment and the Corporation in the East Asian Miracle', UNCTAD, Geneva, Study No. 9. Subsequently published in the *Journal of Development Studies*, 34 (6): 112–37. Subsequently republished in Y. Akyuz and R. Kozul-Wright (eds), *East Asian Development*, London: Frank Cass.

Singh, A. (1998) 'Liberalisation, the Stock Market and the Market for Corporate Control: A Bridge too far for the Indian Economy?', in I. J. Ahulwalia and I. M. D. Little (eds), *India's Economic Reform and Development*, New Delhi: Oxford University Press: 169–96. Also republished in Sima Motamen-Samadian and Celso Garrido (eds), *Emerging Markets: Past and Present Experiences, and Future Prospects*, London: Macmillan.

Singh, A. and B. Weisse (1998) 'Emerging Stock Markets, Portfolio Capital Flows and Long-term Economic Growth: Micro and Macroeconomic Perspectives', *World Development*, 26 (4) (April): 607–22.

Glen, J., A. Singh, and R. Matthias (1999) 'How Intensive Is Competition in Emerging Markets? An Analysis of Corporate Rates of Return from Nine Emerging Markets', International Monetary Fund Working Paper, No. WP/99/32, Washington, DC.

Singh, A. (1999) 'Should Africa Promote Stock Market Capitalism?', *Journal of International Development*, 11 (3): 343–67.

Singh, A. and R. Dhumale (1999) 'Competition Policy, Development and Developing Countries', Working Paper 7, South Centre, Geneva. Republished in P. Arestis, M. C. Baddeley and J. S. L. McCombie (eds), *What Global Economic Crisis?*, Basingstoke: Palgrave.

Glen, J., K. Lee and A. Singh (2000) 'Competition, Corporate Governance and Financing of Corporate Growth in Emerging Markets', Department of Applied Economics, Cambridge, Discussion Papers in Accounting and Finance, No. AF46.

Singh, A. (2000) 'The Anglo-Saxon Market for Corporate Control, the Financial System and International Competitiveness', Department of Applied Economics, Discussion Paper in Finance and Accounting, No. AF16, 1995. A revised version of this paper was published in C. Howes and A. Singh (eds), *Competitiveness Matters*, Ann Arbor, Mich.: University of Michigan Press.

Singh, A., A. Singh and B. Weisse (2000) 'Information Technology, Venture Capital and the Stock Market', Department of Applied Economics, Cambridge, Discussion Papers in Accounting and Finance, No. AF47.

Singh, A. and J. A. Zammit (2000) 'International Capital Flows: Identifying the Gender Dimension', *World Development*, 28 (7): 1249–68.

Glen, J., K. Lee and A. Singh (2001) 'Persistence of Profitability and Competition in Emerging Markets', *Economics Letters*, 72: 247–53.

Glen, J., K. Lee and A. Singh (2001) 'Intensity of Competition in Emerging Markets and in Advanced Economies', *Viertejahrsheft zur Wirtschaftsforschung*, 2: 70.

Singh, A. (2001) 'Financial Liberalisation and Globalisation: Implications for Industrial and Industrialising Economies', in K. S. Jomo and S. Nagraj (eds), *Globalisation versus Development*, Basingstoke: Macmillan.

Singh, A. and B. Weisse (2001) 'Mergers and Acquisitions', in Jonathan Michie (ed.), *Reader's Guide to the Social Sciences*, vol. 2, London: Fitzroy Dearborn.

Glen, J., K. Lee and A. Singh (2002) 'Corporate Profitability and the Dynamics of Competition in Emerging Markets: A Time Series Analysis', Working Paper No. 248, Working Paper Series, Centre for Business Research, University of Cambridge. A revised version published in *Economic Journal*, 113 (November) 2003: F465–F484.

Singh, A. (2002) 'Competition and Competition Policy in Emerging Markets: International and Developmental Dimensions', Working Paper No. 246, Working Paper Series, Centre for Business Research, University of Cambridge (2002). Also available in the G-24 Discussion Paper Series, No.18, UNCTAD, and Center for International Development, Harvard University, September.

Singh, A. (2002) 'Corporate Governance, the Big Business Groups and the G-7 Reform Agenda: A Critical Analysis', *Seoul Journal of Economics*, 15, (2): 103–48.

Singh, A. (2002) 'Competition, Corporate Governance and Selection in Emerging Markets', Working Paper (247, Working Paper Series, Centre for Business Research, University of Cambridge. A revised version of this paper published in *Economic Journal*, 113 (November) 2003): F443–F464.

Glen, J. and A. Singh (2003) 'Capital Structure, Rates of Return and Financing Corporate Growth: Comparing Developed and Emerging Markets', Working Paper No. 265, Centre for Business Research, University of Cambridge. A revised version published in Robert E. Litan, Michael Pomerleano, V. Sundararajan (eds), *Future of Domestic Capital Markets*, Washington, DC: Brookings Press, (2003): 373–416.

Singh, Ajit., Alaka Singh and Bruce Weisse (2003) 'Corporate Governance, Competition, the New International Financial Architecture and Large Corporations in Emerging Markets', Working Paper No. 250, Working Paper Series, Centre for Business Research, University of Cambridge, 2002. A revised version published subsequently in UNCTAD (ed.), *Management of Capital Flows*, Geneva: UNCTAD: 1–70.

Singh, A. (2003) 'Corporate Governance, Corporate Finance and Stock Markets in Emerging Countries', Working Paper No. 258, Working Paper Series, Centre for Business Research, University of Cambridge. A revised version published in *Journal of Corporate Law Studies*, 3, Part 1 (April): 41–72.

Singh, A. (2003) 'The New International Financial Architecture, Corporate Governance and Competition in Emerging Markets: New Issues for Developing Economies', in Ha-Joon Chang (ed.), *Rethinking Development Economics*, London: Anthem Press: 377–403.

Glen, J. and A. Singh (2004) 'Comparing Capital Structures and Rates of Return in Developed and Emerging Markets', *Emerging Markets Review*, 5 (2): 161–92.

Glen, J. and A. Singh (2004) 'Corporate Governance, Competition and Finance: Re-thinking Lessons from the Asian Crisis', CBR Working Paper No. 288, June. Subsequently published in *Eastern Economic Journal*, 31(2) (Spring) 2005: 219–42. The paper won an honourable mention in the Otto Eckstein competition for the best article in the journal for the two years 2004–2006.

Singh, A. (2004) 'Corporate Social Responsibility': A Developmental Perspective', *Oil, Gas and Energy Law Journal* (Special Issue on Business and Human Rights). Available at: www.gasandoil.com/ogel

Singh, A. (2004) *Multilateral Competition Policy and Economic Development. A Developing Country Perspective on the European Community Proposals*, UNCTAD Series, on Issues in Competition Law and Policy, United Nations, New York and Geneva (UNCTAD/DITC/CLP/2003/10).

Singh, A. and R. Dhumale R. (2004) 'Competition Policy, Development and Developing Countries', in P. Arestis, M. Baddeley and J. McCombie (eds), *What Global Economic Crisis?*, Paperback edn, Basingstoke: Palgrave Macmillan: 122–45.

Singh, A., J. Glen, A. Zammit, R. De Hoyos, Alaka Singh and B. Weisse (2005) 'Shareholder Value Maximisation, Stock Market and New Technology: Should the US Corporate Model Be the Universal Standard?', *Asia–Europe Papers*, Discussion Paper No.1, July. Also published as CBR Working paper No. 315. Subsequently published in *International Review of Applied Economics*, 19 (4) (October) 2005: 419–37.

Singh, A. (2006) 'Stock Market and Economic Development', in David Alexander Clark (ed.), *The Elgar Companion to Development Studies*, Cheltenham: Edward Elgar: 584–90.

Singh, A. and A. Zammit (2006) 'Corporate Governance, Crony Capitalism and Economic Crises: Should the US Business Model Replace the Asian Way of Doing Business?, Working Paper No. 329, June, Working Paper Series, Cambridge Centre for Business Research, Cambridge. Subsequently published in *Corporate Governance: An International Review*, July 2006.

Singh, A. (2007) 'Economic Crisis and the Asian Way of Doing Business', *Business Economist*, 38 (2): 9–21. This paper was short-listed for the Rybczynski Prize.

Fagernas, S., P. Sarkar and A. Singh (2007) 'The Legal Protection of Investors and Stock Market Development', Working Paper, 343, 2007, Working Paper Series, Cambridge Centre for Business Research, Cambridge. Forthcoming in Gugler, K. and B. Yurtoglu (eds), *The Economics of Corporate Governance and Mergers: Essays in Honour of Dennis Mueller*, London: Edward Elgar.

Armour, J., S. Deakin, P. Sarkar, M. Siems and A. Singh (2007) 'Shareholder Protection and Stock Market Development: An Empirical Test of the Legal Origins Hypothesis', Working Paper 358, 2007, Working Paper Series, Cambridge Centre for Business Research, Cambridge. Also available as ECGI – Law Working Paper No. 108/2008.

In relation to the contributions above, my long-term research programme has been to investigate the workings of the financial markets and examine their implications for the real economy. I have focused increasingly during the last ten years or more on emerging markets. The current themes of the research programme are (a) issues of stock market, corporate control and corporate governance, including those related to the financial crisis in East Asia; (b) analyses of micro- as well as macroeconomic aspects of foreign capital flows into these economies. I am carrying out research projects on these subjects at the Cambridge Endowment for Research in Finance (CERF) at the Judge Business School, Cambridge, in collaboration with colleagues from the IFC (World Bank) and Universities of Leicester, Birmingham and Vienna. The research programme has been consolidated and extended to include work on law and finance at the Centre for Business Research (CBR) in Cambridge. The latter project is being carried out in collaboration with Professor Simon Deakin of the Law Faculty, Cambridge, and Professor John Armour of the Law Faculty at Oxford. The project is funded to the tune of £200,000 by the ESRC. The project has also been awarded additional funding of £30,000 by the Newton Trust.

I am also carrying out other research under the auspices of the Centre for Business Research, Cambridge, investigating questions relating to the state of competition in product and capital markets in the UK and other industrial countries.

Deindustrialization and Long-term Structural Changes in the United Kingdom and other Advanced Economies; North–South Competition and Issues of Employment and Unemployment in the North and the South; Liberalization and Globalization of Financial and Product Markets

Singh, A. (1977) 'UK Industry and the World Economy: A Case of De-Industrialisation?', *Cambridge Journal of Economics*, 1 (2). Also published in A. P. Jacquemin and H. W. de Jong (eds), *Welfare Aspects of Industrial Markets*, Nijenrode Studies in Economics, vol. 2, The Hague, 1977. Also republished in C. H. Feinstein (ed.), *The Managed Economy: Essays in British Economic Policy and Performance since 1930*, Economic History Society, Oxford: Clarendon Press, 1983.

Singh, A. (1979) 'North Sea Oil and the Reconstruction of UK Industry', in F. Blackaby (ed.), *De-industrialisation*, National Institute of Economic and Social Research, Economic Policy Paper No. 2, London: Heinemann.

Singh, A. (1980) 'De-industrialisation in the UK and Investment Planning', in W. Hafkamp and G. Reuten (eds), *Investment and Unemployment: Perspectives on Policy and Planning*, Brussels/Alphen aan de Rijn: Samson.

Singh, A. (1980) 'Industrial Policy and the Economics of Disequilibrium: A Reply to Professors de Jong and Van der Zwan', in W. Hafkamp and G. Reuten (eds), *Investment and Unemployment: Perspectives on Policy and Planning*, Brussels/ Alphen aan de Rijn: Samson.

Singh, A. (1981) 'Third World Industrialisation and the Structure of the World Economy', in D. Currie, D. Peel and W. Peters (eds), *Microeconomic Analysis: Essays in Microeconomics and Economic Development*, London: Croom Helm.

Singh, A. (1981) 'Uncertainty, Multiple Objectives and Optimal Regulation: The Regulation of the Petroleum Industry in Norway', Comment on Mr Ekbo's paper in T. Barker, and V. Brailovsky (eds), *Oil or Industry?*, London: Academic Press.

Singh, A. (1982) 'Structural Changes in the UK Economy: A Long-Term Structural Analysis of the UK's Trade with Less Developed Countries and its impact on the UK Economy', Vienna : UNIDO.

Singh, A. (1984) 'Long-Term Structural Disequilibrium of the UK Economy: Employment, Trade and Import Controls', in R. Parboni (ed.), *L'Europa Nella Crisi Economica Mondiale*, Milan: Franco Agnelli. Also published in G. Sjostedt and B. Sunderlius (eds), *Free Trade – Managed Trade? Perspectives on a Realistic International Trade Order*, London: Swedish Institute of International Affairs/ Westview Press 1986.

Singh, A. (1985) 'The World Trading and Payments System, Economic Growth and Structural Change', *Economic and Political Weekly*, XX (1) (January).

Singh, A. (1987) 'Manufacturing and De-industrialisation', *The New Palgrave: A Dictionary of Economics*, London: Macmillan.

Singh, A. (1989) 'Third World Competition and De-Industrialisation in Advanced Countries', *Cambridge Journal of Economics* (March) 1989. Republished in T. Lawson, J. G. Palma and J. Sender (eds), *Kaldor's Political Economy*, London: Academic Press.

Glyn, A., A. Hughes, A. Lipietz and A. Singh (1990) 'The Rise and Fall of the Golden Age: A Historical Analysis of Post-War Capitalism in the Developed Market Economies', in S. Marglin and J. Schor (eds), *The Golden Age of Capitalism: Re-interpreting the Post-War Experience*, Oxford: Clarendon Press.

Singh, A. (1990) 'Global Rules and a New Golden Age: Southern Competition, Labour Standards and Industrial Development in the North and the South', in *Labour Standards, Development and the Global Economy*, US Department of Labor, Washington, DC.

Singh, A. (1991) 'International Competitiveness and Industrial Policy', in Irfan Ul Haque (ed.), *International Competitiveness*, DC: EDI Seminar Series, World Bank, Washington.

Singh, A. (1991) 'Labour Markets and Structural Adjustments: A Global View', in Guy Standing and Victor Tokman (eds), *Towards Social Adjustment: Labour Market Issues in Structural Adjustment*, Geneva: ILO.

Singh, A. (1992) 'Industrial Policy in the South: Alternative Perspectives for the 1990s', in Keith Cowling and Roger Sugden (eds), *Current Issues in Industrial Strategy*, Manchester: Manchester University Press.

Singh, A. (1992) 'Comment: The Political Economy of Growth', in J. Michie (ed.), *The Economic Legacy 1979–1992*, London: Academic Press.

Chang, H. and A. Singh (1993) 'Public Enterprises in Developing Countries and Economic Efficiency: Analytical, Empirical and Policy Issues', *UNCTAD Review*, No. 4.

Singh, A. (1994) 'Global Economic Changes, Skills and International Competitiveness', *International Labour Review*, 133 (2): 167–83.

Singh, A. (1994) 'Growing Independently of the World Economy: Asian Economic Development Since 1980', *UNCTAD Review*, September 1994: 91–106.

Singh, A. (1994) 'Industrial Policy in Europe: Implications for Developing Countries', in P. Bianchi, K. Cowling and R. Sugden (eds), *Europe's Economic Challenge*, London: Routledge: 60–78.

Howes, C. and A. Singh (1995) 'Long-term Trends in the World Economy: The Gender Dimension', *World Development*, 23 (11) (November): 1895–911.

Singh, A. (1995) 'Institutional Requirements for Full Employment in Advanced Economies', *International Labour Review*, 135 (4–5) (December).

Singh, A. (1995) 'Review of Adrian Wood', *North–South Trade Employment and Inequality, Economic Journal*, 105 (432) (September): 1287–9.

Singh, A. and J. A. Zammit (1995) 'Employment and Unemployment: North and South', in J. Grieve-Smith and J. Michie (eds), *Managing the Global Economy*, Oxford: Oxford University Press: 93–110.

Singh, A. (1996) 'Expanding Employment in the Global Economy: The High Road or the Low Road', in P. Arestis, G. Palma and M. Sawyer (eds), *Essays in Honour of Geoff Harcourt*, London: Edward Elgar.

Singh, A. (1996) 'Supporting the South's Industrial Revolution After the Cold War: Developing Countries and the Emerging New International Economic Order', in D. Bourantonis and M. Evriviades (eds), *A United Nations for the Twenty-first Century: Peace, Security and Development*, The Hague: Kluwer Law International: 287–306.

Singh, A. (1996) 'The World Economy Under the Market Supremacy Model and Third World Industrialisation', Malcolm Adiseshiah Memorial Lecture, 1995 Annual Meeting of the Indian Economic Association, published in the *Indian Economic Journal*, 44 (1) (July–September).

Singh, A. (1996) 'The Post-Uruguay Round World Trading System, Industrialisation, Trade and Development', in *Expansion of Trading Opportunities to the Year 2000 for Asia-Pacific Developing Countries*, Geneva: United Nations.

Chang, H.-J. and A. Singh (1997) 'Can Large Firms be run Efficiently Without Being Bureaucratic? Some Critical Comments on Bureaucrats in Business', *Journal of International Development*, 9 (6): 865–75.

Singh, A. (1997) 'Liberalisation and Globalisation: An Unhealthy Euphoria', in Jonathan Michie and John Grieve-Smith (eds), *Employment and Economic Performance*, Oxford: Oxford University Press.

Singh, A. (1997) 'Catching Up With the West: A Perspective on Asian Economic Development and Lessons for Latin America', in Louis Emmerij (ed.), *Economic and Social Development into the XXI Century*, Washington, DC: Inter-American Development Bank.

Singh, A. (1998) *Financial Crisis in East Asia: The End of the Asian Model?*, ILO Discussion Paper No. 24, Geneva, November.

Singh, A. and J.A. Zammit (1998) 'Foreign Direct Investment: Towards Co-operative Institutional Arrangements between the North and the South?', in J. Michie and J. Smith (eds), *Globalisation, Growth and Governance*, Oxford: Oxford University Press: 30–49.

Chang, H.- J. and A. Singh, (1999) 'Lessons from the Asian Crisis', *South Letter*, 1 and 2 (33): 5–8.

Howes, C. and A. Singh (1999) 'National Competitiveness, Dynamics of Adjustment and Long Term Economic Growth: Conceptual, Empirical and Policy Issues', DAE Discussion Papers in Finance and Accounting, No. AF43, University of Cambridge.

Singh, A. (1999) 'Asian Capitalism and the Financial Crisis', in Jonathan Michie and John Grieve-Smith (eds), *Global Instability and World Economic Governance*, London: Routledge. Also published in John Eatwell and Lance Taylor (eds), *International Capital Market: Systems in Transitions*, Oxford: Oxford University Press, 2002.

Singh, A. (1999) 'Asian Crisis: What Really Happened in Asia?', *Economic Bulletin*, National Institute for Economic Policy, 1 (1): 13–16.

Singh, A. (1999) 'Global Unemployment, Long-run Economic Growth and Labour Market Rigidities: A Commentary', Special contribution in B. Dibroy (ed.), *Perspectives on Globalization and Employment*, Office of Development Studies Discussion Paper Series, UNDP: 50–69.

Singh, A. and B. Weisse (1999) 'The Asian Model: A Crisis Foretold?', *International Social Science Journal*, 160: 203–15.

Howes, C. and A. Singh (2000a) (eds) *Competitiveness Matters: Industry and Economic Performance in the US*, Ann Arbor, Mich.: University of Michigan Press.

Howes, C. and A. Singh (2000b) 'Competitiveness Matters: An Introduction', in Howes and Singh (2000a): 1–30.

Singh, A. (2000) Foreword to Michael Kitson and Jonathan Michie, *The Political Economy of Competitiveness*, London: Routledge.

Singh, A. and A. Zammit (2000) *The Global Labour Standards Controversy: Critical Issues for Developing Countries*, South Centre, Geneva, ISBN 929162 0130; ISSN 1607-5323.

Singh, A. (2001) 'Income Inequality in Advanced Economies: A Critical Examination of the Trade and Technology Theories and an Alternative Perspective', Working Paper No. 219, Centre for Business Research, University of Cambridge. Subsequently published in Jayati Ghosh and C. P. Chandrasekhar (eds), *Work and Well-Being in the Age of Finance*, New Delhi: Tulika Books (2003): 349–63.

Singh, A. and B. Weisse (2001) 'Deindustrialisation', in Jonathan Michie (ed.), *Reader's Guide to the Social Sciences*, vol. 1, London: Fitzroy Dearborn.

Singh, A. and B. Weisse (2001) 'Asian Model of Capitalism', in Jonathan Michie (ed.), *Reader's Guide to the Social Sciences*, vol. 1, London: Fitzroy Dearborn.

Singh, A. and J. A. Zammit (2003) 'Globalisation, Labour Standards and Economic Development', Working Paper No. 257, Centre for Business Research, University of Cambridge. Subsequently published in revised form in Jonathan Michie (ed.), *The Handbook of Globalisation*, Cheltenham: Edward Elgar, 2003: 191–215.

Singh, A. (2003) 'Capital Account Liberalisation, Free Long-term Capital Flows, Financial Crises and Economic Development', Centre for Business Research Working Paper No. 245, University of Cambridge, December. Subsequently published in a revised form in the *Eastern Economic Journal*, 29 (2) (Spring) 2003: 191–216. Also published in P. Arestis, M. Baddeley and J McCombie (eds), *Globalisation, Regionalism and Economic Activity*, Cheltenham: Edward Elgar, 2003: 15–46.

Singh, A. and J. A. Zammit (2003) 'Labour Standards and the "Race to the Bottom": Re-thinking Globalization and Workers' Rights from Developmental and Solidaristic Perspectives', Centre for Business Research Working Paper No. 279,

University of Cambridge, March. A revised version subsequently published in the *Oxford Review of Economic Policy*, 20 (1), (Spring) 2004: 85–104.

Singh, A. (2004) 'Introductory Note to the Prebsich Report', *Recalling UNCTAD I at UNCTAD XI*, South Centre, Geneva, June.

Singh, A. (2004) 'Corporate Profitability and Competition in Emerging Markets', in M. Luthra (ed.), *Tapping UK's Diversity to Connect With Emerging Markets with Special Reference to India and China. A Consultation Day Seminar Report on the White Paper – Globalisation, A Force for Good*, London: UK Department of Trade and Investment.

Singh, A. and R. Dhumale (2004) 'Globalisation, Technology, and Income Inequality: A Critical Analysis', in C. A. Cornea (ed.), *Inequality, Growth, and Poverty in an Era of Liberalization and Globalisation*, UNU-WIDER Studies in Development Economics, Oxford: UNU-WIDER and UNDP/Oxford University Press: 145–65.

Dasgupta, S. and A. Singh (2005) 'Will Services Be the New Engine of Indian Economic Growth?', Working Paper No. 310, Centre for Business Research, University of Cambridge, September. Subsequently published in *Development and Change*, 36 (6): 1035–57.

Singh, A. (2005) 'IED, Globalizacion y Desarrollo Economio: Hacia la Reforma de las Reglas del Juego Nacionales e Internacionales', in *Ekonomiaz*, Eusko Jaurlaritza Gobierno Vasco, (55): 14–39.

Singh, A. (2005) 'Special and Differential Treatment: The Multilateral Trading System and Economic Development in the Twenty-first Century', in Kevin P. Gallagher (ed.), *Putting Development First*, London: Zed Books: 233–63.

Singh, A. (2005) 'Globalisation and the Regulation of FDI: New Proposals from the European Community and Japan', *Contributions to Political Economy*, 24: 99–121.

Singh, A. (2005) 'FDI, Globalisation and Economic Development: Towards Reforming National and International Rules of the Game', Centre for Business Research Working Paper No. 304, University of Cambridge, March.

Dasgupta, Sukti and Ajit Singh (2006) 'Manufacturing, Services and Premature De-Industrialisation in Developing Countries: a Kaldorian Empirical Analysis', Working Paper No. 327, Centre for Business Research, University of Cambridge, June. Subsequently republished in George Mavrotas and Anthony Shorrocks (eds), *Advancing Development: Core Themes in Global Economics*, Palgrave Macmillan in association with the United Nations University-World Institute for Development Economics Research (UNU-WIDER): 435–56.

Fagernas, S. and A. Singh (2006) 'Globalisation, Instability and Economic Insecurity', Working Paper No. 328, Centre for Business Research, University of Cambridge, June.

Singh, A. (2006) 'William Brian Reddaway 1913–2002 Memorial', *Proceedings of the British Academy*, 138, London: British Academy: 285–306.

Singh, A. (2007) 'Capital Account Liberalization, Free Long-Term Capital Flows, Financial Crises and Economic Development' in Anwar Shaikh (ed.), *Globalization and the Myths of Free Trade*, Oxford: Routledge: 259–87.

Singh, A. (2007) 'Legacy – Lal Jayawardena: Crafting Development Policy', in George Mavrotas and Anthony Shorrocks (eds), *Advancing Development: Core Themes in Global Economics*, Palgrave Macmillan in association with the United Nations University-World Institute for Development Economics Research (UNU-WIDER): xxxv–xxxviii.

Singh, A. (2007) 'Does Integration of India and China with the World Economy Harm the US Workers? A Commentary on the Freeman Thesis', *Indian Journal of Labour Economics*, 50 (3) (July–September): 457–66.

Singh, Ajit (Forthcoming) 'The Past, Present and Future of Industrial Policy in India: Adapting to the Changing Domestic and International Environment' in M. Cimoli, G. Dosi and J. Stiglitz (eds), *Policies and Development*, Oxford University Press. Forthcoming.

Industrialization, Economic Development and Economic Policy in Emerging Markets

Paine, S. H. and A. Singh (1973) 'The Shanghai Diesel Engine Factory', *Cambridge Review*, 94, June.

Singh, A. (1973) 'Die Politische Ökonomie der Sozialistischen Entwicklung in China seit 1948', lecture delivered in 1972 at the University of Heidelberg and subsequently published in P. Hennicke (ed.), *Probleme des Sozialismus und der Uebergangsgesellschaften*, Frankfurt am Main. Published in English in *Economic and Political Weekly*, VIII (47).

Singh, A. (1975) *An Essay on the Political Economy of Chinese Development*, Thames Papers in Political Economy, London.

Singh, A. (1979) 'The "Basic Needs" Approach to Development and the New International Economic Order: The Significance of Third World Industrialisation', *World Development*, 7, June.

Eatwell, J. L. and A. Singh (1981) 'Is the Mexican Economy Overheated? Some Issues of Short- and Medium-Term Economic Policy', *Economia Mexicana*, Analisis y Perspectivas, No. 3, Centro de Investigacion y Docensia Economicas, AC (CIDE), Mexico.

Eatwell, J. L. and A. Singh (1981) 'Is the Mexican Economy Overheated? A Further Note on Imports and Capacity Utilisation', *Economia Mexicana*, Analisis y Perspectivas, No. 3, Centro de Investigacion y Docensia Economicas, AC (CIDE), Mexico.

Singh, A. (1981) 'Mexican Economy at the Crossroads: Policy Options in a Semi-Industrial Oil Exporting Country', a Commentary on Mr Brailovsky's paper', in T. Barker and V. Brailovsky (eds), *Oil or Industry?*, London: Academic Press.

Singh, A. (1982) 'Industrialisation in Africa: A Structuralist View', in M. Fransman (ed.), *Industry and Accumulation in Africa*, London: Heinemann.

Singh, A. (1982) 'Foreign Aid for Structural Change: Industrial Development Policy Issues in Lesotho', in M. Fransman (ed.), *Industry and Accumulation in Africa*, London: Heinemann.

Singh, A. (1982) 'The Present Crisis of the Mexican Economy From a Mexican Perspective', *South*, October.

Singh, A. (1982) 'Basic Needs and Industrialisation', in ILO, *Basic Needs in Danger: A Basic Needs Oriented Development Strategy for Tanzania*, Addis Ababa: ILO.

Singh, A. (1983) 'Ante Un Mundo En Desequilibrio, El Neoliberalismo No Podra Dar Recomendaciones Adecuadas: Quienes las Sigan Marcharan Por Mal Comino', in Sohel Riffka (ed.), *Los Modelos de la Crisis*, Ecuador: Ildis: 141–50.

Singh, A. (1984) 'The Present Crisis of the Tanzanian Economy: Notes on the Economics and Politics of Devaluation', *African Development*, IX (2). Also published in JASPA/ILO, *The Challenge of Employment and Basic Needs in Africa*, Nairobi: Oxford University Press 1986.

Singh, A. (1984) 'Deceleration in World Economic Growth and Industrial Development in the Third World: UNCTAD Twenty Years on', *Bulletin of the Institute of Development Studies*, University of Sussex, 15 (3) (July).

Singh, A. (1984) 'The Interrupted Industrial Revolution of the Third World: Prospects and Policies for Resumption', *Industry and Development*, 12. Also published in G. Sjostedt and B. Sunderlius (eds), *Free Trade – Managed Trade? Perspectives on a Realistic International Trade Order*, London: Swedish Institute of International Affairs/Westview Press, 1986.

Singh, A. (1985) 'The Continuing Crisis of the Tanzanian Economy: The Political Economy of Alternative Policy Options', *African Development*, X (1/2).

Singh, A. (1986) 'Crisis and Recovery in the Mexican Economy: The Role of the Capital Goods Sector', in M. Fransman (ed.), *Machinery and Economic Development*, London: Macmillan.

Singh, A. (1986) 'Tanzania and the IMF: The Analytics of Alternative Adjustment Programmes', *Development and Change*, 17 (3) (July): 425–54.

Singh, A. (1986) 'The Great Continental Divide: The Asian and Latin American Countries in the World Economic Crisis', *Labour and Society*, 1 (3) (September).

Singh, A. (1986) 'The IMF–World Bank Policy Programme in Africa: A Commentary', in P. Lawrence (ed.), *The World Recession and the Food Crisis in Africa*, London: James Currey/Review of African Political Economy.

Singh, A. (1986) 'The World Economic Crisis, Stabilisation and Structural Adjustment: An Overview', *Labour and Society*, 1 (3) (September).

Singh, A. (1987) 'Exogenous Shocks and De-Industrialisation in Africa: Prospects and Strategies for Re-Industrialisation', in RISNODEC, *African Economic Crisis*, New Delhi.

Singh, A. (1988) 'Employment and Output in a Semi-Industrial Economy: Modelling Alternative Policy Options in Mexico', in M. Hopkins (ed.), *Employment Forecasting*, London: Pinter.

Singh, A. (1988) 'Industrial Policy in Developing Countries: The Foreign Exchange Cost of Exports', *Industry and Development*, 23.

Singh, A. (1988) 'La Révolution Industrielle Inachevée du Tiers Monde', *Revue Tiers-Monde*, XXIX (115) (July–September).

Singh, A. and J. Ghosh (1988) 'Import Liberalisation and the New Industrial Strategy: An Analysis of their Impact on Output and Employment in the Indian Economy', *Economic and Political Weekly*, XXIII (45, 46 and 47), Special edition.

Singh, A. and H. Tabatabai, (1990) 'Facing the Crisis: Third World Agriculture in the 1980s', *International Labour Review*, 129 (4).

Hughes, A. and A. Singh (1991) 'The World Economic Slow-Down and the Asian and Latin American Economies: A Comparative Analysis of Economic Structure, Policy and Performance', in T. Banuri (ed.), *Economic Liberalisation: No Panacea*, Oxford: Clarendon Press.

Singh, A. (1991) 'The Role of the Government in Indian Industrial Development', in Irfan Ul Haque (ed.), *International Competitiveness: Interaction of the Public and the Private Sectors*, EDI Seminar Series, Washington, DC: World Bank.

Singh, A. (1992) 'Urbanisation, Poverty and Employment: The Large Metropolis in the Third World', *Contributions to Political Economy*, 11.

Singh, A. (1992) 'The Actual Crisis of Economic Development in the 1980s: An Alternative Perspective for the Future', in A. Dutt and K. Jameson (eds), *New Directions in Development Economics*, London: Edward Elgar.

Singh, A. and H. Tabatabai (1992) 'Agriculture and Economic Development in the 1990s: A New Analytical and Policy Agenda', *International Labour Review*, 131.

Singh, A. (1993) 'Asian Economic Success and Latin American Failure in the 1980s: New Analyses and Future Policy Implications', *International Review of Applied Economics*, 7 (3).

Singh, A. (1993) ' "Close" vs. "Strategic" Integration with the World Economy and "Market-Friendly Approach to Development" vs. an "Industrial Policy"', University of Duisburg, *INEF Report*, 4.

Singh, A. and H. Tabatabai (eds) (1993) *Economic Crisis and Third World Agriculture*, Cambridge: Cambridge University Press.

Singh, A. and H. Tabatabai (1993) 'Third World Agriculture in a Crisis Environment: Analytical and Policy Issues', in *Economic Crisis and Third World Agriculture*, Cambridge: Cambridge University Press.

Singh, A. and H. Tabatabai (1993) 'The World Economic Crisis and Third World Agriculture in the 1980s', in *Economic Crisis and Third World Agriculture*, Cambridge: Cambridge University Press.

Dutt, A., K. Kim and A. Singh (eds) (1994) *The State, Markets and Development*, London: Edward Elgar.

Dutt, A., K. Kim and A. Singh (1994) 'The State, Markets and Development: An Introduction', in A. Dutt, K. Kim and A. Singh (eds), *The State, Markets and Development*, London: Edward Elgar: 3–21.

Singh, A. (1994) 'State Intervention and the Market-Friendly Approach to Development: A Critical Analysis of the World Bank Theses', in A. Dutt, K. Kim and A. Singh (eds), *The State, Markets and Development*, London: Edward Elgar, London: 38–61.

Singh, A. (1994) 'Openness and Market-Friendly Approach to Development: Learning the Right Lessons from Development Experience', *World Development*, 22 (12) (December): 1811–23.

Singh, A. (1994) 'The Present State of Industry in the Third World: Prospects and Policies for the Future', in G. K. Chadha (ed.), *Sectoral Issues in the Indian Economy: Policy and Perspectives*, New Delhi: Har-Anand Publications.

Singh, A. (1994) 'From the Plan to the Market: Controlled Reform in China' (in French), *Revue Tiers-Monde*, XXXV, (139) (July–September): 659–84.

Singh, A. (1995) 'The State and Industrialisation in India: Successes and Failures and Lessons for the Future', in H. Chang and R. E. Rowthorn (eds), *The Role of the State in Economic Change*, Oxford: Clarendon Press: 170–86.

Singh, A. (1995) 'Asia y America Latina Comparidos: Divergencias Economicas en los años '80', *Dessarollo Economico, Revista de Ciencias Sociales*, 34 (136) (January–March): 513–32.

Singh, A. (1995) *How Did East Asia Grow so Fast? Slow Progress Towards an Analytical Consensus*, UNCTAD Discussion Paper No. 97, Geneva, February. Republished as an Occasional Paper by RIS Publications in Delhi, 1995.

Singh, A. (1995) 'Competitive Markets and Economic Development,' *International Papers in Political Economy*, 2 (1): 1–40. Republished in P. Arestis and M. Sawyer (eds), *Political Economy of Economic Policy*, London: Macmillan, 1998.

Singh, A. (1995) 'The Causes of Fast Economic Growth in East Asia', *UNCTAD Review*, Geneva): 91–127.

Singh, A. (1996) 'The Plan, the Market and Evolutionary Economic Reform in China', in Abu Abdullah and Azizur, Rahman Khan (eds), *State, Market and Development: Essays in Honour of Rehman Sobhan*, Dhaka University Press. Republished in Spanish as 'El Plan, el Mercado, y la Transicion Gradual en China', in *Revista de Estudios Asiaticos*, 3, July–December 1996.

Singh, A. (1999) 'Growth, Its Sources and Consequences', in G. Thompson (ed.), *Economic Dynamism in the Pacific Region: The Growth of Integration and Competitiveness*, London/New York: Routledge/Open University: 55–82.

Singh, A. (1999) 'Review article on M. Aoki, H.-K. Kim and M. Okuno-Fujiwara' (eds), *The Role of Government in East Asian Economic Development, Journal of Development Economics*, 59: 565–72.

Singh, A. (2000) *Global Economic Trends and Social Development*, Occasional Paper 9, United Nations Research Institute for Social Development, Geneva, June. ISBN: 92-9085-030-2.

Singh, A. (2000) 'Contribution to Free Trade and the "Starving Child" Defence: A Symposium', *Nation*, 24 April.

Singh, A. and R. Dhumale (2000) 'Competition Policy, Development and Developing Countries, *South Letter*, 2 (36): 13–15.

Singh, A. (2001) 'What Role South–South Cooperation: A 50-year Overview', *South Letter*, 1 and 2 (37): 5–10.

Singh, A. (2002) 'Aid, Conditionality and Development', *Development and Change*, 33 (2): 295–305. Subsequently published in J. P. Pronk *et al.* (eds), *Catalysing Development? A Debate on Aid*, Oxford: Blackwell: 77–88.

Singh, A. (2003) 'South–South Co-operation: A Historical Perspective', in *South Centre High Level Policy Forum*, Geneva: South Centre: 95–112, ISBN 92 9162 023 8.

Singh, A. (2004) 'Standing on the Crossroads: The Indian Economy in the 21st Century', *Annual Report*, Bank of Luxembourg: 21–7.

Singh, A. (2005) 'Lal Jayawardena: Crafting Development Policy', *Development and Change*, 36 (6): 1219–23.

Singh, A. (2006) 'Foreword', in 'Independent Social Scientists' Alliance of Turkey', *On Economic and Social Life in Turkey in 2005*: 1–2.

Singh, A. (2007) 'Globalization and Industrial Revolutions in India and China: Implications for Advanced and Developing Economies and for National and International Policies', Working Paper 81, Policy Integration Department, International Labour Organisation, March 2007.

Index